THE TIMES

LIVES BEHIND THE MUSIC

Published by Times Books

An imprint of HarperCollins Publishers
Westerhill Road
Bishopbriggs
Glasgow G64 2QT
www.harpercollins.co.uk

HarperCollins Publishers
39/40 Mayor Street Upper
Dublin 1, D01 C9W8
Ireland

First edition 2024

ISBN 978-0-00-869964-2

10 9 8 7 6 5 4 3 2 1

© This compilation Times Media Ltd
2024

The Times® is a registered trademark
of Times Newspapers Ltd

Printed in the UK using 100% Renewable
Electricity at CPI Group (UK) Ltd

The contents of this publication are
believed correct at the time of printing.
Nevertheless the Publisher can accept
no responsibility for errors or omissions,
changes in the detail given or for any
expense or loss thereby caused.

The Publishers acknowledge that views
around language and sensitivity in
journalism are continually changing.
However the language, style and format
of the obituaries in this book have been
preserved from when they originally
appeared in the newspaper and should
be read in that context.

A catalogue record for this book is
available from the British Library.

Typeset by Davidson Publishing Solutions

Our thanks and acknowledgements go
to Joanne Lovey and Robin Ashton
at News Licensing and, in particular,
at *The Times*, Ian Brunskill and,
at HarperCollins, Harley Griffiths,
Marta Kizym, Kerry Ferguson,
Kevin Robbins and Rachel Weaver.
With special thanks to News UK Archives.

If you would like to comment on any
aspect of this book, please contact us
at the above address or online.
E-mail: times.books@harpercollins.co.uk
www.timesbooks.co.uk

MIX
Paper | Supporting
responsible forestry
FSC™ C007454

This book is produced from independently certified FSC™ paper
to ensure responsible forest management.

For more information visit: www.harpercollins.co.uk/green

THE ✦ TIMES

LIVES BEHIND THE MUSIC

ERA-DEFINING OBITUARIES
OF ROCK AND POP ICONS

EDITED BY NIGEL FARNDALE

TIMES BOOKS

CONTENTS

INTRODUCTION

INTRODUCTION

Nigel Farndale

"I believe they are a beat combo, m'lud." That, supposedly, was the answer given by a barrister towards the end of the Swinging Sixties when a judge asked in court "Who are the Beatles?" The exchange seems improbable now, but that doesn't mean it didn't happen then. And if it did, I can guess the reason. Around that time there was a famous ad campaign with the slogan "Top people read *The Times*". Those top people will have included members of the judiciary.

And who might those top people have expected to read about when they opened their paper of choice? In the obituaries section it would have been the great and the good: archbishops, captains of industry and ambassadors, several thousand words on each. And war heroes, of course, the Battle of Britain "Few" and so on. Figures from high culture would be covered too, but when it came to music this would mean opera sopranos, classical composers and conductors. The low culture of rock and pop? Not so much.

When Buddy Holly died in a plane crash in 1959, he didn't merit an obituary in *The Times* at all. *Buddy. Holly.*

By the late 1960s, pop stars were starting to get *Times* obituaries but almost begrudgingly, in a perfunctory and formal way. Mr Brian Jones, as he was styled, got a modest and dry 500 words in 1968, even though the news that the Rolling Stones founder and guitarist had been found dead in a swimming pool was making front pages around the world.

By contrast, when Charlie Watts, the Stones' drummer, died in much less dramatic fashion in 2021, I, as the obituaries editor of *The Times*, allotted him 3,000 words. I also thought we could probably, on balance, get away with dropping the "Mr".

What was behind this cultural change of heart? Well, *The Times* has always taken seriously its role as "the newspaper of public record", and back then it took the role very seriously indeed, so seriously it didn't even introduce bylines for writers until the mid-1960s and certainly didn't include anything as frivolous as a colour supplement full of lifestyle features, diet tips and celebrity interviews.

It was the broadsheet of the establishment, and the establishment wore suits and listened to classical music. They didn't wear kaftans and listen to pop. You can get a sense of these "two cultures" when you watch YouTube footage of the Beatles' rooftop concert in 1969. That beat combo is up there with their long hair, flares, and Afghan coats while down in the streets below, looking up in bemusement, are the top people, the city types with their bowler hats and furled umbrellas.

Not everyone, it seems, got the memo about the youth-driven cultural revolution that was the Swinging Sixties. Another illustration: *Sgt Pepper's Lonely Hearts Club Band* may have been the biggest-selling album of 1967, but it wasn't the biggest of the decade. That would be – yes, you haven't guessed it – *The Sound of Music*.

The tone of the obituaries was quite stuffy and obfusc back then too, and this continued into the next decade. Consider the way the obituary for Mr Keith Moon in 1978 requires quote marks around "The Who", then as now one of the most famous bands in the world. Sometimes the terminology jars with what is deemed acceptable today and is considered offensive indeed. The obituary for Mr Elvis Presley, for instance, earnestly notes the "Negro" roots of his style of rock'n'roll.

Also then as now, *Times* obituaries were unsigned, but if you had to guess who wrote Mr John Lennon's from 1980, you might say it was the paper's classical music critic, such is its lofty, slightly patronising tone. It makes no mention of bed-ins, LSD or *Imagine* but it does include the sizzling line: "… the Cavern club in Liverpool, one of the foci of the new Merseyside sound".

Private lives tend not to be mentioned either, just careers. The obituary for Dennis Wilson, who died in 1983, is fascinating for what it doesn't say. He was one of the most colourful figures in pop history, yet there is no mention of the mysteries surrounding his death, nor his heroin addiction and epic sexual promiscuity. The $100,000 he donated to the Charles Manson "family"? Not a whisper.

His obituary doesn't even acknowledge that he was the only member of the Beach Boys who surfed.

These drier, shorter early obituaries, then, are portals to a bygone age, a reminder that the past is another country. I've included a handful of them in this collection to demonstrate what I mean: Mr Jim Morrison and Miss Janis Joplin feature, for example, as well as another member of the infamous "27 Club", Mr Jimi Hendrix. No mention is made of his assiduous drug taking or his legendary performance at Woodstock, but rather sweetly the obituary does note that his music was "awesomely loud".

By the time Kurt Cobain and Amy Winehouse joined that club of pop stars who died at the tender age of 27, not only had the titles been dropped but the obituaries were getting a bit longer and more in depth, covering the sex and drugs as well as the rock'n'roll.

Yet even theirs aren't the most dramatic stories of rock-star excess you will find collected in these pages. Take Glen Campbell's. He may have been a country music star but, my goodness, his lifestyle was pure destructive, hedonistic rock god.

In a strong field, though, it is Ginger Baker, the drummer of Cream, who was the maddest, baddest and most dangerous rock star to know. Against all the odds, he lived to a ripe old age, dying in 2019.

Nowadays obituaries of rock and pop stars are more like long-form features: writerly, full of lively anecdotes, wry. And we hear the subject's voice through quotation. I was tempted to expand some of the older pop obituaries not styled in this way, such as that for Freddie Mercury, but I've kept them as written at the time, on the grounds that they intrigue more as undisturbed time capsules, as first drafts of history.

Inevitably, perhaps, we on the obituaries desk have come to think of those rock stars who did manage to survive the excesses of the Sixties and Seventies as "the new few". This, after all, is a profession where, as "The Who" memorably put it, people hoped to die before they got old. Alongside the de rigueur drug overdoses, the causes of death listed in these pages include suicides, murders and car crashes. But all too often it is something more commonplace. David Bowie choreographed his own departure beautifully, releasing his final single and video, *Lazarus*, as a moving self-epitaph on his 69th birthday in 2016. It was extraordinarily artful, and in complete contrast to the cause of his death two days later, which could scarcely have been more ordinary. Cancer.

Traditionally obituaries for stars of his stature would always be run in print the next day, but now there is an additional need for speed. Digital. *The Times* obituary for Charlie Watts appeared online within minutes of his death being announced one afternoon. It performed well on the website, driving traffic and adding new subscribers. And we know such obituaries are popular with our readers because thanks to the latest technology we can see how long they are spending over each story. Obituaries that appear online quickly have a long "dwell" time, because sometimes the thing you most want to read when someone famous dies – out of shock or nostalgia – is a short biography with a satisfying narrative arc, a clear beginning, middle and end.

Print still matters too. News of Olivia Newton-John's demise in 2022 was less kind in terms of timing, as it broke at 8pm and our print deadline meant her two pages would have to be designed and "revise subbed" by 9pm – but we managed, thanks to one of the worst-kept secrets in journalism, namely that we on the obituaries desk spend a lot of our working day prepping the "household names" in advance. They are called stocks, as in stockpile, and we usually have around 3,500 of them in a fairly up-to-date state.

Who we prepare in advance often has more to do with fame than age or ill health. Big names such as Elton John, Rod Stewart and Keith Richards are all teed up, for example. And Mick Jagger, of course. He, incidentally, once asked to see his. (Hello? Control freak.) We declined to show him, and he accepted our reasoning with good grace.

Paul McCartney's was first prepared for *The Times* in 1967 by none other than Hunter Davis when he was spending a year with the Beatles writing their authorised biography. His obituary for McCartney was the then standard 500 words. The latest iteration, written by our chief music obituaries writer, Nigel Williamson, is 3,000 words long.

Nigel, an author, music critic and veteran interviewer of pop stars, has been doing this job for quite a few years now and recalls that Ian Brunskill, one of my predecessors as obituaries editor, was "the ultimate ambulance chaser. A celeb only had to sneeze and Ian commissioned a stock. His best line was 'I saw Lou Reed on the *Old Grey Whistle Test* at the weekend. He looked a bit peaky. You'd better do him.' To which I replied: 'Lou Reed has been looking peaky since 1966, when he was only 24. It's called heroin.'"

Inevitably there wasn't room for all the fallen rock and pop stars from the past six decades, but I've tried to include a good mix of male and female, British and American, Black and White. I've also gone for a cross section of genres, from rock'n'roll, psychedelic, prog, glam and heavy metal, to disco, punk, C&W, new romantic, ska and grunge (but not jazz and classical, as that felt like a different book).

One omission you may notice is Sid Vicious, the Sex Pistols' bass player and singer, who died of a heroin overdose at the age of 21 in 1977, after murdering his girlfriend, Nancy. That's because this legend of popular culture was not deemed a suitable subject for an obituary back then. But times change, and *The Times* changes with them. Nowadays he would be a double-page spread.

LIVES BEHIND
THE MUSIC

DAVID CASSIDY

●

Anguished teen idol who made his name on television as a member of
The Partridge Family and had a string of hits in the Seventies

The Times, November 22, 2017

David Cassidy was playing in the Broadway production of *Joseph and the Amazing Technicolor Dreamcoat* when he first met a youthful billionaire named Donald Trump, who invited him to a party on his yacht. Many years later, when Trump was making his bid for the Republican presidential nomination, Cassidy recalled the occasion. "First thing when I stepped on his yacht, he said, 'So, David, where's the broads?' And I went, 'Oh, no.'"

The story perhaps reveals much about Trump, but also about Cassidy. It was 1983 and he had spent the previous dozen years as an androgynously good-looking pop star whose concerts provoked more screaming hysteria from his youthful female audience than had been heard since the heyday of the Beatles.

If Trump was disappointed that Cassidy did not turn up with a posse of willing and nubile teenage fans in tow, he had misunderstood his guest. By then Cassidy had come to hate his pop past and was attempting to reinvent himself as a serious singer and actor.

His success as a teeny-bop heart-throb had been spectacular. At his peak in the Seventies, Cassidy was the world's highest-paid live entertainer, earning $50,000 a night (about £225,000 today). His official fan club – 99 per cent of whom were teenage girls – had the largest membership in pop history, exceeding those of Elvis Presley and the "Fab Four".

"I am grateful for it, because without them I might be pumping gas," he once said – and yet he spent most of his adult life attempting to shake off his pin-up image. "I had no life. As a human being I was quite emotionally stunted. I never sought the fame and I was always trying to hide from it," he insisted.

There seemed to be no escape. "I'm exploited by people who put me on the back of cereal boxes," he complained at the height of his fame. "I asked my housekeeper to buy a cereal and when she came home there was a huge picture of me on the back. I can't even eat breakfast without seeing my face."

He was particularly popular in Britain, where between 1970 and 1975 he had five Top 20 hits with the Partridge Family and seven Top 20 solo hits, including the No 1s *How Can I Be Sure* and *Daydreamer*. In one week in 1973 there were six sell-out shows at Wembley Stadium and the word "Cassidymania" entered the language.

Frustrated with his bubble-gum image, Cassidy gave an interview in 1972 to *Rolling Stone* in which he talked about his fondness for drink, drugs and sex and posed naked for Annie Leibovitz on the cover. The accompanying story, headlined "Naked Lunch Box", did not, however, attract the more mature audience he craved.

Cassidymania turned sour in 1974 when more than 600 fans were injured during a stampede of teenage girls at a show at the White City Stadium in London. Thirty were taken to hospital and one, Bernadette Whelan, 14, died without regaining consciousness. The singer announced that the tragedy would "haunt" him until he died. He quit *The Partridge Family*, the TV show that had been the foundation of his success, gave up touring and tried to reinvent himself as a serious singer-songwriter.

He had one further big hit with *I Write the Songs*, although the song had been written by Bruce Johnston of the Beach Boys, which just entrenched the view that he was nothing more than a teeny-bop fake. He later claimed that he had received only $15,000 from the estimated $500 million made from merchandising during his heart-throb years after signing away most of the rights.

By the Eighties he was in the throes of another reinvention as he moved into musical theatre. His appearance in George M Cohan's musical *Little Johnny Jones* was a disaster and negative reviews of his performance led to his replacement before the production reached Broadway. Even worse, the part went to Donny Osmond, his main rival for poster space on teenage bedroom walls during the Seventies.

Joseph and the Amazing Technicolor Dreamcoat was better received. It led to him taking over from Cliff Richard in the West End production of *Time* and returning to Broadway in *Blood Brothers* alongside Petula Clark and his half-brother, Shaun Cassidy. There were long stints on stage in Las Vegas.

His personal life was complex and he struggled to find domestic happiness. There were two failed marriages, first to the actress Kay Lenz, whom he wed in 1977 and divorced six years later, and then to the South African-born horse breeder Meryl Tanz. They had met in 1974 and married ten years later, but separated when he had a daughter with the model Sherry Williams Benedon. Their child, Katie Cassidy, who was born in 1986, became an actress. He married again in 1991 when the songwriter Sue Shifrin became his third wife. The couple had a son, Beau, who became a singer. Cassidy and Shifrin separated in 2013.

Over the years Cassidy had psychotherapy and struggled with drugs and alcohol, which, he admitted, he used to "numb" himself. "It became a struggle not to drink and it became a habit. I was sitting at home drinking wine on my own till 4am," he said. He was arrested more than once for drink-driving. Despite having sold 25 million records, he filed for bankruptcy in 2015. Two years later, after falling on stage, he announced that he was suffering from dementia and retired from performing.

He was born David Bruce Cassidy in 1950 into a showbusiness family in New York. His father was Jack Cassidy, a singer and actor, and his mother was Evelyn Ward, an actress. David was brought up by his maternal grandparents because his parents were constantly away in touring productions.

When he was six he found out from a neighbour's children that his parents had divorced two years earlier. The news only came out because his father had then married the actress Shirley Jones, who had just become a star in the film *Oklahoma!*

He went to live with them in California and his relationship with Jones was loving. "She was a role model on how to deal with fame and success," he said. "She's one of the best human beings I've ever known. She was a great help to me in my difficult relationship with my dad and served as a great buffer."

He admitted struggling to gain the approval of his father, who he suggested became "tormented" when his son became more famous than him. "I loved him and admired him, but I just couldn't find a way for it to be OK with him," he said. "It was a rough one for us."

When his father died in a fire at his Hollywood apartment in 1976, Cassidy had not spoken to him for nine months. His mother, who suffered from Alzheimer's disease, died in 2012. "Seeing such a vibrant woman reduced to this is really just heartbreaking. It's such a cruel and debilitating disease," he said at the time.

He made his Broadway debut in 1969 in a musical, *The Fig Leaves Are Falling*, which closed after four performances, but then passed a screen test with Universal Studios and returned to Los Angeles. After small parts in the TV series *Ironside*, *Marcus Welby, M.D.* and *Bonanza* he was cast in the musical sitcom *The Partridge Family* as Keith, the eldest of five fictional children of a widowed mother, played by his real stepmother, Shirley Jones. The show was a huge success, as were the spin-off hit records credited to the Partridge Family, the first of which, *I Think I Love You*, topped the American singles chart in 1970.

The show also launched Cassidy's solo career, but even at the height of his success he craved recognition as a "serious" rock musician. In interviews he created a persona who loved garage rock and the blues and cited Jimi Hendrix, the Doors and John Lennon as his heroes. He became friends with Lennon after the former Beatle moved to New York in the Seventies and claimed that David Bowie had once offered to produce an album of him singing songs written by Lou Reed.

In later years Cassidy continued to perform for a small fan base that had grown up with him. Thankfully, they had at least learnt to stop screaming, he noted. On TV he appeared in a "where are they now?" show and was reunited with Trump on the future president's reality show *Celebrity Apprentice*. He was the first contestant to be ousted, but claimed that his rustication came as a huge relief. "When The Donald said, 'Fired!' I went, 'Thank God!'"

David Cassidy, singer and actor, was born on April 12, 1950. He died of liver and kidney failure on November 22, 2017, aged 67

LEMMY

●

The frontman of the metal band Motörhead, who, in a milieu devoted to sex and drugs, was idolised for playing loudest and living hardest

The Times, January 3, 2016

Even by rock'n'roll standards, the commitment of Lemmy to the sex and drugs lifestyle was dedicated and unrepentant. The heavy-metal noise he made with Motörhead provided a ferocious soundtrack to an appetite for excess that defined him in the public mind as one of rock music's most notorious hell-raisers.

Dressed in black denim and leather with biker boots, cowboy hat and a Nazi Iron Cross around his neck, Lemmy drank a bottle of Jack Daniel's every day for almost 40 years. He admitted to having slept with more than 1,000 women. Mythic bacchanalian stories surrounding him included a Playboy model allowing him to tie her to a bed for three days.

The drug intake was on a similarly industrial scale. "He's a living, breathing, drinking and snorting legend. No one else comes close," said Dave Grohl, of Nirvana and later Foo Fighters.

While many rock'n'roll "legends" died young – including the Sex Pistols' bass player Sid Vicious, whom Lemmy recalled trying to teach the instrument, "unsuccessfully" – the Motörhead frontman continued to swagger on stage in his seventh decade.

His rebellious nature may have been a reaction to being the son of an RAF chaplain, yet in reality neither church nor military affected his life. He was born Ian Fraser Kilmister in 1945 in Burslem, Staffordshire. His father left his mother when he was three months old. Lemmy described him as a "nasty little weasel".

When his mother remarried, Lemmy spent his secondary school years in Anglesey, where he earned his nickname, allegedly derived from the phrase "Lend me [lemmy] a quid till Friday", owing to his habit of borrowing money to feed his addiction to slot machines.

School was not a happy experience. His escape came in music and the early records of Little Richard, Jerry Lee Lewis and Chuck Berry. "Rock'n'roll sounded like music from another planet," he recalled. He noticed that when a fellow pupil took his guitar to school, he was "surrounded by chicks", and so he resolved to learn how to play. "In those days just having a guitar was enough. That was it," he said.

After playing with the Manchester band the Rockin' Vickers, Lemmy moved to London in 1967 and shared a flat with Noel Redding, bassist with the Jimi Hendrix Experience. The association led to a brief stint as a procurer of drugs and roadie for the group, a taxing task given Hendrix's prodigious intake of LSD and a tendency to destroy his equipment.

Lemmy went on to join the space rockers Hawkwind, whom he got to know as fellow squatters in west London. Switching from guitar to bass, he sang the lead vocal on the band's biggest hit, Silver Machine. "It was like Star Trek, except with long hair and drugs," he said. "We used to lock the doors so people couldn't get out."

He was fired from Hawkwind in 1975 after being arrested in Canada for possession of cocaine. While his former bandmates continued their North American tour, Lemmy returned to Britain and systematically set about sleeping with their wives and girlfriends. He claimed success with all but one of them.

He then formed Motörhead, which was driven by Lemmy's machinegun-style bass-playing and snarly vocals. Lemmy said: "I've got what you call a low tonal register, which loosely translated means I sound like a gorilla on Valium."

Lemmy left Britain in 1990 for Los Angeles, where he lived for the rest of his life in a modest apartment, which he claimed never to have cleaned. It was full of his vast collection of Nazi memorabilia. He denied sympathies with the Third Reich, insisting that he just "liked the clobber – the bad guys always have the best uniforms". He described himself as a libertarian anarchist, believing that "government causes more problems than it solves", although he once proclaimed himself a Thatcherite.

In later years he delighted in surprising interviewers with his views and tastes. He enjoyed reading history books as well as the novels of PG Wodehouse and said that he was a staunch believer in the sanctity of marriage, which is why he never entered it. "I never saw a chick that could stop me looking at all the others," he said, before adding: "If you're going to get married, get fucking married and that's it."

Eventually, the hell-raising caught up with him. Diagnosed with diabetes, he gave up his daily bottle of Jack Daniel's in 2013. He switched to a bottle of vodka instead.

Lemmy, musician, was born on December 24, 1945. He died of cancer on December 28, 2015, aged 70

PRINCE

———————•———————

*Pop superstar who transcended musical genres but remained
a maverick enigma to his fans*

The Times, April 22, 2016

In a song on his landmark *Purple Rain* album, Prince slyly teased his listeners by singing, "I am something that you just can't understand." He spent the next three decades ensuring that it remained that way and there were few who claimed fully to comprehend some of the maddening choices and quixotic pronouncements that made him pop music's most enigmatic and eccentric superstar.

Yet there was universal recognition of a lavish and often thrilling talent that enabled him to sell more than 100 million albums and produced enduring hits such as: *Let's Go Crazy, 1999, Purple Rain, When Doves Cry, Little Red Corvette, The Most Beautiful Girl in the World* and *Nothing Compares 2 U*, which was memorably covered by Sinéad O'Connor.

He was once asked by an interviewer if there was anything he could not do. He appeared puzzled. Eventually he replied: "Anything I can't do? Yeah. I can't cook." Had he applied his attention to the kitchen rather than the studio, he would probably have become a master chef, for musically there appeared to be nothing that was beyond him.

At the age of 19 he was credited on his debut album with playing 27 different instruments. "Produced, arranged, composed and performed by Prince," ran a sleeve note. He seldom worked with other musicians, for his self-confidence and audacity were such that he believed that he could do the job better himself.

He mastered a myriad of musical styles, from rock to funk to jazz to psychedelia. His records were as poptastically danceable as the hits of Michael Jackson, with whom he had an intense rivalry. However, like David Bowie, every album was expansive, experimental and never the same as its predecessor, as he balanced artistic and commercial imperatives with a rare astuteness.

He was a magnetic performer, a provocative sex symbol, and combined the flamboyance of James Brown with the theatricality of Madonna. Like Jimi Hendrix before him, he liquidated the conventional boundaries between White and Black music."Can you keep up?" he often asked during his concerts. The answer was invariably an ear-shattering "Yes" from his fans, but sometimes it wasn't easy.

A prolific songwriter, he sang about sex and seduction and flirted with the listener outrageously. It was Prince's lascivious lyrics – including, "If you're tired of the masturbator/Come on over 2 my neighbourhood" on *Jack U Off* – which provoked Tipper Gore, wife of the American politician Al Gore, to launch the campaign that led to the introduction of "Parental Advisory: Explicit Lyrics" stickers on CDs. Yet his songs also addressed serious social concerns and delved into arcane areas of mysticism and mapped out strange sci-fi visions.

The one subject he seldom sang about was himself. When he did, it tended to be in throwaway lines such as, "I don't wanna die, I'd rather dance my life away."

The paradox of the arrogant, self-assured global superstar, who was at the same time intensely private, was one of the many dualities that drove his art and sustained his sphinx-like mystique. He seldom gave interviews and, when he did, gave little away. His last encounter with journalists before his death was conducted from behind a piano and tape recorders; mobile phones and cameras were forbidden. If he did not like the question, he shook his head and played the tense theme tune from *The Twilight Zone*.

His eccentricities were legendary, from his obsession with the colour purple to his idiosyncratic spelling, using "U" for "you" and "2" for "two" many years before the advent of textspeak. Then there was the battle with his record company over copyright, which led to him appearing at the Brit awards in 1995 with the word "Slave" written on his cheek in felt tip pen. "If I can't do what I want to do, what am I?" he said. He renounced his name and insisted that he should be known as an unpronounceable emblem that he had designed and which had nothing to do with any of the 26 letters of the alphabet, but approximated to a combination of the scientific symbols for male and female.

The gesture was designed to throw his record company, Warner Bros., into confusion but caused consternation in the media too. Broadcasters were unable to pronounce it and newspapers were stymied because the symbol did not exist on any keyboard, and so he was called "The Artist Formerly Known as Prince", sometimes shortened simply to "The Artist". When *The Times* refused to go along with this, and continued to refer to him as Prince, he ordered his British PR company to ban the newspaper from attending his Wembley concert during his 1998 tour of Britain. Nigel Williamson, *The Times* reviewer, bought a ticket from a tout outside the venue and his piece ran on the front page. Despite the review being surprisingly positive under the circumstances, Prince was furious and fired his press officer.

Two years later, he announced that he was resuming the use of his original name, which led critics to refer to him, rather waggishly, as "The Artist Formerly Known as 'The Artist Formerly Known as Prince'". Having regained ownership of his copyright, he then took on the internet, fighting to keep his music offline. "The internet's completely over," he prophesied somewhat prematurely in 2010. "I don't see why I should give my new music to iTunes or anyone else. Anyway, all these computers and digital gadgets just fill your head with numbers and that can't be good for you."

Like Michael Jackson, he used his wealth to create his own fantasy world in which the rules and values of conventional society did not apply. Just as Jackson built his bizarre private theme park, Neverland, the physical manifestation of "Prince world" was Paisley Park, the "fun factory" that he built at Chanhassen, near Minneapolis.

Named after a song of the same title – the lyrics of which declared "Love is the colour this place imparts, there aren't any rules in Paisley Park" – the huge 70,000 sq ft site resembled an industrial complex or a branch of Ikea. Within were his private living quarters, a recording studio, a hair salon, a concert hall and even his own nightclub with velvet circular sofas, a dancefloor, balcony and chrome stairway and two 20ft-high screens showing his own videos.

Several rooms were decorated all in purple with purple toy clowns and music boxes and the famous unpronounceable symbol hanging everywhere. A purple garage housed his purple cars and even the lavatories were purple. The corridors were lined with platinum discs and decorated with murals of the singer. One end of the building housed a permanent team of tailors, employed to make bespoke clothes for his band and girlfriends and, of course, the singer himself.

Dubbed the "peacock of rock" for his use of androgynous costumes to subvert gender stereotypes, he could be clad in motorcycle leathers one minute, and the next in pink feathered shoulder pads. "He can wear lace and still have women chasing after him," said one girlfriend. On stage there might be seven wardrobe changes a night, from matador to white flares to his purple suit. "I get attacked for the clothes I wear. It would be nice if everyone were nude. We could be the same," he said.

The one glaring absence in Paisley Park was a bar; he was teetotal and a vegan and guests reported being offered glasses of water and sliced melon and raw vegetables. However, if the victuals were sparse, spiritual nourishment was in more plentiful supply: there was a "Galaxy Room" for meditation, illuminated by ultraviolet lights and painted with planets, and a library labelled the "Knowledge Room", and filled with Bibles and other religious books reflecting his faith as a Jehovah's Witness.

That such a libidinous figure who wrote and sang some of the raunchiest, most carnal songs in pop – one of which boasted about "23 positions in a one night stand" – should become a devotee of a conservative, even puritanical sect was another of the paradoxes that made Prince such an enigma. "I know those paths of excess, drugs, sex and alcohol – all those experiences can be funky, but they're just paths, a diversion, not the answer," he said.

He was raised as a Seventh Day Adventist but became a Jehovah's Witness in 2001 when he was recruited to the church by Larry Graham, formerly the bass player with Sly and the Family Stone. He began attending meetings at a local Kingdom Hall and a Minneapolis newspaper reported he was knocking on doors asking, "Would you like to talk about God?" and offering copies of *The Watchtower*.

One orthodox Jewish couple found him ringing their doorbell on Yom Kippur, but recognised him and invited him in for a religious discussion. "Sometimes people act surprised, but mostly they're really cool about it," Prince noted.

His faith reportedly led him to refuse hip-replacement surgery because Jehovah's Witnesses do not accept blood transfusions and resulted in his opposition to same-sex marriage: "God came to earth and saw people sticking it wherever and doing it with whatever, and he just cleared it all out. He was, like, 'enough'."

One critic described him becoming a Jehovah's Witness as "the least fashionable religious awakening of all time", but his biographer, Touré, in his 2013 book, *I Would Die 4 U: Why Prince Became an Icon*, attempted to square the carnal/spiritual dichotomy: "Prince intended sexuality to be linked to the worship of God, and he filled his music with classic Christian messages," he wrote.

The multimillionaire rock star was once a quiet, doe-eyed schoolboy. He was born in 1958 in Minneapolis, Minnesota. His father, John Lewis Nelson, was a jazz pianist and used the stage name Prince Rogers; his mother, Mattie Della Shaw, was a jazz singer. His father entered the name Prince Rogers Nelson on the birth certificate "because I wanted him to do everything I wanted to do", but he was known to his friends as "Skipper".

He had a difficult boyhood: he suffered from epilepsy and his parents separated when he was ten. He lived first with his mother, but after fighting with his stepfather he lived briefly with his father, who he watched perform. "It was great, I couldn't believe it," he later recalled. "People were screaming. From then on, I think I wanted to be a musician." While still in his early teens he was given a home by the family of a schoolfriend, André Cymone, with whom he formed his first band – named Grand Central – when he was 15.

By then, he had already stopped growing at 5ft 2in and wore stack heels to compensate throughout his life; according to his first wife, he even wore them around the house. His diminutive stature was further emphasised by his 6ft 8in bodyguard, "Big Chick" Huntsberry, who seldom left his side.

By 1977 Prince was with a group called 94 East and the word was out that the outfit's singer, multi-instrumentalist and writer was destined to be "the next big thing". The bidding war was won by Warner Bros., which granted him artistic control over his recordings, an unprecedented clause in a first contract for an unproven artist who was not even out of his teens.

What followed was often described as Prince's "imperial phase". A string of 1980s albums that included *Dirty Mind, 1999, Purple Rain, Around the World in a Day, Parade, Sign o' the Times* and *Lovesexy* put him in a "triumvirate of titans" alongside Michael Jackson and Madonna as the defining artists of the decade.

Not even being booed and pelted off stage when invited to perform as the support act to the Rolling Stones on their 1981 tour could halt his rise. Among the items hurled at him on stage was a bag of chicken giblets.

What sparked the audience's ire was not clear but perhaps he was just too full-on, even for Stones fans. While Mick Jagger worked his double entendres on *(I Can't Get No) Satisfaction*, Prince sang openly about oral sex and threesomes on libidinous songs such as *Head, Do It All Night* and *Sexuality*. He shrugged it off: "I've always written real explicit. ... I don't think sex is dirty at all. I think it can be described as anything just as soccer can be described." He populated Paisley Park with starlets, backing singers, supermodels, girlfriends and hangers-on, many of whom he seemed to fashion and shape to his own tastes, Warhol-style. Among them were the singers Vanity, Susan Moonsie, Sheila E and Carmen Electra, whose careers he directed and with whom he was romantically involved.

His 1984 touchstone album *Purple Rain* – the opener *Let's Go Crazy* had the pulpit introduction: "Dearly beloved, we are gathered here today to get through this thing called life" – was accompanied by a somewhat absurd semi-autobiographical film of the same name, in which Prince played a rock star known simply as "The Kid". The album spent six months at No 1 in the US and sold more than 13 million copies.

With celebrity came the first signs of his eccentric behaviour, which was not always endearing. He was monosyllabic at the award ceremonies that fêted him and ended his 1985 world tour by announcing that he was retiring to go and "look for the ladder". It was all nonsense, of course, and he continued producing music at a prolific rate, ending the decade by recording the soundtrack for Tim Burton's 1989 film *Batman* and duetting with Madonna on *Like a Prayer*.

The 1990s were less happy, due to the "slave" dispute. However, his fanbase remained huge and loyal, both in the US and in Britain: in 2007, he sold out 21 nights at the O2 Arena in London. In 2014, he rejoined Warner Bros. as the undoubted master.

He was engaged in the mid-1980s to his backing singer Susannah Melvoin, about whom he wrote *Nothing Compares 2 U*. Later, Sinéad O'Connor was not impressed when she met the song's writer. "We had a fist fight," O'Connor alleged. "He summoned me to his house to tell me that he didn't like me swearing in my interviews. I told him to go fuck himself and it went downhill from there. I ended up having to escape from his house at six o'clock in the morning. ... He's a very frightening person. His windows are covered in tin foil because he doesn't like light."

There were relationships with Madonna, Kim Basinger and Susanna Hoffs of the Bangles, whose hit *Manic Monday* was written by Prince. Then in 1996 he married another backing dancer, Mayte Garcia, who was 15 years his junior. She was already pregnant but their son, Boy Gregory, died from Pfeiffer syndrome, a rare defect of the skull, when he was a week old. The couple appeared on *The Oprah Winfrey Show* and maintained a pretence that he was still alive.

Garcia became pregnant again but had a miscarriage and the double loss tore the couple apart. They divorced in 1999. "I think I'm now screwed for life because my first relationship was the most bizarre relationship ever," she said several years later. Their marriage had coincided with him renouncing his name: "Technically, I was married to the Symbol. Our house was full of them, but I just couldn't say the word. I don't think in the whole time we were together I called him anything, which I guess is a bit weird."

In 2001, he married Manuela Testolini, whom he met while she was working for his charitable foundation. They divorced in 2006. There was also a relationship with the interior designer Charlene Friend, who unsuccessfully attempted to sue him for emotional distress in 2003. She claimed to have been an 18-year-old virgin when she met him and in her deposition said: "His staff were not allowed to look at me and I was not allowed to look at them."

Prince confessed to difficulty sleeping at night. "I always wanted to be really famous," he once said. "But now, just like Elvis, I find myself a prisoner of my fame." In recent years he reopened his mansion to host his infamous parties where he would jam with 20 instruments and invite fans from his mailing list.

Unlike Bowie – to whom he sang a tribute in one of his final shows – he had no time to prepare for his end. More prolific than ever, he had recorded four albums in the past 18 months, and was writing a memoir. He kept a vault of unheard songs and said he recorded every day: "If I didn't make music, I'd die."

After recent hospitalisation, he announced that he was going to throw a dance party at Paisley Park with tickets priced at just $10 and dismissed concerns about his health, saying: "Wait a few days before you waste any prayers."

Prince, musician, was born on June 7, 1958. He died of an accidental overdose of painkillers on April 21, 2016, aged 57

ASTRUD GILBERTO

———•———

*Bossa nova singer whose signature track propelled her to
international fame*

The Times, June 6, 2023

Astrud Gilberto did not come from Ipanema and it was never intended that she should sing the song with which she became synonymous.

The "accident" that changed her life happened one day in March 1963 in a New York studio, where her husband João Gilberto was recording an album with the American jazz saxophonist Stan Getz.

The record was destined to become one of the biggest-selling jazz albums of all time and turned the world on to the sound of the bossa nova rhythms of Brazil. Astrud had never sung on a record before and was merely there to support her husband.

One of the songs they planned to record was *Garota de Ipanema.* It had been written by the Brazilian pianist Antônio Carlos Jobim with lyrics in Portuguese by the singer Vinícius de Moraes about a beautiful teenage girl, called Heloísa Pinheiro, whom the two men had admired passing by as they drank at the Veloso Bar on Rio de Janeiro's Ipanema beach.

The lyrics were translated into English by Norman Gimbel, who came up with the song's unforgettable opening lines: "Tall and tan and young and lovely/ The girl from Ipanema goes walking/ And when she passes, each one she passes goes, 'ahhh'."

When the album's producer, Creed Taylor, decided that they should record the song with its English lyrics, he immediately realised he had a problem. João Gilberto spoke no English and neither did any of the other professionals in the studio.

"Astrud was in the control room and Creed said he wanted to get the song done right away and looked around the room," recalled Phil Ramone, who engineered the session. "Astrud volunteered, saying she could sing in English. Creed said, 'Great.' She wasn't a professional singer, but she was the only victim sitting there that night."

She took the lyric sheet with trembling hands and in what she called "a little bit of fate" proceeded to sing in a dreamily romantic and sensual voice that fitted the song like a silk glove. Taylor later said he knew *The Girl from Ipanema* was going to be a smash "from the moment Astrud came in with her little voice and sang with that accent".

Yet when the record was released as a single in 1964, her name did not even appear in the credits, although that changed when *The Girl from Ipanema* became an international hit, won a Grammy award for record of the year and earned Astrud a nomination for best female vocal performance.

The song was also used as the opening track on the 1964 album *Getz/Gilberto* and she sang a second song on the record, *Corcovado (Quiet Nights of Quiet Stars)*.

The album went on to become a million-seller and spent almost two years in the American charts. "It was Astrud Gilberto who made the album a smash hit," Bryan McCann wrote in his 2018 book *Getz/Gilberto*. "Astrud provided the ineffable allure that made the album irresistible."

The men around her were more concerned with arguing about who should take the plaudits for "discovering" her. Taylor, her husband and Jobim all claimed it had been their idea to get her to sing. So did Getz. "She was just a housewife and I put her on that record because I wanted *The Girl from Ipanema* sung in English, which João couldn't do. That was a lucky break for her," he claimed with more than a whiff of condescension.

The remark rankled the singer. "The funny thing is that after my success, stories abound as to Stan Getz or Creed Taylor having 'discovered me', when in fact, nothing is further from the truth," she said. "I guess it made them look important to have been the one that had the 'wisdom' to recognise potential in my singing. I suppose I should feel flattered by the importance that they lend to this, but I can't help but feel annoyed that they resorted to lying."

Every bit as galling was that she went unpaid for her definitive version of what is said to be the second-most recorded song in popular music behind the Beatles' *Yesterday*. Frank Sinatra, Amy Winehouse and Madonna are among the hundreds of singers to record *The Girl from Ipanema*, which has also featured in numerous films and television programmes, including *The Simpsons* and *The Sopranos*.

In the 2003 book *Bossa Nova: The Story of the Brazilian Music That Seduced the World*, the author Ruy Castro revealed that João Gilberto got $23,000 for his work on the album while Getz pocketed a sum estimated to be not far short of $1 million, with which he bought himself a 23-room mansion in Irvington, New York. Astrud earned only the musicians' union scale rate for a night of session work – a paltry $120 – and there is some doubt as to whether even that was ever actually paid. By the time *The Girl from Ipanema* became a hit, she had also separated from her husband, who was having an affair with a young student, later to find fame as the singer Miúcha.

Astrud toured America with Getz and his band but it was a difficult time. "Besides being in the midst of a separation and dealing with the responsibilities of being a single mother and a brand new, demanding career, I was also coping with being on my own for the first time in my life, in a foreign country, travelling with a child, having financial difficulties and totally naive," she said. Additionally, she suffered from chronic stage fright and attended classes at the Stella Adler School of Acting in New York to combat her fear.

The press reported that she had an affair with Getz during the tour and she was subjected to the objectification that was the lot of too many female singers at the time. One reviewer wrote that she "evoked every straight man's daydream of an exotic, submissive woman in a bikini". Yet she proved to be remarkably resilient and after leaving Getz's band she built a successful career. She made her solo debut in London in 1965 and over the next six years made eight albums, earning another Grammy nomination. She also worked with such jazz luminaries as the pianist Gil Evans, the saxophonist Stanley Turrentine and Quincy Jones, although she insisted she was not a jazz singer. "I've been told that my phrasing is jazz-influenced but I prefer simplicity," she said.

It was perhaps her reluctance to be pigeonholed that led her in 1977 to record a disco version of the song that made her famous on an album titled *That Girl from Ipanema*. Replacing the lilting rhythm of the original with a banging dancefloor beat was undeniably crass, but it did not excuse the way she was mistreated once again by the record industry. "It was the second instance she would record the song, and never be paid for it," said her son Marcelo Gilberto, who played in her band for 15 years and acted as her manager. "She believed in people and was trusting. They took advantage of her good nature, her trust and her desire to make music."

She is survived by her son Marcelo, from her marriage to Gilberto, and by her younger son, Gregory Lasorsa, a guitarist in her band, from her second marriage to Nicholas Lasorsa. Both marriages ended in divorce.

Although she was an international star, oddly the one country where she went uncelebrated was her native Brazil. The reasons for the hostility towards her were never entirely clear but she made no secret of the fact that what she called the "harsh criticism and unwarranted sarcasm" of the Brazilian media left her "very hurt". She was so upset that in 1965 she declared that she would never perform in the country of her birth again. She kept her promise and declined to attend the opening ceremony of the 2016 Olympic Games in Rio de Janeiro at which *The Girl from Ipanema* was played. After divorcing Gilberto, she lived for the rest of her life in the United States.

Having announced her retirement in 2002, she spent her time painting, studying philosophy and campaigning for animal rights, but was reported to lead a reclusive existence.

She was born Astrud Evangelina Weinert in 1940 in Salvador, Brazil, more than 750 miles north from Ipanema. Her Brazilian mother Evangelina Neves Lobo was a teacher who sang and played the violin and the Portuguese mandolin (known as the bandolim). Her German-born father Fritz Wilhelm Weinert was a professor of languages at Bahia State University. She grew up fluent in German, French, Italian, Spanish, Portuguese – and, of course, English.

In her teens she hung out with a group of Brazilian singers and songwriters that included Carlos Lyra, Roberto Menescal, Ronaldo

Bôscoli and Nara Leão, who introduced her to João Gilberto. He was a decade older than her and they married when she was 19.

Although she sometimes sang at home while her husband was composing on the guitar, she expressed no ambition to sing professionally and admitted that at the time she was content to play the role of a devoted Brazilian housewife. By the time of their marriage her husband was already one of the brightest stars in Brazilian music.

The year before he had arranged what is widely acknowledged as the first bossa nova song, *Chega de Saudade* (or *No More Blues*), for the singer Elizbeth Cardoso and swiftly followed with his own debut solo recording, which became a bossa nova landmark.

The popularity of his gentle rhythms spread to North America and he was making his debut along with other Brazilian artists at New York's Carnegie Hall in 1962 when he was introduced to Getz. The idea of fusing Brazilian bossa nova with American jazz was born and four months later the two men got together in the studio to record the *Getz/Gilberto* album.

The success of *The Girl from Ipanema* meant that Astrud was immediately signed up to perform her hit song in the 1964 MGM film *Get Yourself a College Girl*, appearing alongside the Animals and the Dave Clark Five. Stand-out moments in her later career included singing with George Michael and a "virtual duet" with Frank Sinatra, when their two versions of *Fly Me to the Moon* were edited together for the soundtrack of the 2003 romcom – *Down with Love*.

Even in her old age, in the public's imagination she remained the girl from Ipanema, the sound of her voice able in an instant to banish the cares of the world by conjuring visions of a land of suntanned, youthful bliss.

Astrud Gilberto, "the girl from Ipanema", was born on March 29, 1940. She died on June 5, 2023, aged 83

DAVID BOWIE

Rock superstar who had a profound impact on popular music and culture during 50 years of continuous artistic innovation

The Times, January 12, 2016

To describe David Bowie as one of pop music's most influential figures only begins to hint at his significance in the cultural firmament. With his constant shapeshifting, endless innovation and restless determination always to look forward rather than back, he was often described as a chameleon.

Yet he was more than that, for a chameleon changes in order to blend in with its surroundings. Bowie spent the greatest part of his career dictating trends and creating new, avant-garde landscapes in music, fashion and popular culture for others to follow. From the cosmic folk of *Space Oddity*, through the glam rock of *Ziggy Stardust* and the blue-eyed funk of *Young Americans*, to the electronic dance experimentation of *Heroes* and the synth-pop of *Ashes to Ashes*, his music changed the fabric of pop music and challenged his fans to keep pace with his ability to embrace new sounds.

When it was put to him that these frequently brilliant artistic metamorphoses were the work of a genius, he self-deprecatingly joked that it was "more a case of attention deficit disorder", putting his creative ingenuity down to an inability to concentrate on one thing for any length of time.

In truth, this refusal to repeat himself was signalled in one of his earliest songs, *Changes*, in which the 24-year-old Bowie had sung: *"Turn and face the strange ch-ch-changes, /Oh look out now you rock'n' rollers /Pretty soon now you're gonna get older."*

Several years later he spoke of a desire to make music "so incredibly uncompromising" that he would have no fans left. In that, at least, he failed and perhaps his greatest achievement was that he not only managed to make cutting-edge art that was constantly evolving, but also succeeded in taking a mainstream audience with him. Over the course of his career, it was estimated that he sold almost 150 million albums.

His ambition, he once said, was to make pop music a "wider receiver" that could "incorporate ideas from other arts". His success in this aim was evident in 2013, when the V&A Museum in London curated an exhibition dedicated to his career containing more than 300 objects – spanning handwritten lyrics, stage costumes, fashion, photography, film, music videos and set designs.

The breadth of his impact was evident in the list of those who paid tribute to his personal influence: his fellow musicians were joined by Tony Blair, David Cameron, JK Rowling, Whoopi Goldberg, the British astronaut Tim Peake and even the German Foreign Office, which thanked him for "helping to bring down the wall" and posted a link to his song *Heroes*.

Written while he was living and working in Berlin in the late 1970s, the lyric told of love across the brutality of the East-West divide: *"I can remember standing by the wall,/And the guns, shot above our heads/And we kissed, as though nothing could fall /And the shame, was on the other side."*

Among the most theatrical of all rock stars, he adopted a string of flamboyant alter egos including his most famous creation, Ziggy Stardust, named after a tailor's shop and the Stardust Cowboy – and whom he described as "a cross between Nijinksy and Woolworths".

Bowie's first appearance as Ziggy on *Top of the Pops*, dressed as an androgynous alien with orange hair and outrageous make-up, and with his arm draped around guitarist Mick Ronson, was the defining moment in the emergence of glam rock as a teenage fashion. It launched thousands of Ziggy-lookalikes on every high street.

With its self-referential rock'n'roll theme and blurring of fiction and reality, the accompanying album – *Ziggy Stardust and the Spiders from Mars* – has since been hailed as "the first postmodern pop record".

When he announced the death of Ziggy from the stage at the Hammersmith Odeon in 1973, fans mourned as if it was a genuine bereavement. Bowie hosted a post-show retirement-party-cum-wake at the Café Royal, attended by Mick and Bianca Jagger, Paul and

Linda McCartney, Lou Reed and Barbra Streisand. More sinister was the persona he adopted three years later when, taking a line from the title song of his *Station to Station* album, he became the Thin White Duke: a character who had a dangerous fascination with Nazism. Describing Adolf Hitler as "one of the first rock stars", he opined that "Britain could benefit from a fascist leader" and argued that "people have always responded with greater efficiency under a regimental leadership".

In April 1976, he was detained by border police in eastern Europe and questioned about his possession of Nazi memorabilia. The following month, looking pale and emaciated due to the ravages of his cocaine addiction, he appeared to give a Nazi salute at Victoria Station from an open-topped Mercedes. Together with some equally unfortunate anti-immigrant comments by Eric Clapton, his pro-fascist remarks led other musicians and grass-roots activists to set up Rock Against Racism. Forced into a hasty retreat by the outcry, he blamed his comments on the cocaine that had left him "out of my mind, totally, completely crazed".

By 1977, he was carefully insisting in interviews that he was totally "apolitical" and – apart from a cryptic message of opposition to Scottish independence at the time of the 2014 referendum – he eschewed, for the most part, further political comment throughout the rest of his career.

The look and character of the Thin White Duke had, in part, been borrowed from his first major film role, playing an alien in Nicolas Roeg's *The Man Who Fell to Earth*. The diversity of his musical persona was matched by the versatility that he showed in his parallel screen career: prominent roles included playing a prisoner-of-war in *Merry Christmas, Mr Lawrence*; a goblin king in *Labyrinth*; Pontius Pilate in *The Last Temptation of Christ*; an FBI agent in *Twin Peaks: Fire Walk with Me*; and Andy Warhol in Julian Schnabel's biopic of Jean-Michel Basquiat. He also spent a year in the title role of the Broadway production of *The Elephant Man*.

His shapeshifting as an artist was reflected, too, in the gender-bending of his personal life. There were a string of early girlfriends, including the dancer Hermione Farthingale, who was "the girl with the mousy hair" in *Life on Mars,* and Mary Finnigan, to whom he was first lodger and then lover. Finnigan organised a famous music festival in a Beckenham park in 1969 at which he played; it was later commemorated in his song *Memory of a Free Festival.*

In 1970, he married the 20-year-old Angie Barnett, a brash American who grew up in Cyprus and went to a Swiss finishing school. She claimed that, on their wedding day, they had enjoyed a three-in-a-bed romp; she gave birth a year later to Bowie's son, whom they named Zowie, but who is now known as the film director Duncan Jones. Bowie had by then already posed dressed as a woman on the cover of his album *The Man Who Sold the World,* and in 1972 – just as he was launching his androgynous Ziggy Stardust persona – he used a *Melody Maker* interview to announce that he was gay.

Some suspected it was a publicity stunt designed to shock prevailing moral prejudices, and he clouded the issue in later years by first confirming that he was bisexual and then issuing a quasi-denial in which he said he had always been "a closet heterosexual". Finnigan also claimed that Bowie was more into women than men, and that "homosexuality with him was more opportunist and contrived".

Yet, according to Angie Bowie in her salacious 1993 memoir *Backstage Passes – Life On The Wild Side With David Bowie,* she and her husband operated a wildly promiscuous open marriage and swung both ways as "the best-known bisexual couple ever".

She reported that they had both enjoyed affairs with the singer Dana Gillespie and that she had once found Bowie in bed with Mick Jagger. She also claimed that he had seduced Bianca Jagger. "David made a virtual religion of slipping the Lance of Love into almost everyone around him," she wrote. "He did a lot of cavorting but I was not going to be humiliated, so I made sure I did plenty of cavorting myself because that meant the playing field was levelled," she said later. By the mid-1970s, the couple were starting to lead separate lives, both with dangerously out-of-control drug habits, while their son was largely brought up by nannies before being sent to board at Gordonstoun.

They divorced in 1980; she left the marriage with a £500,000 settlement and a ten-year gagging clause. She did not fight for custody and remained bitter towards her ex-husband, whom she accused of "poisoning" her son against her. Only days before Bowie's death, she gave an interview in which she claimed that listening to his music made her "nauseous".

Over the years he was equally uncomplimentary about his first wife, claiming that their relationship had been like "living with a blowtorch" and that she had "as much insight into the human condition as a walnut, and a self-interest that would make Narcissus green with envy".

He married – more happily – the Somali-American model Iman Abdulmajid in 1992; his son acted as best man. Their daughter, Alexandria "Lexi" Zahra Jones, was born in 2000 and Bowie took pains to be a more dutiful father second time around. "I don't want to start doing what I unfortunately did with my son, inasmuch as I spent an awful lot of time on tour when he was a young child. I really missed those years, and I know he did too." Her birth also persuaded him to give up his 60-a-day smoking habit and take up meditation. He kept his main home in New York City but also owned properties in London and Sydney.

Always a master of controlling his image and manipulating his mystique, he grew increasingly private – even reclusive – in his mature years. He refused to give interviews or promote his records and abandoned the concert stage; his last tour took place in 2003 and his final performance came in 2006.

There were occasional guest appearances on recordings by other artists and even rarer public sightings – he was seen as a proud father in 2009 at the premiere of *Moon*, his son's debut as a film director.

Rumours emerged of further health issues following surgery in 2004 for an acutely blocked coronary artery. He was said to be enjoying the simple pleasures of being with his family; watching box sets of his favourite TV shows, which reportedly included *Downton Abbey*; and reading the novels of Martin Amis and Ian McEwan. *The Times* was his daily newspaper of choice. Most believed that he had retired from the fray for good, although his absence only seemed to enhance interest in him.

Out of the blue, in 2013, his website announced the imminent release of *The Next Day* – his first album in ten years. No explanation for why he had decided to return was offered. The record's producer, Tony Visconti, described as Bowie's "voice on Earth", talked to the media on his behalf.

His surprise return generated something close to hysteria, with at least one front-page headline hailing "the comeback of the century". Five-star reviews followed and the album went straight to No 1 – the first time Bowie had topped the charts in 20 years.

Three years later came another flurry of unannounced activity with an off-Broadway musical and another album, *Blackstar*. Released days before his death, the record included a song titled *Lazarus*, which Visconti – one of the few who knew that Bowie had received a diagnosis of cancer 18 months ago – described as his "parting gift" to the world.

The video for the song featured a blindfolded, fragile-looking Bowie lying in bed singing – "Look up here, I'm in heaven, I've got scars that can't be seen." It seemed that he was stage-managing his career right up until his final departure. "His death was no different from his life – a work of art," Visconti wrote on Facebook.

David Robert Jones was born in 1947 in Brixton, south London. His father, John, had served with the 8th Army in north Africa during the Second World War; he had a penchant for the bottle and gambling, and ran a failed piano bar before taking an administrative job with the Dr Barnardo's children's charity. His mother, Peggy, who had a son by a previous relationship, worked as a cinema usherette and had allegedly been a supporter of Oswald Mosley's Blackshirts in the 1930s. Whether she had any influence on her son's later flirtation with fascism is not known. She did, however, reveal in a 1985 interview that, as a child, David had taken an unusual interest in her cosmetics bag, and at the age of three had daubed himself in eyeliner and face powder.

Mental illness ran in the family. Bowie's half-brother, Terry Burns, was committed to a psychiatric hospital, from which he escaped in 1985 and lay on the tracks in the path of an oncoming train. Bowie did not attend the funeral but left a wreath and a card, saying: "You've seen more things than we could imagine but all these moments will be lost, like tears washed away by the rain."

Themes of alienation were prominent in his songwriting, which he admitted was his form of therapy. "Most of my family have been to an analyst," he said. "My parents went, my brothers and sisters went and my aunts and uncles and cousins. They ended up in a much worse state. I thought I'd write my problems out."

When he was six, the family moved to the leafier suburb of Bromley, Kent, where he enjoyed a relatively comfortable lower middle-class upbringing. It provided the perfect paradigm of mundanity for his future escape. He failed his 11-plus and went to Bromley Technical High School, where he fell in love with the early rock'n'roll records of Little Richard and Elvis Presley.

Teaching himself to play the ukulele and tea-chest bass, he joined a skiffle group called George and the Dragons – led by George Underwood, who remained a lifelong friend despite punching Bowie in the left eye during a fight over a girl. Bowie needed a series of operations to save his sight, leaving him with a dilated pupil, which made it seem as though his eyes were different colours.

By the time he left school in 1963 with only O-level passes in art and woodwork to show for his education, he had added first guitar and piano to his repertoire – and then saxophone, after his half-brother had introduced him to the jazz records of John Coltrane.

The standard R&B of his first bands, which included the Kon-Rads, the King Bees, the Mannish Boys and the Lower Third, offered little hint of what was to come. By 1966, he had gone solo and changed his name – after the American frontiersman who died at the Alamo and gave his name to the popular bowie knife.

Throwing himself into the bohemian world of London hippiedom, he took lessons in mime and dance from Lindsay Kemp at the London Dance Centre; flirted with Buddhism; developed an interest in aliens and UFOs; and set up an "Arts Lab" at the Three Tuns pub "deep in the heart of – God forbid – Beckenham".

After several false starts, including an early novelty single, *The Laughing Gnome*, on which he sounded uncannily like Anthony Newley, his first hit came in the summer of 1969 with *Space Oddity*, which was released to coincide with the first *Apollo* Moon landing.

It was followed by the album *Hunky Dory*, with songs such as *Life on Mars*. Then came Ziggy Stardust – and nothing was ever the same again.

The next album was intended to be a concept album based on George Orwell's *1984*, a plan that was thwarted by the author's estate, although several of the songs appeared on the chart-topping album *Diamond Dogs*; he also produced a concert album, *David Live*, but he was by now so strung out on drugs that he later suggested it should have been titled "David Bowie Is Alive and Well and Living Only in Theory".

After moving to America, there came another change of direction as he melodramatically announced that rock music was dead and embraced black dance music on *Young Americans*. The album included *Fame*, co-written with John Lennon; it gave Bowie his first US No 1.

While managers, middlemen and record companies grew rich on the back of his record sales, Bowie himself was close to bankruptcy despite his success. Like many of his contemporaries, he had signed contracts early in his career without reading them and a long legal battle ensued as he tried to rid himself of the leeches.

It provided a lesson that he never forgot. In later years his business affairs were managed carefully and, in 1997, he became the first rock star to launch shares in his back catalogue with the "Bowie Bond", which generated him £37.5 million. *The Sunday Times* Rich List in 2015 calculated his worth at £120 million.

To help kick a drug habit that by 1976 had grown "astronomic", he left America to take up residence in tax-friendly Switzerland (another example of his newly-acquired financial acuity). The change of view unleashed a prolific period of creativity. Working with Brian Eno and recording in Berlin in a studio next to the infamous wall, he came up with a trilogy of dark, densely synthesised albums in *Low*, *Heroes* and *Lodger*. Ever the shapeshifter, he also collaborated with Bing Crosby on *The Little Drummer Boy* and narrated a version of Prokofiev's *Peter and the Wolf*.

The 1980s brought more hits and changes of direction with *Ashes to Ashes*, *Let's Dance* and a duet with Mick Jagger, *Dancing in the Street*, before he took the surprising decision at the end of the decade to dissolve his solo career and form the band Tin Machine. Less surprisingly, he soon found group democracy painfully restrictive and by 1993 had resumed his solo career.

Subsequent projects included composing the soundtrack for the television adaptation of *Buddha of Suburbia* (written by his friend Hanif Kureishi) and an excursion into late 1990s dance, techno and drum'n'bass styles.

Bowie reportedly turned down an appointment to CBE and a knighthood. He said his main regret in life was that he had never written a book. Asked how he hoped to be remembered, he replied: "Nice trousers, I think I'm supposed to say. Or silly haircuts. Oh fuck, don't do this to me."

David Bowie, singer and actor, was born on January 8, 1947. He died of cancer on January 10, 2016, aged 69

KIRSTY MACCOLL

Singer who wrote scathingly witty songs about the inadequacies of men, but found fulfilment in the joyousness of Latin music

The Times, December 20, 2000

Kirsty MacColl was a reluctant pop star. She made only five albums in a career of more than two decades and worked in a variety of styles. Her most recent records were heavily influenced by her love of Cuban music, but in everything she did she brought a much needed dash of wit and urbanity to the art of popular song – leading U2's Bono to call her "the Noel Coward of her generation".

Though she was the daughter of the stern traditional folk singer Ewan MacColl, she did not grow up with her father, who left her mother Jean soon after she was born. For years she denied that his strong musical personality had had any influence on her, but eventually paid him an indirect tribute: "I think I did learn something from him, which was that you can have a successful career as a songwriter regardless of pop fashion. If you've got good songs, it doesn't matter if you've got a crap haircut."

Dropping out of school, she signed to Stiff Records as a 17-year-old in 1978, when the label was in the vanguard of the punk and New Wave explosion. She nearly had a hit single the following year with the first self-written release *They Don't Know*, but somehow missed out. It was later taken into the charts by Tracey Ullman's inferior version.

She had to wait until 1981 for her first hit single with the memorably witty *There's a Guy Works Down the Chip Shop Swears He's Elvis*, a song that established her droll style. "Vitriol and misery have always been far easier to express in song," she said some years later. "People seem to think that humour implies you're not serious about the music, but I don't buy that."

In 1984 she married the producer Steve Lillywhite, with whom she was to have two children. One of the first records he produced for her was a version of Billy Bragg's *A New England*, a Top 20 hit in early 1985. There was demand for her as a backing singer, too, on records by the Rolling Stones, Simple Minds, Robert Plant, the Smiths, Talking Heads, Van Morrison and Morrissey. But it was a collaboration with Shane MacGowan and his band the Pogues, that produced her biggest hit, *Fairytale of New York*, which reached No 2 at Christmas 1987.

She admitted to suffering from writer's block for long periods, but professed herself untroubled by them and advised others that "if you've got nothing to say, it's better just to shut up". She also suffered acutely from stage fright, and for most of the 1980s she refused to perform.

Yet her stop-start career gathered new impetus with two well-received albums in quick succession around the turn of the decade, when she also returned to the stage to sing. Her 1989 album *Kite* included the hit singles *Free World* and *Days* (a version of the old Kinks song). Two years later *Electric Landlady* found her co-writing with Johnny Marr of the Smiths and Mark E Nevin of Fairground Attraction.

The album also included *My Affair*, a song recorded in New York with top Cuban session musicians. She described the experience as "the most fun I'd ever had in a recording studio", and it established her future musical direction. She made her first visit to Cuba in 1992 and began taking lessons in Spanish. At her language classes she met a teacher who also gave her Portuguese lessons in return for lodgings in her spacious Ealing home.

When she and Lillywhite separated she first made what she called her "sad divorce album", *Titanic Days* (1994), after which she made increasingly regular trips to Cuba, continuing her love affair with Latin music. "I was completely consumed by it because it was so outside my own upbringing and different to everything else you hear," she later said.

When Virgin Records released her greatest hits album *Galore* in 1995, it featured a picture of her in a Castro-style military cap lighting a huge Cuban cigar with an American dollar bill. Her name became a fixture at Cuban Solidarity Campaign benefits, and she returned from her regular visits to Havana with suitcases full of records. Her interest in Latin rhythms also soon extended to Brazil, which she visited.

These trips eventually led to her last album *Tropical Brainstorm*, released in 2000. She toyed with the idea of working with Latin musicians and attempting to produce an authentic Cuban album in the vein of the Grammy-winning Buena Vista Social Club, but instead opted to fuse the salsa rhythms she had heard on her travels with her own typically quirky and very British style of songwriting. "It's an Anglo-Latin hybrid pop record that reflects some of the things I love about Cuban and Brazilian music," she said on its release in April.

In recent months she had been working on a six-part series on Cuban music which she was due to present for BBC Radio 2. When the programmes were finished at the beginning of December she took her children to Mexico for a two-week scuba-diving holiday. It was there that she was killed in an accident.

Kirsty MacColl, singer and songwriter, was born on October 10, 1959. She died in a boating accident in Mexico on December 18, 2000, aged 41

VANGELIS

Reclusive, Oscar-winning composer who disdained the world of showbusiness his music propelled him into

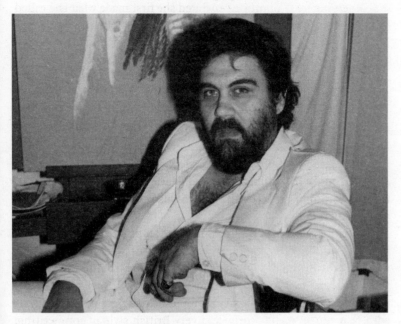

The Times, May 20, 2022

When Vangelis was four, he opened the lid of his parents' grand piano and placed nails, chains, cutlery and other alien objects on the strings. It was not the whim of a recalcitrant child but a conscious attempt to experiment with the sounds he could coax from the instrument.

"I drove that piano crazy, but I never smashed the strings or broke anything," he said. "It was all for the sound." It was the beginning of a lifelong fascination with sonic innovation as a one-man orchestra using a vast array of synthesisers, sequencers and modulators to conjure undulating waves of sound.

Most famously of all, it led to the pulsating synth beats and soaring melody that accompanied the opening, slow-motion sequence of a 1981 film showing a group of athletes running on a Scottish beach. The piece of music was officially called *Titles* but the world came to know it as *Chariots of Fire* after the film's own title, and it was an enduring if unofficial anthem for the Olympic Games.

The film, directed by Hugh Hudson, told the story of Eric Liddell, the Scottish runner who would not race on Sunday because of his Christian faith, and Harold Abrahams, the Jewish athlete who ran to overcome prejudice. Vangelis's majestic theme perfectly reflected the nobility of the two men, who refused to compromise their principles as they trained for the 1924 Olympics. "The story of these runners is full of magnificent and profound messages and that's what inspired me," the composer said.

The theme topped the American charts and was a Top 20 hit in Britain, and the score won Vangelis an Academy award in 1982. Not that he was there to receive it – when his win was announced, he was several thousand miles away, asleep at his home in Marble Arch, London. With characteristic disdain for showbusiness and the cult of celebrity, he had refused to attend, claiming a fear of flying. Offered a first-class Atlantic crossing on Queen Elizabeth 2, he turned that down too.

When he was told he had beaten John Williams's score for *Raiders of the Lost Ark* to emerge as the winner, he denounced the idea that music was a "competition". His theme was just "another piece of music", he insisted.

Indeed, at times he seemed resentful that the ubiquity of *Chariots of Fire* risked overshadowing much of the rest of his prolific output, which encompassed solo albums, ballet scores, a choral symphony and soundtracks for another dozen movies, including, most hauntingly, Ridley Scott's sci-fi dystopia *Blade Runner*.

With the film set in a sinister future version of Los Angeles, Vangelis's soundscape of bleakly malevolent synth passages mixed with lush ambient interludes was arguably even more influential on electronic film composition than *Chariots of Fire*. "It has turned out to be a very prophetic film – we're living in a kind of *Blade Runner* world now," Vangelis noted in 2005.

Other notable film scores included the Palme d'Or-winning *Missing* (1982), directed by his compatriot Costa-Gavras; the Mel Gibson and Anthony Hopkins drama *The Bounty* (1984) and Roman Polanski's *Bitter Moon* (1992).

The movies he turned down were even more numerous. "Half of the films I see don't need music. It sounds like something stuffed in," he said.

He guarded his privacy fiercely and in later years rarely appeared in public. Burly and bearded, with a mane of hair and benign green eyes, a journalist who was granted a rare interview likened him to Aslan from CS Lewis's *The Chronicles of Narnia*.

Fame, he protested, was the enemy of creativity and success was "sweet and treacherous". Once he had found it, he spent the rest of his life trying to "get out of it", noting that you could sell a million records and feel a failure but that you could sell nothing at all and feel artistically satisfied. "I compose for myself. I don't want to be successful. I want to be me," he said.

His dislike of the music industry and the star system was palpable. "The more successful you become, the more you become a product of something that generates a lot of money, instead of being able to move forward freely and do what you wish," he said. "Freedom is a need of every human being, which the system methodically fights against."

He lived variously in Athens, Paris and London and was married at least twice, to Veronique Skawinska, a French photographer, and to Vana Veroutis, a Greek singer who appeared on some of his recordings. There were no children. "Because of the amount of travelling I do and the nonsense of the music business, I couldn't take care of a child," he said.

He was born Evangelos Odysseas Papathanassiou in 1943 in Agria, on Greece's Aegean coast, and grew up in Athens. His father, Odysseas Papathanassiou, was a property magnate who had been an amateur sprinter in his youth. He died shortly before *Chariots of Fire* was released and Vangelis dedicated the music to him.

School was "awful and I didn't learn anything", although he later enjoyed studying painting at the Athens School of Fine Arts.

Youthful music lessons were also a flop and when asked by his tutor to perform, he played from memory while pretending to sight-read. Musical notation was a skill he never acquired and when he composed a piece for a 400-piece orchestra and choir, he recorded the composition and then handed the disc to the conductor, who had it transcribed.

"People ask how I can compose if I can't read or write music but you can't teach someone to be a composer. Great musicians are not great because they study. They are great because they are great," he said, not unreasonably.

By 1963 he had formed a group, the Formynx, playing ballads and Beatles covers, with Vangelis playing the Hammond organ. They scored hit records in Greece but the arrival of a military junta in 1967 led him to head for London.

Along the way he became stranded in Paris by work permit problems, a transport strike and the industrial and student unrest of 1968. While stuck in France he formed Aphrodite's Child with the singer Demis Roussos and had a hit with *Rain and Tears*. Not for the last time, he balked at its popularity. "We had a million seller, then another. I hate it if a project I am involved in and don't like becomes successful. I did some things I couldn't bear at the time," he later said.

The group went on to make the psychedelic double album *666*, based on the Book of Revelation and which has since become a cult classic. At first their record company refused to release it on the grounds that it was uncommercial and the album sat ignored in the vaults. On the first anniversary of its completion, Vangelis threw a birthday party. "I booked the studio in which we had made the record, bought a big chocolate cake and a candle and invited friends and journalists to a party, where we listened to the album."

Among those in attendance was Salvador Dalí, who declared it to be a work of genius. Eventually the record company acceded and *666* was belatedly released at the end of 1971. Yet by then Vangelis had grown tired of waiting and Aphrodite's Child had broken up.

Three years later he moved to London, where he built his own recording studio and recorded a series of solo works, including 1975's extraordinary *Heaven and Hell*, on which his synthesisers combined with the voices of the English Chamber Choir and Jon Anderson, the lead singer with Yes. Invited to replace Rick Wakeman in Yes, he declined, although he went on to record five albums with Anderson as the duo Jon and Vangelis.

He was approached to score *Chariots of Fire* after Hudson heard the music he had composed for a documentary directed by Frédéric Rossif. Around the same time he was also asked by the astronomer Carl Sagan to provide the music for his TV series *Cosmos*. His interest in space led to a long association with both Nasa and the European Space Agency (ESA), which adopted his music for various missions. In 2018 the ESA broadcast into space a musical tribute he had composed on the death of Stephen Hawking and his final album, *Juno to Jupiter* (2021), was inspired by Nasa's Juno probe and featured recordings of its launch and the sounds it had picked up in space. He also had a minor planet named after him.

His compositional method was a mix of scientific discipline and new age mysticism. He believed that "music is implanted in us all and we are all part of a collective memory". To tap into it he emptied his mind of all thoughts. "Nothing is pre-programmed. Composition, orchestration, musical direction and recording happens simultaneously. If you ask me how, the answer is I do not know. But I use the first impression which comes into my head. I've done all my film scores like this and it's a very liberating way to work."

Accused of having plagiarised the main theme from *Chariots of Fire*, he set up his banks of synthesisers in the courtroom and showed his "simultaneous" methods to the judge. He won the case. "Every time a sound comes it is always instinctive," he said. "I don't have any preconceived ideas, plans or construction. I follow this flow until the music doesn't need me any more."

Vangelis, electronic composer, was born on March 29, 1943. He died of heart failure on May 17, 2022, aged 79

CHUCK BERRY

———●———

Founding father of rock'n'roll who lit the flame of teenage rebellion in 1950s America and was himself never far from trouble

The Times, March 20, 2017

One of the greatest testaments to Chuck Berry's status as the progenitor of rock'n'roll occurred in the 1985 film *Back to the Future*, in which Marty McFly, played by Michael J Fox, travels back in time and performs a futuristic vision of popular music at a 1955 high-school hop.

Robert Zemeckis realised that if they wanted to represent convincingly the moment in which rock'n'roll guitar-playing was born, one song fitted the bill above all others – Berry's signature tune *Johnny B Goode*, performed by Fox complete with the guitarist's trademark "duck walk".

John Lennon made a similar point more succinctly. "If you tried to give rock and roll another name, you might call it Chuck Berry." Keith Richards concurred: "I've stolen every lick he ever played."

On songs such as *Roll Over Beethoven, Sweet Little Sixteen, No Particular Place to Go* and, above all, *Johnny B Goode*, Berry created a set of riffs that remain the core building blocks of rock guitar-playing. He combined them with smart, sassy, sly and playful lyrics that painted incisive vignettes of teenage life. The result was a series of perfect three-minute pop masterpieces built around themes of fast cars, erotic discovery and escape from parental authority, which not only captured the mood of 1950s American youth but defined the spirit of teenage rebellion the world over for generations to come.

As he boasted in the title of one of his hits, Berry was also a "brown-eyed handsome man" with a devilish twinkle in his eye that women across the racial divide found irresistible. It was an appeal that, in his younger days, often led him into trouble.

As musical tastes changed, the hits dried up. The pop world of the 1960s was the province of youth and Berry was approaching 40 by the time the Beatles and the Rolling Stones emerged. Both groups paid homage to him and covered his songs, yet they were also his nemesis by unintentionally making Berry sound "old hat".

With the exception of the playground innuendo of *My Ding-a-Ling,* which unexpectedly returned him to No 1 in Britain and America in 1972, there would be no more chart entries. By 1979 he had stopped bothering to make new records and made his money from touring, demanding that promoters paid him in suitcases full of cash before he took the stage – a practice that subsequently led to a prison sentence for tax evasion.

If he spent his later career resting on his laurels, he could afford to do so. While other more ephemeral hit-makers of the 1950s were forgotten and faded into obscurity, Berry's influence was profound, permanent and ineradicable. It would be an exaggeration to say that without him there would have been no Beatles or Rolling Stones, and no Jimi Hendrix or Led Zeppelin, but they would at the very least have sounded considerably less potent.

Yet he remained an enigma. He was described as "the least biddable man in showbusiness" and his life was conflict-strewn. "Every 15 years it seems I make a big mistake," he noted in a candid autobiography. Most of them were big enough to involve custodial sentences.

His first taste of prison life came when he was still in his teens after he went on a crime spree in Kansas City with two friends, robbing stores at gunpoint and hijacking a car. At the height of his success in 1960 he was sentenced to five years after having sexual intercourse with a 14-year-old waitress, Janice Escalante, and illegally transporting her across state lines to work at his nightclub in St Louis, Missouri.

He appealed successfully on the grounds that the trial judge had made racist comments that had prejudiced the jury against him. The cultural historian Martha Bayles later wrote that Berry's "brown-eyed handsome man" image, which attracted so many white female fans, had caused outrage in the segregated South, provoking a "lynch-mob atmosphere surrounding his arrest".

A retrial resulted in a shorter prison sentence and he served two years, re-emerging in late 1963, just as Beatlemania was about to go into overdrive. It was a critical break in the momentum of his career.

A third prison sentence for tax evasion followed in 1979. Somewhat more embarrassing was the suspended sentence he received in 1990 after police found incriminating videotapes at his home, taken with a camera he had installed in the ladies' toilet at a restaurant he owned in Missouri. A class action settlement with 59 women cost him an estimated $1.2 million, with additional legal fees.

Despite the times when romantically he preferred the road less travelled, he was married to Themetta (known as "Toddy"), for almost 70 years. They had four children: Darlin Ingrid Berry-Clay, Melody Exes Berry-Eskridge, Aloha Isa Lei Berry and Charles Berry, sometimes known as Chuck Jr.

Ingrid and Charles performed in his band at the monthly concerts he gave at the Blueberry Hill club in St Louis. The basement dancehall where he played was named the Duck Room, after his famous stage walk, which he first performed in 1959 because his suit was creased yet threw his audience into instant rapture.

He lived for more than half a century on an estate outside St Louis that he named Berry Park and which he designed as a private version of the Whites-only country clubs from which he was excluded when he was growing up in the days of segregation. In later years he spent his time there quietly, playing chess and croquet and mowing his many acres on a tractor, sculpting crop circles into the greensward.

Significant birthdays were celebrated in jubilee style as if they were rock'n'roll's equivalent of state occasions. On Berry's 60th birthday, Keith Richards and Eric Clapton visited him and played a celebratory concert in St Louis. Characteristically, he got into an ugly row with Richards, who later confessed that meeting his ultimate musical hero had been a "big disappointment".

On his 90th birthday he announced that he was recording his first new album since 1979. Simply titled *Chuck*, the record is due for release in June. It features his son, Charles Jr, on guitar and his daughter Ingrid on harmonica.

Early in his career he complained bitterly that he had been misrepresented by the press and he spent most of his life shunning mainstream media. He was famous enough without it, he argued, and in later years those requesting interviews were peremptorily told to read his autobiography.

Published in 1987, it was written without the help of a "ghost" after he had learnt to type during one of his prison sentences. A curious yet compelling book that mixed prurient confessions and elegant accounts of his early years, he conveyed the sexual anecdotes with a poetical degree of circumlocution. A woman engaged in oral sex was described as "paying personal homage to his magnitude".

He was born Charles Edward Anderson Berry in 1926 in St Louis. His father, Henry, was a carpenter and Baptist church deacon and his mother, Martha, was a school principal. One of six children, Chuck learnt to play the family piano, sang in the church choir and was a well-regarded pupil at Sumner High School, but went off the rails in his teens and ended up in a youth reformatory for armed robbery.

While in detention he formed a vocal quartet. Released on his 21st birthday, he worked on a car assembly line and trained as a hairdresser and beautician. By 1950 he was doing well enough to buy a house in St Louis, which is now a listed historic monument.

Nights were spent playing in local bars and clubs under the name "Chuck Berryn", a thin disguise to protect his God-fearing parents from the shame that their son was playing "the Devil's music". Modelling himself on influences that ranged from Nat King Cole to Muddy Waters and even mixing in country styles, local audiences came to dub him the "black hillbilly".

His breakthrough came in 1955 when he travelled to Chicago and met Waters, who introduced him to Chess Records. His first recording for the label, *Maybellene*, topped the R&B charts and made No 5 in the pop listings. This success also gave Berry his first taste of the crooked machinations of the record industry. It was the days of "payola" and when he received his first royalty statement he discovered that he was sharing the payment with two others, including the disc jockey Alan Freed, who were credited as co-authors, despite having had nothing to do with writing the song.

Berry was incensed and, having been stung once, he took great pains never to be cheated again, gaining a reputation for excessive meanness. On tour in Britain, not even Don Arden could intimidate

Berry. In fact he told the bruising promoter that he was upping his fee just before going on stage.

In concert he became infamous for checking his watch in mid-song: he was not going to perform for a minute longer than the time for which he had been contracted.

Maybellene was followed by *Roll Over Beethoven*, an anthem of rebellion that was inspired by childhood memories of his sister playing *Für Elise* on the family piano, and by *Johnny B Goode*, which went on to become one of the most covered songs.

By the end of the decade he had reeled off a dozen more hits, including *School Days* and *Sweet Little Sixteen*, which tapped into the teenage *Weltanschauung*, articulating adolescent passions in worldly, streetwise poetry, acutely aware of the need to reach White as well as Black listeners.

Then came the enforced hiatus of jail, where he took courses in business law and accountancy, and wrote songs such as *No Particular Place to Go*, *You Never Can Tell* and *The Promised Land*, which provided him with a stream of hits when he was released.

When these dried up he took to touring prolifically, maximising his income by not employing a permanent backing band, but using a cheap pick-up group at each venue. Unsurprisingly, this led to an alarming lack of quality control. Sometimes the pick-up musicians were outstanding and a young Bruce Springsteen and Steve Miller were among those who backed him on one-night stands. When the musicianship was of a lesser standard, the results were often dire, not helped by his refusal to rehearse.

He was asked in 2002 why he had written hardly any new songs since his initial glorious hits in the Fifties. "I felt it might be ill-mannered to try and top myself," he answered. As excuses went, it was not a bad one – and as long as he played *Johnny B Goode* every night, nobody really cared.

Chuck Berry, rock'n'roll musician, was born on October 18, 1926. He died on March 18, 2017, aged 90

BOB MARLEY

———•———

*Reggae singer, songwriter and guitarist considered one of
the pioneers of the genre*

The Times, May 13, 1981

Bob Marley, the singer and composer of reggae music who died
on May 11, was the figure most responsible for disseminating the
popular music of Jamaica around the world during the 1970s. His
uncompromising songs, style and attitudes provided a rare and
powerful example for young West Indians, particularly those living in
Britain, to whom he presented the elements of a cultural identity. It was
a position he never abused, and last week he was awarded the Jamaican
Order of Merit by his country's Prime Minister, Mr Edward Seaga.

Robert Nesta Marley was born in the parish of St Ann, near
Kingston, in 1945; his mother was a Jamaican woman, his father,
whom he remembered meeting only twice, a serving captain in the
British Army. During his adolescence, Marley gravitated quickly

towards music and made his first record at the age of 19. In 1965 Marley formed a group, the Wailers, with his fellow singers and composers Bunny Livingstone and Peter Tosh; they became popular within the Jamaican market, singing a light, lilting variation of the local idiom known as ska music.

They became the first Jamaican artists to achieve fame abroad when, in 1972, they signed a recording contract with Island Records, the London-based company. Careful promotion, modern recording facilities and the energetic proselytising efforts of high-profile English musicians such as Mick Jagger and Eric Clapton brought their music, and reggae in general, into fashion with the rock audience.

Although Livingstone and Tosh left the group, Marley reconstituted it and went on to even greater success, touring around the world and achieving enormous record sales in America, Africa and Europe. At home, he exerted such a hold on the popular imagination that politicians habitually attempted to elicit his endorsement, which he resolutely withheld. Nevertheless, in 1977 he was wounded by gunshots on his house in an attack which was said to have been politically motivated.

He considered his finest hour to have been his appearance at the Zimbabwe independence celebrations, to which he was expressly invited by Dr Robert Mugabe.

Whether on stage or on record Marley conveyed a vivid intensity heightened by his use of the fiery biblical texts appropriated by the Jamaican cult of Rastafarianism, of which he was a prominent disciple. He was a deeply expressive singer and a composer whose range extended from the melodic lament of *No Woman No Cry* to inspiring and politically loaded dance tunes such as *Exodus* and *Zimbabwe*. He came to be seen as the embodiment of reggae, but possessed an originality which would have ensured his pre-eminence in any type of popular music. Reggae will survive the loss of his unique vision, but it may never have another spokesman of such eloquence and broad appeal.

Bob Marley, singer and songwriter, was born on April 6, 1945. He died of cancer on May 11, 1981, aged 36

OLIVIA NEWTON-JOHN

Known for her role as the wholesome Sandy, she became one of the world's biggest-selling female artists

The Times, August 9, 2022

Olivia Newton-John should have been far too old to play the chaste teenage prom queen Sandy Olsson in the film *Grease*. She was 29 when the movie was made and yet the image of her dancing with John Travolta at a high-school hop came to epitomise adolescent fantasy in which wholesome and innocent schoolgirls fall for leather-clad bad boys and together find that true love conquers all.

"I was worried I was too old so I asked if I could do a screen test to make sure I looked appropriate," she said. "But John wanted me for the role and in the screen test it really worked between us. There was an attraction that kept the chemistry going."

Adapted from the Broadway musical of the same name and set in 1950s America, *Grease* was the peak of her acting success. There were further lead roles, including a reprise of her partnership with Travolta in 1983's *Two of a Kind*. But in the public's imagination she was forever cast as *Grease*'s eternal teenager, seen first in a demure frock with fringe and bob and then in black spandex pants with an extravagant bubble perm as the film tracked a time-honoured youthful rite of passage.

The enduring appeal of the film meant that on the opening weekend of its 20th anniversary rerelease in 1998, only *Titanic* did better at the box office.

That she never repeated the movie success of *Grease* did not bother her, for Newton-John regarded herself as primarily a singer rather than an actress. The two came serendipitously together when the movie's soundtrack gave her three top-five hits in *You're the One That I Want*, *Hopelessly Devoted to You* and *Summer Nights*.

While her post-*Grease* movie career stalled, her success as a recording artist soared as she went on to become one of the biggest-selling female artists of all time. Her record sales eventually topped an estimated 100 million and until the emergence of Kylie Minogue she was said to be Australia's most famous female singer since the operatic soprano Nellie Melba. She was made an OBE in 1979 and a dame in 2020.

Although an Australian citizen and an American resident for much of her life, she was born in England, in Cambridge, in 1948. Her mother, Irene, was the daughter of the Jewish Nobel prize-winning atomic physicist Max Born, who left Germany for Britain with his family before the Second World War to escape the horrors of Nazism. Her Welsh father, Brinley "Bryn" Newton-John, was an MI5 officer who worked on the Enigma project at Bletchley Park, spoke fluent German and was charged with taking Rudolf Hess into custody after Hitler's deputy had flown to Scotland on his bizarre peace mission in 1941.

She remembered her father keeping a pistol in his pocket, but said: "He never talked about what he did. He wasn't allowed to. Just before he died he gave us tapes in which he talked a little about it but he was still pretty guarded. I wish I'd known more when he was still alive so I could have asked him about it."

The family emigrated to Australia when she was six, after her father retired from government service and was appointed master of Ormond College at the University of Melbourne. Three years later her parents separated. "We went from living in the college to my mother and I living on our own. That was pretty traumatic. In those days divorce wasn't so common; telling my friends was awkward," she recalled.

In adult life her own personal relationships were similarly complex. Her first serious relationship was with Ian Turpie, the Australian actor and television presenter, who was five years her senior. In the 1970s she was engaged to Bruce Welch of the Shadows but they never married. She described Travolta as "very sweet, handsome and charming" and he confessed to having had a "crush" on her; but she denied that they ever slept together.

She also denied rumours that she was a lesbian and in 1984 married the actor Matt Lattanzi, whom she met on the set of *Xanadu*. They had a daughter, the singer and actress Chloe Lattanzi who appeared on stage with her mother from an early age.

Her marriage to Lattanzi was annulled in 1994 and she had an 11-year relationship with the cameraman Patrick McDermott until his disappearance during a fishing trip off the Californian coast in 2005. There were rumours of foul play and a suggestion that he may have staged his own disappearance in order to avoid alimony payments to his ex-wife, the actress Yvette Nipar.

Newton-John, who was in Australia at the time, refused to comment on the speculation but was severely shaken and spent several months on antidepressants. A US Coast Guard investigation eventually concluded three years later that he had been lost at sea.

In 2008, she secretly wed John Easterling, owner of a company specialising in new age remedies. After an Inca ceremony staged at sunrise on a mountain in Peru, a more conventional wedding took place in Florida although no guests were invited and only her daughter knew of the marriage.

Newton-John's older sister Rona, who died from brain cancer in 2013, was also an actress and was married for a while to the actor Jeff Conaway, who co-starred in *Grease*.

In her early years in Australia her chief passion was horse riding and she harboured ambitions to be a vet; but at the age of 15 she won a television talent contest. "My mum wanted me to finish my education but suddenly I was being offered all these TV opportunities," she recalled. "There was even a controversy in the papers when I was offered a job on a kids' show –'should she take it or should she finish her schooling?'" She took the job and appeared on the show as "Lovely Livvy".

Part of the prize for winning the talent show was a trip to London, but she delayed taking it up for a year until she was 16. "I found it totally overwhelming and I wanted to go home and see my boyfriend. I kept booking my flight home and my mother kept cancelling it."

Her mother wanted her to enrol at Rada but she was more interested in singing than acting. Cliff Richard was an early champion and she appeared regularly in his TV show, but she had been in London for six years before she scored her first chart hit in 1971 with an easy listening, country-tinged version of Bob Dylan's *If Not for You*.

She was chosen to sing the British entry in the 1974 Eurovision Song Contest, *Long Live Love*, but only came fourth. Reinventing herself as a country singer, she topped the American charts with *I Honestly Love You* and *Have You Never Been Mellow*. Her success persuaded her to move to the US, where she appointed the Hollywood impresario Allan Carr as her manager. He then put up six million dollars to produce *Grease* and ensured that his client was cast in the lead female role.

However, the follow-up, *Xanadu*, in which she danced with Gene Kelly, flopped so badly that the film inspired the creation of the Golden Raspberry awards. *Xanadu* scooped seven of them at the inaugural ceremony, although it didn't stop the film's soundtrack giving Newton-John three major hits, including *Magic*, which went to No 1.

The raunchily carnal lyrics of her 1981 hit *Physical*, which topped the American charts for ten weeks, found her leaving behind her "girl next door" image, although an aerobics video in which she appeared in leotard and headband and which accompanied the song made an unconvincing attempt at pretending at a more innocent kind of physicality.

At the peak of her chart success, she took several years out while bringing up her daughter before returning in the late 1980s with an album produced by Elton John, only for her career to be put on hold again when in 1992 she was diagnosed with breast cancer, on the same weekend that her father died from the disease.

Her own treatment meant that she was unable to attend his funeral but she made a full recovery, an experience that sparked an intense interest in yoga, meditation and other alternative and new age therapies. "I think we find strength we don't expect to have. I made a decision that I was going to be alright and after that I had a deep-down belief that I would be," she said.

After her treatment she returned to Australia and announced she had "a mind to retire". But the new age bug had bitten and instead, she wrote a set of songs that chronicled her illness and recovery and released them as a kind of spiritual self-help manifesto on the album *Gaia: One Woman's Journey*. "My whole cancer journey was so I could help people. I don't regret it because I see the experience of going through it and coming out of it as a gift," she said with a piety that seemed almost too good to be true.

Olivia Newton-John, actress and singer, was born on September 26, 1948. She died of breast cancer on August 8, 2022, aged 73

MICHAEL JACKSON

---•---

*Global figure in popular culture who started out as a child star, broke record
sales, invented the moonwalk and later became embroiled in controversy
regarding his eccentric private life*

The Times, June 26, 2009

He liked to be known as the King of Pop, and only a handful of
performers – Presley, Sinatra, the Beatles – could challenge Michael
Jackson for the title of most successful popular music entertainer of
all time.

Although ill health dogged his career in later years, and his
reputation was irrevocably tarnished by the allegations of child
abuse levelled against him in 1993 and again in 2004, the sheer scale
of Jackson's achievements remains undiminished. With sales of
about 53 million copies, *Thriller*, his magnum opus, released in 1982,
remains by far the bestselling album ever released. The follow-up, *Bad*,
from 1987, has sold 28 million copies and sales of *Dangerous* (1991)

stand at 29 million. His total record sales were estimated by his Sony Music label to be in excess of 750 million. These staggering figures mark only some of the peaks of a career begun at the age of five.

Born in 1958, in Gary, Indiana, Michael was the seventh of nine children to Joe Jackson and his wife Katherine (née Scruse). Joe was a steel mill worker who in his spare time played guitar in an R&B group called the Falcons. Katherine, a devout Jehovah's Witness who played clarinet, piano and sang, worked as an assistant in a department store.

Under Joe's strict tutelage and with encouragement and support from Katherine, five of the brothers formed a group called the Jackson 5 with Michael as the lead singer. The sixth, Randy, was still too young but eventually joined the line-up much later on, while of the sisters, LaToya enjoyed limited success as a solo act in adult life, and Janet eventually became a star in her own right.

"I was so little when we began to work on our music that I don't remember much about it," Jackson mused in his autobiography *Moonwalk*, published in 1988. "When you're a showbusiness child, people make a lot of decisions concerning your life when you're out of the room." The book's title was a reference to the distinctive and deft foot-shuffling dance that he performed on stage and made his own.

Joe Jackson managed the group with a rod of iron and in later life Michael spoke regretfully of the rift which developed and was never healed between him and his father. Nevertheless, Jackson Sr successfully steered the group from talent competitions and a residency in the local striptease parlour to a recording contract with Tamla Motown records, signed in 1969 reputedly for a dismal 2.7 per cent cut of the royalties.

Success with Motown was instantaneous and spectacular, as the group's first four singles – *I Want You Back*, *The Love You Save*, *ABC* and *I'll Be There* – all went to the top of the US chart, each title selling over a million copies. Michael was 11 when he first saw his own face on the cover of *Rolling Stone* magazine. In 1971, two years after the Jackson 5's first hit, Michael was signed separately to Motown as a solo act and immediately sallied forth with a string of his own hits

– *Got to Be There, Rockin' Robin, Ben* and others – which were released in tandem with his work as a member of the group.

In 1975, frustrated by the Motown supremo Berry Gordy's unwillingness to let them write or produce their own material, four of the Jackson 5, including Michael, joined the exodus of acts from the ailing label. Changing their name to the Jacksons for contractual reasons, they signed to Epic, where they teamed up with the celebrated writing and production team of Kenny Gamble and Leon Huff. The results were mixed. The single *Show You the Way to Go* was the group's first and only UK No 1 in 1977, but the album *Goin' Places*, released later the same year, failed to reach the US Top 60.

In 1979 Jackson accepted an offer to co-star with his longstanding friend and mentor Diana Ross in *The Wiz*, a version of *The Wizard of Oz*. While working on the film he met the veteran producer Quincy Jones and invited him to produce his next solo album, *Off the Wall*. This was the collection which marked the start of Jackson's passage to the super league, and took his success as a solo artist into realms beyond anything achieved by the Jacksons. It has sold 19 million copies to date. Even so, no one was fully prepared for the epoch-making success of *Thriller*.

Again produced by Jones, the album yielded an incredible total of seven Top Ten hit singles in America. Retailers reported that *Thriller*'s appeal reached far beyond the normal strata of record buyers, attracting people who had never previously visited a record shop in their lives. Even a documentary, *The Making of Michael Jackson's Thriller* (1984), quickly became established as the bestselling music video ever released.

Quite why Jackson should have been so phenomenally successful at this point is difficult fully to explain. Musically, he was not a great innovator like Elvis Presley or Bob Dylan, nor was he a role model for a generation like the Beatles or the Rolling Stones had been before him. But he emerged as a spectacularly talented all-rounder at a time when pop music was taking over as the world's primary mainstream entertainment. He was as good a dancer as he was a singer and he employed the new technology to make videos that were as full of stylish impact as his music. The appeal of his impossibly slick and electrifying song-and-dance routines transcended barriers of age, race, class and nationality.

Above all, Jackson was a stringent perfectionist. He explained why it had taken five years to release *Bad*, the follow-up to *Thriller*: "Quincy and I decided that this album should be as close to perfect as humanly possible. A perfectionist has to take his time. He can't let it go before he's satisfied. He can't. When it's as perfect as you can make it, you put it out there. That's the difference between a No 30 record and a No 1 record that stays No 1 for weeks."

Bad was very much in the latter category, as was Jackson's next album, *Dangerous*, released in 1991. And even *HIStory – Past, Present and Future – Book 1*, an unwieldy double album combining 15 greatest hits and 15 new songs released after the torrent of bad publicity surrounding the first allegations of child abuse in 1993, had achieved global sales of 18 million copies by the time of his death.

Jackson did not react well to the relentless barrage of (frequently prurient) media attention which was generated by success on such a grand scale. "Success definitely brings on loneliness," he wrote in *Moonwalk*. "People think you're lucky, that you have everything. They think you can go anywhere and do anything, but that's not the point. One hungers for the basic stuff."

In Santa Barbara county, California, Jackson built himself a fantasy ranch called Neverland – a reference both to JM Barrie's Peter Pan (perhaps significantly, the boy who never grew up) and to Elvis Presley's Graceland home in Memphis, Tennessee – where he created a zoo, a miniature railway and a Ferris wheel.

But as he became an increasingly reclusive and secretive figure, so reports of his eccentricities became ever more lurid and fantastic. In Britain, *The Sun* newspaper posed the question that came to dominate popular reportage of his private life: "Is Jacko Wacko?" He was known to have kept snakes and a pet chimpanzee called Bubbles, who, it was said, slept in the same room as Jackson. He attempted to buy the bones of Joseph (John) Merrick, the so-called Elephant Man, after seeing the movie starring John Hurt. He was photographed wearing a face mask, to ward off germs, and sleeping in an oxygen chamber, a practice which he apparently believed would help to prolong his life to 150.

He was known to have had a nose job and a cleft put in his chin, but Jackson categorically denied persistent allegations that he had had his whole face restructured and his skin tinted a shade lighter than its natural tone. As he got older, though, his features became oddly contorted and he took on a distinctly unhealthy pallor.

"I have a skin disorder which destroys the pigment of my skin," he told Oprah Winfrey in February 1993. "It's in my family. We're trying to control it. I am a Black American."

When his *Bad* tour reached England in 1988, Jackson's constant companion was the American television child actor Jimmy Safechuck. In London, the pair paid an after-hours visit to the Regent Street toy shop Hamleys. It seemed as if Jackson, having started his career so young, had been forced to stretch his childhood well into adult life.

"I believe I'm one of the loneliest people in the world," he wrote, in what was to become the most frequently quoted remark from his *Moonwalk* book.

But as he approached middle age, it was Jackson's abiding interest in children which was his undoing. In August 1993 the Los Angeles Police Department announced that he was under criminal investigation after allegations by a Beverly Hills dentist that Jackson had molested his 13-year-old son, Jordan Chandler. The story provoked a prolonged "feeding frenzy" among the world's media, and Jackson eventually settled out of court, paying the Chandlers a sum believed to be in the region of $26 million to drop the case, while continuing vigorously to protest his innocence. The announcement, some months after the event, that on May 26, 1994 Jackson had been married to Lisa Marie Presley, the daughter of the late Elvis Presley, was initially greeted with disbelief and subsequently derided as a cynical public relations ploy, designed to repair Jackson's tattered image. But at least neither partner could be accused of marrying for a stake in the other's fortune. Their combined worth was said to be close to half a billion dollars. The marriage lasted only 17 months.

In 1997 Jackson was married to Debbie Rowe, a 37-year-old nurse, who bore him two children, Prince Michael I and Paris Michael Katherine before leaving him (and the children), and filing for divorce in 1999.

It was ironic that a near-fanatical interest in fitness was in itself the cause of concern about Jackson's health. Rail-thin all his life, he was a strict vegetarian who put himself through various punishing regimes involving days of fasting and long spells of obsessive dance practice. In 1979, while working on *The Wiz*, he burst a blood vessel in his lung. In 1988 he collapsed onstage during one of the *Bad* shows in Europe, and in 1990 much was made of a suspected heart attack which turned out to be an inflamed rib cartilage, damaged through excessive exercise.

He cancelled the last six dates of the European leg of the *Dangerous* tour in 1992, because of "throat problems", and in 1993 publicity surrounding the child abuse allegations reached a peak, the South-East Asian leg of the same tour collapsed in disarray and Jackson retired to undergo treatment for an addiction to painkillers. It was not until December 1995 that he attempted a return to live performance. But disaster struck again when he collapsed during rehearsals for a show that was to have been televised worldwide from New York. He was rushed to hospital suffering from low blood pressure, dehydration and a suspected virus affecting his heart.

Jackson's next full-length album, *Invincible* (2001), was a creditable collection of R&B songs which sold six million copies, a huge success if judged by any standards other than those of Jackson's earlier work. A greatest-hits compilation, *Number Ones* (2003), sold well over a million copies in Britain alone, despite the almost continual controversy that by now surrounded him. Almost a year earlier, after fathering another son, Prince Michael II, with an unidentified surrogate mother, he dangled the baby perilously over the balcony of a Berlin hotel. The pictures, circulated around the world, prompted questions about his suitability as a parent.

There was further cause for concern when a TV interview with the documentary film-maker Martin Bashir, first screened in Britain in 2003, revealed a middle-aged man trapped in a child's mindset. More disturbingly, Jackson's admission in the same interview that he routinely slept with children in his room created further lurid speculation and led to his arrest by the Santa Barbara police, who charged him with molesting a 13-year-old boy. Jackson's lawyers promised that there would be "no quarter" given in their efforts to defend him, and fans were vocal in protest. "His life has been about peace," insisted Jackson's elder brother Jermaine.

The case opened on January 31, 2005, and the huge media circus outside the Santa Maria court was not disappointed as Jackson provided it with an almost daily supply of dramatic stories. Even before the jury had been sworn in, he announced a list of star witnesses that included Diana Ross, Elizabeth Taylor and Stevie Wonder, although in the event none was actually called to the stand and nor was Jackson required to testify. Even so, the strain on him took its toll, visibly so. He twice sought medical attention, once for flu-like symptoms and once for back pain. At one point, Judge Rodney Melville threatened to revoke the singer's $3 million bail and lock him up for the rest of the trial after Jackson shuffled in weakly, more than an hour late, wearing his pyjamas.

On June 14, almost five months after the trial began, Jackson was sensationally acquitted of all ten charges of child abuse, charges which carried a maximum sentence of more than 18 years in prison. Hundreds of fans who had kept a vigil outside the courthouse celebrated with abandon. But for Jackson, grim-faced and by now extremely fragile, there was only relief that the ordeal was over and that he still had his freedom. In the aftermath of the trial he sought refuge from the public eye in Bahrain, where it was reported that he had bought a property close to the palace of his friend Sheikh Abdullah bin Hamad al Khalifa.

Yet another greatest hits compilation – *The Essential Michael Jackson* – sailed to No 2 in the UK chart, but could only limp into the American chart at No 128, a disastrous showing for the man who once reigned supreme as the King of Pop.

Jackson's last years were marked chiefly by stories of financial difficulties brought on by years of extravagant spending. He moved out of Neverland and at the time of his death was living with his children in a mansion in Bel Air, Los Angeles, which he was renting for $100,000 a month.

His fans remained loyal, however. The singer's death came only weeks before he was due to begin an unprecedented series of 50 concerts in London at the O2 arena in Greenwich. When the performances were announced there was a strong suggestion that they might be Jackson's last, and that he would retire when they were over. The dates sold out at once. Ominously, the first four concerts, beginning on July 13, were postponed because Jackson needed more time to rehearse.

The pop star had come to look increasingly frail and had long been erratic in his behaviour. What his true character was like is difficult to say, it being heavily camouflaged by music industry public relations hype and lurid media speculation. He had spent almost his entire life in the showbusiness spotlight.

Michael Jackson, pop singer, was born on August 29, 1958. He died on June 25, 2009, aged 50

CHAS HODGES

———————————— • ————————————

Pianist and singer who as one half of Chas and Dave stormed the charts
with cheeky Cockney anthems about life in the East End

The Times, September 24, 2018

After Chas Hodges's father committed suicide the day before his fourth birthday, his mother Daisy took to playing piano in the pubs of north London as her only means of putting food on the table.

If losing his father in such circumstances was a shattering experience, his mother's enterprise was an inspiration that signposted his way to fame and fortune as the Joanna-bashing half of Chas and Dave on such singalong hits as *Rabbit, Gertcha, Ain't No Pleasing You, London Girls* and *Snooker Loopy*.

Sung chirpily in Cockney geezer rhyming slang over Hodges's thumping pub piano chords, Chas and Dave's trademark sound was full of such distinctive wit that when Ronnie Corbett and Ronnie Barker essayed a parody of the duo on the TV show *The Two Ronnies*, it hardly even sounded like a spoof.

A mix of music-hall humour, beery bonhomie, Cockney variety act and rock'n'roll, the style became known as "rockney". By the early 1980s they were so popular that they were given their own show on ITV titled *Chas and Dave's Knees Up*. It was set, naturally, in a studio mock-up of an East End pub.

They also recorded a Christmas special featuring Eric Clapton and the comedian Jim Davidson, which was still being repeated on Christmas Day more than 30 years later.

As a stereotypical portrayal of working-class London, Hodges and his partner Dave Peacock were perhaps the musical equivalent of the Trotter brothers in *Only Fools and Horses* or the more menacing Mitchell siblings in *EastEnders*. They had no time for *EastEnders*, complaining that the programme "completely misses the sense of humour in the East End", but were great admirers of *Only Fools and Horses*, in which Hodges's wife, Joan, once appeared.

Invited to record the show's theme song, they reluctantly declined as they were in Australia on tour at the time, although they did record theme tunes for *Crackerjack*, *In Sickness and in Health*, and the children's cartoon series *Bangers & Mash* as well as a series of jingles for Courage beer.

Suspicions that their act was a "mockney" fake were unfounded. Both Hodges and Peacock were genuine "geezers" and the uninitiated were often left mystified by the liberal use of rhyming slang between them. A famous American record producer was concerned when Hodges turned to his partner in the studio and said, "Give us an oily, Dave." Convinced it was code for some kind of illegal substance, he was much relieved when Hodges explained to him that all he wanted was a simple cigarette (oily rag = fag).

"Some people assumed we couldn't be real Cockneys and we must be putting it on because it was such an unusual thing to do," Hodges said. "But we simply became ourselves, singing in the way we speak about things we know about. Before that I did Jerry Lee Lewis take-offs in an American accent. I thought, 'You're being a fraud, you should sing in your own accent.'"

Away from music his passions included football and growing vegetables on his allotment, which led to a book, *Chas and His Rock'n'Roll Allotment*, and a weekly column in the *Sunday Express*.

A lifelong Tottenham Hotspur fan, he and Dave also wrote and recorded two Top 20 hits with the great Glenn Hoddle-era Spurs team of the early 1980s to mark the club's two consecutive appearances in the FA Cup final. One of them was titled *Ossie's Dream* in honour of the club's Argentine star Ossie Ardiles and included such lines as "Ossie's going to Wembley/His knees have gone all trembly". They also wrote a line for Ardiles to sing, intended to poke mild fun at his South American accent in which "'Tottenham" was invariably rendered as "Tottingham".

On the day of the recording Ardiles arrived at the studio and proudly announced that he had been practising and had learnt to say the word properly. "'No, you don't understand – we want you to say 'Tottingham'," Hodges told the baffled footballer.

He liked to joke that the highlight of his career came not in tandem with Dave, but was when he became a Beatle for the night at a party thrown by Eric Clapton. "There was a marquee set up in the grounds with a stage, amps and drum kit in case anyone felt like getting up and having a jam," he recalled. "I started singing some rock'n'roll stuff, looked up and there was Ringo Starr sitting there smiling at me. The next thing I knew Paul McCartney was plugging in his bass and George Harrison was slipping on a guitar. And there's me in the middle thinking, 'I'm the fourth flippin' Beatle 'ere. Chas, Paul, George and Ringo.' We played for about half an hour and finished with *Get Back*."

To Hodges's disappointment no photographic evidence of this historic jam session has ever come to light, but his wife was present as his witness.

Charles Nicholas Hodges was born in 1943 in Edmonton, north London, the younger of two brothers. His father, Albert, was a lorry driver and moved the family to rural Kent in 1947. Several months later he turned a shotgun on himself. The family never discovered what caused him to do it. "We returned to London to live with my grandparents and I realised that not only had I lost my dad, but this beautiful part of Britain had been taken away from me, too," Hodges recalled.

Times were hard and Hodges earned pocket money by collecting empty beer bottles and waste paper and made his own bicycle from parts scavenged from a dump.

His mother encouraged him musically and by the age of 13 he was playing guitar in a skiffle band. He took up the piano after seeing Jerry Lee Lewis performing *Great Balls of Fire* on stage at the Edmonton Regal in 1958.

After a brief spell working as an apprentice to a clock repairer, by the age of 16 he had become a professional musician, playing a summer season at a Butlin's holiday camp and working as a session player at Joe Meek's studio on hits such as *Johnny Remember Me* by John Leyton and *Just Like Eddie* by Heinz.

He spent much of 1963 touring as the bass player for his hero, Lewis, which was a sharp learning curve: "I'd spend each night standing beside him watching his hands move on the keys, taking mental notes, so I always tell people that Jerry Lee Lewis taught me piano, he just didn't know it."

He then joined Cliff Bennett and the Rebel Rousers, supporting the Beatles on their last European tour in 1966 and recording a cover version of *Got to Get You Into My Life*, written and produced by McCartney, which reached No 6 in the singles chart.

By 1970 he had joined the country-rock band Heads Hands and Feet and it was while touring America with them two years later that the musical ideas that would propel Chas and Dave to fame took shape.

The pair had first met in 1963 when Peacock picked up Hodges when he was hitching home from a girlfriend's house. They had kept in touch and on his return from America, Hodges called him to suggest that they formed a duo.

They were to remain partners for the next 45 years, "writing songs about things we know about and singing them in our own accent", said Hodges.

Rabbit (from rabbit and pork = talk) was about Hodges's garrulous wife while *Ain't No Pleasing You* was inspired by a row between his brother and his sister-in-law. "He was putting up some curtains and his missus said they weren't straight. He said, 'There ain't no fucking pleasing you, is there?' So it was planted in my head. They ended up splitting up."

Hodges stayed with his wife until his death. A former Playboy bunny and actress, Joan married him in 1966. They had three children: Juliet, Kate, a singer and songwriter, and Nik, who played the drums for Chas and Dave after the retirement of long-time sideman Mick Burt in 2011.

When it was put to him that there might have been a hint of misogyny about Chas and Dave, Hodges conceded that women had tended not to come off well in their songs, but insisted it was because they were "too embarrassed to write love songs".

Peacock announced his retirement after his wife died from cancer in 2009, but was coaxed back by the ever-persuasive Hodges and in 2013 the duo released *That's What Happens*, their first studio album in 18 years.

On the afternoon that his death was announced, Tottenham Hotspur won 2-1 at Brighton with their fans singing a paean to Hodges as "one of our own".

Chas Hodges, musician, was born on December 28, 1943. He died of oesophageal cancer on September 22, 2018, aged 74

JONI SLEDGE

Sister Sledge singer who sang We Are Family *for a pope, a president and at a gay pride festival in Brighton*

The Times, March 13, 2017

"We are family," sang Sister Sledge in their 1979 disco anthem. And they were family: Debbie, Joni, Kim and Kathy, although Kathy left in 1989 to pursue a solo career. "No matter how many times we sing *We Are Family*, it always has some kind of freshness to it, I think, because so many people identify – because we all have families or want to be a part of one if we don't have one," Joni said of the song's enduring popularity.

Disco music had taken hold with John Travolta's 1977 hit *Saturday Night Fever* and Sister Sledge's song became a classic of the era, although Joni disliked the term "disco", saying: "It conjures up all these mechanical studio gimmicks." *We Are Family* had a distinctive disco beat, but its message was a step beyond the usual disco sentiments, with its rousing call for community, unity and spirit. They received a big boost when *We Are Family* was appropriated by the Pittsburgh Pirates baseball team on their way to a World Series championship win in 1979, with Sister Sledge singing the US national anthem at the opening game.

The sisters sang for everyone from President Clinton to Pope Francis, and everywhere from Zaire, where they were part of a warm-up concert for the Rumble in the Jungle, the 1974 boxing match between Muhammad Ali and George Foreman, to Glastonbury, where they lit up the Pyramid Stage in 2005. Their rousing hit became an anthem for many, ranging from LGBT groups around the world to supporters of Hillary Clinton in the 2016 US presidential election campaign.

Joni Sledge was born in 1956, a third-generation Philadelphian and the third of five daughters of Edwin Sledge, a Broadway tap dancer, and his wife Florez (née Williams), a former chorus girl.

They divorced in 1964. Carol, the eldest sister, did not take up singing and became a teacher. The girls owed their vocal training to Viola Williams, their maternal grandmother, who was a former opera singer and protégée of Mary McLeod Bethune, the civil rights activist. Viola had them singing at their local episcopal church. "She wouldn't let us get away with just shouting," Joni recalled in 1994. "She'd say, 'Oh no! Sing that note there.'"

By the age of three or four they were known as Mrs Williams' Grandchildren, gaining experience at any tea party or charity event that their grandmother could find. They soon became the Sledge Sisters but at one event the MC had been enjoying too much sauce and introduced them as Sister Sledge. "We just looked at each other backstage and said, 'Hey! That's kind of cool,'" Joni recalled. They prepared for stardom by spraying old 45s with gold paint and hanging them on their walls.

As teenagers they did session work at Sigma Sound, one of the main studios in Philadelphia, and before leaving high school they had some success with *Time Will Tell* (1971), *Mama Never Told Me* (1973), which reached the Top 20 in Britain in 1975, and *Love Don't You Go Through No Changes on Me* (1974), a hit in Japan. "We were just average kids, and that weekend we went to Tokyo," Joni said. "We got off the plane and there were hundreds of Japanese kids in the airport with posters of us."

Mother Sledge, who held down several waitressing jobs to pay the bills and would later drive the group's tour bus up and down the east coast, made sure they did not neglect their education. "She's been involved in every facet of our career," said Joni. "We probably could never have done this without her." In the mid-1970s, even while their careers were blooming, the sisters graduated from Temple University, making them one of the best-educated big female groups in pop-music history.

Yet although their first album, *Circle of Love*, had been released in 1975, the big time was eluding them. "The four of us had been in the music business for eight years and we were frustrated," Joni told *The Guardian*, adding that they seriously considered abandoning music and going to law school. "We'd been working in Atlantic City, four in the afternoon to four in the morning, six sets … but our record company, Atlantic, didn't quite know what to do with us." She told how the label boss had made paper dolls of them in his search for inspiration: "We were all looking at each other, like … nah."

Eventually they teamed up with Nile Rodgers and Bernard Edwards, who had made their band Chic into a top-selling group, with disco songs such as *Dance, Dance, Dance.* Soon came Sister Sledge's album *We Are Family,* with its anthemic title track and songs such as *He's the Greatest Dancer, Lost in Music* and *Thinking of You.* "Working in the studio with those guys was a good feeling," Joni said. "It convinced us not to give up." *Lost in Music* reached No 4 in the UK, only to be bettered by *Frankie,* which took the No 1 slot for four weeks in 1985.

Meanwhile, Joni's marriage to her home-town sweetheart had ended in divorce. She had a son, Thaddeus, who studied at Arizona State University and is now an independent contractor. By the 1990s she was living in a gated community in Scottsdale, Arizona. Her home was something of a romantic refuge, with long white curtains over large windows and neutral furnishings that served as a canvas for the accessories that she had acquired on her travels, such as a wedding kimono from Kyoto, a courtyard painting from Italy and a hand-painted tapestry from Zimbabwe.

Kathy's departure in 1989 to pursue a solo career led to litigation, which made the lyrics of their most famous song ("I got all my sisters with me") seem rather hollow. Debbie, Joni and Kim, who was also an ordained minister, continued as Sister Sledge and during the 1990s enjoyed a number of British successes, including a remix of *We Are Family* that reached No 5 in 1993.

By the turn of the century Sister Sledge were disco royalty; they performed at Bill Clinton's final Christmas party at the White House, rerecorded *We Are Family* with Diana Ross and Patti LaBelle for a 9/11 benefit record and made regular appearances in Britain, including at Brighton Pride, the LGBT festival, last summer. They entertained the Pope when he visited the World Festival of Families in Philadelphia in September 2015, with film of nuns dancing in the street to *We Are Family* going viral. "We're not Catholics, but we believe in the Pope," quipped Joni.

Joni Sledge, disco singer, was born on September 13, 1956. She died on March 10, 2017, aged 60

Joni Sledge (top right) with sisters and bandmates, Debbie, Kim and Kathy Sledge

JOE STRUMMER

—●—

Lead singer of the Clash, the band that helped launch punk and inspired a riot in Bournemouth

The Times, December 24, 2002

Outspoken and uncompromising, Joe Strummer was the epitome of punk. A gung-ho but big-hearted rebel, with his band the Clash he made sharp-edged, angry music which struck blows against what he saw as the complacency of the political and musical establishments.

His only rival as the main spokesman for the punk revolution which transformed British youth culture in the late 1970s was Johnny Rotten. Yet unlike the Sex Pistols' singer, Strummer maintained his punk radicalism. When he was interviewed in *The Times* a year before his death, the writer observed that he was "the only rock star of his generation who hasn't mellowed with age". Only last month, he was to be found playing a benefit gig for the striking Fire Brigades Union with his new band, the Mescaleros.

John Graham Mellow, as he was born, was the son of a British diplomat. He spent his early years living variously in Turkey, Mexico, Germany and Egypt and was educated at a boarding school in Surrey. Art college followed, along with a spell busking on the London Underground. After this he formed his first band, the 101ers, playing amiable R&B on the mid-1970s London pub-rock circuit.

But he was frustrated by what he saw as the stagnation of the music scene of the time. In April 1976, the 101ers were supported at a London date by an emerging group called the Sex Pistols. Their volatile and nihilistic garage rock sounded crude and unrehearsed. Yet Strummer became convinced that the energy of the emerging punk movement could be harnessed to revolutionise British music. Within two months he had teamed up with the guitarist Mick Jones, the bass player Paul Simonon and the drummer Nicky "Topper" Headon to form the Clash.

Managed by Bernie Rhodes, an associate of the Sex Pistols' manager Malcolm McLaren, they swiftly built a following at punk venues such as London's 100 Club. Then, late in 1976, they joined the Sex Pistols on their "Anarchy in the UK" tour. With punk already making front-page headlines for its alleged violence and moral threat to the nation's youth, all but three of the 19 planned dates were cancelled by anxious promoters.

Such notoriety only enhanced punk's appeal. Leading record labels were soon jumping on the bandwagon and after making some demos for Polydor, in January 1977 the Clash signed to CBS Records. Their first single was the provocatively titled *White Riot*, a raw, aggressive, streetwise song with Strummer's angry lyrics snarled at breakneck speed.

It reached only number 38 but the band's debut album, *The Clash*, made number 12 on its release in the spring of 1977. Taking unemployment, alienation and rebellion as its subject matter and recorded in a matter of days, it remains, along with the Sex Pistols' *Never Mind the Bollocks*, punk's definitive statement.

In many ways, Strummer's songs were responding to the same events and sense of political drift that led to Margaret Thatcher's radical Conservatism. But Strummer moved in the opposite direction and was spotted at gigs wearing a T-shirt supporting Brigade Rosse, the Italian Red Brigades held responsible for the murder of the former Italian Prime Minister Aldo Moro. He also expressed his support for Germany's Red Army Faction, better known as the Baader-Meinhof gang.

Given the group's provocative attitude, trouble inevitably followed them. During their 1977 White Riot tour, Strummer and Headon were arrested and fined for spray-painting "Clash" on a wall. The same pair spent a night in jail in Newcastle, ludicrously charged with stealing a pillowcase from a local Holiday Inn. They responded by calling their next tour "Out on Parole". The group even managed the not inconsiderable feat of inciting a riot when they performed in genteel Bournemouth.

They put their money behind their political convictions, and in April 1978 they headlined a free Anti-Nazi League festival in London, organised by the pressure group Rock Against Racism. But their politics and growing commercial success were always in potential conflict, as Strummer recognised in the single *White Man in Hammersmith Palais*, in which he struggled with the dilemma of punk rockers "turning rebellion into money".

The group's second album, *Give 'Em Enough Rope* appeared in November 1978, and went straight into the charts at number two, kept from the top spot by the soundtrack to the film *Grease*. The recruitment of the top American rock producer Sandy Pearlman smoothed over some of the group's rougher edges but did nothing to lessen their political anger in songs such as *Guns on the Roof* and *Tommy Gun*, which gave them their first British Top 20 single. "Protest songs, that's what you'd call them. Folk songs with an electric guitar," Strummer said at the time.

A four-track EP which included a suitably venomous version of Bobby Fuller's *I Fought the Law* was released in summer 1979 as a holding operation while they broke America and began planning their third album, *London Calling*. Produced by the veteran Guy Stevens, the double album is widely regarded as the group's finest, as reggae and rockabilly tunes take their place alongside raw punk aggression on songs such as *The Guns of Brixton* and *Revolution Rock*.

London Calling, despite having a cover considered one of the most iconic in rock history, reached only number nine in the British charts, but it remains one of the most influential rock albums. Among those to fall under its influence was Bob Dylan's son Jacob, who now leads his own band, the Wallflowers, and recently cited *London Calling* above his father's work as the record that "changed his life".

The group's politically charged fourth album, *Sandinista!,* appeared in 1980. The first to be produced by the group themselves, this sprawling, 36-song triple album was released at a special budget price, after the group agreed to forgo royalties on the first 200,000 copies in return for CBS's co-operation.

In 1982 Strummer mysteriously disappeared for three months, later claiming that he was in Paris where his girlfriend's mother had been in jail. The mystery helped the next album, *Combat Rock,* to number two in the British charts and gave the group their first American Top Ten entry.

Strummer still sounded confrontational and the album produced hit singles in *Rock the Casbah* and *Should I Stay or Should I Go?* Yet paradoxically, it was the beginning of the end for the group. Headon left, and when the Clash joined The Who on their farewell tour of America in late 1982, many felt that the latter-day punk heroes sounded tame in comparison to the 1960s veterans.

The following year Jones, who had not only performed lead vocals on many of the Clash songs but had also co-written them, was unceremoniously evicted from the group. Strummer and Simonon soldiered on with two new recruits, Vince White and Nick Sheppard, and played benefit shows for the striking miners. But after the group's final album *Cut the Crap* was savaged by critics, they called it a day at the end of 1985.

As a rock great who had achieved everything before he was 30, Strummer appeared unsure what to do next. He played on Bob Dylan's album *Down in the Groove,* organised a "Rock Against the Rich" tour, played with Latino Rockabilly War and released the 1989 solo album *Earthquake Wonder.* But that was to be his last album for a decade as he turned to cinema and deployed his chiselled good looks to effect in such films as *Straight to Hell, Sid and Nancy, Mystery*

Train and *Lost in Space*. He also worked on several film soundtracks including John Cusack's *Grosse Point Blank*.

After a brief spell deputising for the equally dentally challenged Shane MacGowan as lead vocalist with the Pogues, Strummer spent much of the 1990s resisting invitations to re-form the Clash as various compilations kept them in the charts and a reissue of *Should I Stay or Should I Go?* became the Clash's first No 1 single, following its use in a Levi's jeans commercial. Strummer reportedly refused an offer of more than £3 million for the group to tour America. "That was never the Clash way of doing things," he later told *The Times*. "We all agreed it would have been sickening to have been playing that music with the pound signs hanging over us."

It was not until 1999 that he returned fully to the fray with a new band, the Mescaleros, and the album *Rock Art and the X-ray Style*. A second Mescaleros album, *Global a Go-Go*, followed within 18 months. "It took ten years to recharge my batteries. I felt isolated and wanted to wait until I'd stopped being the singer from a once-famous group and was this guy who needed help," he said.

Although he moved with his wife to Somerset to bring up their two daughters and his stepdaughter, his political fire remained undimmed. "The spirit of rock'n'roll helped to stop the Vietnam War," he said. "Perhaps it's a bit crazy for me still to feel like that. But I can't help it. Someone's got to keep the faith."

Joe Strummer, rock singer and lyricist, was born on August 21, 1952. He died of a suspected heart attack at his home in Somerset on December 22, 2002, aged 50

JAMES BROWN

—————————•—————————

Singer, dancer and entertainer supreme who became Black music's
most influential artist of the 20th century

The Times, December 26, 2006

The Godfather of Soul, the Hardest Working Man in Showbusiness;
Soul Brother No 1; Mr Dynamite – James Brown was not a modest
man, yet he more than earned the many colourful sobriquets with
which he described himself over the years.

In a career spanning five decades, this tireless consummate
showman with a rasping voice redefined the nature of soul in the
1950s, invented funk in the 1960s, partly inspired the disco revolution
of the 1970s and, thanks to the technological miracle of sampling,
involuntarily contributed excerpts of his work to an estimated two
or three thousand rap recordings of the 1980s and 1990s.

And not just rap: the drum part from his 1970 hit *Funky
Drummer*, for instance, has been recycled endlessly, providing the
basis for songs by Sinéad O'Connor, George Michael, LL Cool J,
Fine Young Cannibals, Public Enemy and many others besides.

A singer, dancer and entertainer supreme, Brown was long
acknowledged as the leading influence on a subsequent generation
of superstar hoofers, notably Michael Jackson, Hammer, Bobby
Brown and Prince.

An ally of successive US presidents and a confrère of Black
Power leaders, his influence in the community was such that his TV
appeals for calm after the assassination of Dr Martin Luther King in
1968 played a vital part in defusing a potentially explosive situation
on the streets of America's inner cities.

Yet his own volatile temperament was less readily contained
and in 1988 he was sentenced to six years' imprisonment after an
incident in which he threatened two policemen with a gun, then
attempted to run them over in his car while under the influence of
the drug angel dust. He was released in March 1991 and put on

parole until October 1993. Further brushes with the law ensued in 1995 when he was arrested and charged with beating up his wife, Adrienne, at their home in Aiken, South Carolina, and in 1998 when he was charged with possession of cannabis and unlawful use of a firearm.

Brown always gave his date of birth as 1933, but this was at odds with the facts, as recorded on the various court documents relating to his run-ins with the American authorities, which give his date of birth as May 3, 1928.

Born in Barnwell, South Carolina, in the woods a few miles from the Georgia state line, James Joseph Brown Jr was shunted off to live in a brothel in Augusta, Georgia, after his parents had separated. In that Black neighbourhood of clapboard shacks, he was looked after by one "Aunt T", when she was around, or else left to fend for himself.

His school attendance was irregular, and he dropped out in his early teens. The seeds of his notoriously fraught relationship with the law were sown at the age of 16 when he was arrested for breaking into cars, a crime for which he served nearly four years in corrective institutions.

He competed in local field sports events and then trained and fought as a bantamweight boxer. He also sang with a local gospel group, the Three Swanees and an R&B band called Bill Johnson and the Four Steps of Rhythm.

In 1954 he co-opted a group called the Gospel Starlighters led by a singer and pianist friend, Bobby Byrd, and converted them into his own group James Brown and the Famous Flames. They came to the attention of Little Richard's manager, Clint Brantley, who secured a contract for them with Syd Nathan's Cincinnati-based King record label. In 1956 Brown scored a hit in the R&B chart with his debut single *Please Please Please*.

Success in the mainstream pop market took a while to come, but by 1963 he had scored his first US Top 20 single with *Prisoner of Love* and powered his way to No 2 in the American album chart with his landmark album, *Live at the Apollo*. This was the recording of a show at that most hallowed of New York venues on October 24,

1962, and its success underlined Brown's phenomenal impact as a stage performer.

With his band drilled to perfection – so much so that individual musicians were fined for any wrong notes or missed cues – Brown performed with the energy of an athlete and a zeal that bordered on the hysterical. He would push the microphone stand away, spin himself full circle and catch it on the rebound; he would shimmy frantically across the stage, drop to one knee, then leap up and do the splits. At the end of a performance he would affect to be overcome by emotion, and a personal assistant would lead him off the stage, a cloak wrapped round his shoulders, like a spent boxer at the end of a gruelling bout. (It was no coincidence that Muhammad Ali used to train to James Brown records – the two were in much the same business.)

Behind the hoopla, though, there was a unique musical genius at work. His early recordings, particularly ballads like *Try Me* and *Bewildered*, took soul to new peaks of gospel-infused intensity. Later, in the 1960s, he stamped his most indelible mark on the musical landscape when as the American critic Dave Marsh put it: "He invented the rhythmic future in which we live today." The record with which James performed this unlikely feat was called *Papa's Got a Brand New Bag* (1965) and what he created was the dance-soul hybrid known as funk.

Based on a relentlessly syncopated, minimalist backing track and overlaid with Brown's intensely passionate, hump'n'grunt style of vocalese, *Papa's Got a Brand New Bag* revolutionised Black (and ultimately all popular) music. It was his first Top 10 hit in America and his first hit of any description in the UK. It marked the beginning of a golden era for Brown, who proceeded to issue a string of classic recordings including *I Got You (I Feel Good)*, *It's a Man's Man's Man's World* and *Get Up (I Feel Like Being a) Sex Machine*.

Brown lost ground in the Seventies as soul music evolved into an easy listening upmarket crossover style, and disco, which was initially inspired by his work, gradually rendered him an unfashionable anachronism.

Brown took this reversal of fortune on the chin, kept on touring and, even when he was at his lowest ebb and without a recording contract in the mid-1980s, never lost faith in his unassailable abilities as a performer. His confidence was vindicated when in 1986 he swept back into the American and British Top 5 with *Living in America*, a song from the soundtrack of the Sylvester Stallone movie, *Rocky IV* (1985). He also made a memorable appearance as a preacher in *The Blues Brothers* (1980).

Although well past his peak, Brown remained active throughout the 1990s. He toured Britain in 1993 and again in 1998, and in 1999 he became, at 70, the oldest solo artist ever to register a new hit single on the British chart, when his song *Funk on Ah Roll* climbed to No 40, his biggest hit of the decade.

Brown is survived by his fourth wife, Tomi Raye Hynie, one of his former backup singers. His third wife, Adrienne, predeceased him in 1996. He had six children.

Authoritatively described by *Billboard* magazine as Black music's all-time No 1 artist, Brown was a performer of colossal and enduring influence. He will be remembered as a dynamic inspiration to those who followed him and as one of the most important popular music entertainers ever.

In 2003 the South Carolina parole board granted Brown a pardon for his crimes in that state.

James Brown, soul singer, was born on May 3, 1928. He died of pneumonia on Christmas Day, 2006, aged 78

CHRISTINE MCVIE

Reserved, intelligent singer and songwriter for Fleetwood Mac,
whose album Rumours *was one of the biggest-selling of all time*

The Times, November 30, 2022

Under normal circumstances, when Christine and John McVie divorced, they would have gone their separate ways. There were no children to consider and nothing to keep them together – except that they were trapped in the same band, forced to see each other each day and share a stage together every night as they toured the world with Fleetwood Mac.

To rub salt into the wounds, after separating from her husband, Christine had started an affair with the group's lighting director while at the same time two other members of the band, Stevie Nicks and Lindsey Buckingham, were also breaking up and Nicks began an affair with the fifth member of the group, drummer Mick Fleetwood.

If one had been writing a rock'n'roll soap opera, the emotional maelstrom of this torrid plot would surely have been rejected as too preposterous. Yet for the participants it was all too real and they dealt with the fallout in the only way they knew how. They wrote songs to each other about their collective trauma.

The songs became the 1977 album *Rumours*, which went on to sell more than 40 million copies worldwide and became one of the biggest-selling albums of all time.

Christine's compositions for the album included *You Make Loving Fun*, addressed to her new lover, and *Don't Stop*, a message to her husband, which was later famously adopted by President Bill Clinton as his campaign theme tune. On both of them, the jilted ex-husband played bass without missing a beat.

McVie was the most reserved member of the group in the saga, although the description is relative in the context of the rock'n'roll madness and tempestuous lifestyles that characterised the times.

She joined Fleetwood Mac in 1970 from the Birmingham blues-rock band Chicken Shack. When she joined, the group was in transition from its roots as a blues band, following the departure of guitarist Peter Green. McVie had guested on piano on the group's early blues-based albums, but after she became a full-time member Fleetwood Mac began to embrace a more mellifluous soft-rock sound, a process which reached its culmination when the American couple Nicks and Buckingham joined the group in 1974.

This was the classic line-up that three years later recorded *Rumours*. By then, not only were the McVies in the throes of a divorce, but Nicks and Buckingham were also breaking up and barely on speaking terms.

Amid this emotional carnage, the group somehow managed to stay together with dogged and perhaps masochistic determination. The songs they wrote to each other resembled pages ripped from their intimate diaries, the edginess heightened by a chronic cocaine addiction that McVie shared with her fellow band members. The result was some of the most compelling and irresistible rock music of its era.

The group's two female singers became great friends, but they also made for an intriguingly contrasting pair, their different personalities evident in concert, where McVie sat demurely to the side behind her keyboards while Nicks took centre stage and strutted her stuff without inhibition.

McVie stayed with Fleetwood Mac until 1998, when she announced her retirement. She sold her house in the US and returned to Britain, where she spent later years living peacefully in the Kent countryside, shunning the spotlight. She refused the entreaties of former bandmates to rejoin Fleetwood Mac on subsequent tours – for a while, at least.

Christine Anne Perfect was born in 1943, in Bouth, a small Lake District village near Ulverston, in Lancashire. She grew up in Smethwick, Birmingham, after her father, Cyril, a concert violinist, took up a post as a lecturer at a Birmingham college. Her mother, Beatrice, was a psychic medium and faith healer and her grandfather had been an organist at Westminster Abbey.

She took piano lessons from the age of four and continued her classical training until the age of 15, when her elder brother bought a Fats Domino songbook and she began playing rock'n'roll and rhythm and blues tunes.

She studied sculpture at art college in Birmingham for five years and during her student years played pub gigs with a band called Sounds of Blue, occasionally also singing with Spencer Davis. After completing her degree and qualifying as a teacher, she joined Chicken Shack, a blues band formed by Stan Webb and Andy Silvester, with whom she had played in Sounds of Blue.

She recorded two albums with the band and made the Top 10 in 1969 with *I'd Rather Go Blind*, a performance that helped her to win the *Melody Maker* poll as best female vocalist in both 1969 and 1970.

As two of the leading bands of the late 1960s British "blues boom", Chicken Shack and Fleetwood Mac often shared gigs and she played piano as a guest musician on the Fleetwood Mac albums *Mr Wonderful* (1968) and *Then Play On* (1969). On *Kiln House* (1970), she not only played piano but also painted the album's cover.

After leaving Chicken Shack and recording a self-titled solo album, in 1970 she married John McVie and officially joined him in the ranks of Fleetwood Mac. It was an uncertain time for the group with a constantly shifting line-up, but she contributed a number of fine songs to the albums *Future Games* (1971), *Bare Trees* (1972), *Penguin* and *Mystery to Me* (both 1973). She also contributed four songs, including the title track, to *Heroes Are Hard to Find* (1974), but by the time it was released the group – which by now had relocated to America, a move made with some reluctance by the singer – was reduced to a core trio of the McVies and drummer Mick Fleetwood.

When Fleetwood recruited the little-known duo of Nicks and Buckingham to the line-up, it seemed to be a last desperate throw of the dice for a band that was reaching the end of the line. Instead, the new arrivals transformed the group's fortunes.

Nicks and Buckingham were fine songwriters, and McVie found their presence invigorating. She contributed three songs to *Fleetwood Mac* (1975), the singles *Warm Ways*, *Over My Head* and *Say You Love Me*, which helped the album to No 1 in the American charts and global sales of eight million.

The follow up, *Rumours*, was an even bigger success, staying at No 1 in the American charts for eight months. McVie's contributions included two Top Ten singles, *Don't Stop* and *You Make Loving Fun*. The next album, *Tusk* (1979), was a more experimental affair, but sales of "only" four million were considered a commercial failure in the light of what had gone before.

The world tour that followed took rock'n'roll excess to new heights. They travelled by private plane with special aides assigned to carry the band's drugs, and when they hit the ground, each member was ferried in a separate stretch limousine, while the world's finest hotels were instructed to repaint hotel suites in certain colours and install grand pianos in them before the band checked in.

Mirage (1982) was a return to their earlier sound, to which McVie contributed the hits *Hold Me* and *Love in Store*. As had become the Fleetwood Mac way, she couldn't help her private life spilling over into her songs, and *Hold Me* was inspired by her tempestuous relationship with the infamous hell-raiser Dennis Wilson of the Beach Boys.

As the band took a five-year hiatus, McVie released an eponymous 1984 solo album, which included the US Top Ten single *Got a Hold on Me*. To Fleetwood Mac's 1987 comeback album *Tango in the Night* she contributed *Little Lies*, one of the group's biggest hits, co-written with her new husband Eddy Quintela. After the release of *Behind the Mask* (1990), McVie announced she was no longer prepared to tour and Nicks also left the band, although both appeared on stage with the group at President Clinton's inauguration gala in 1993 to perform *Don't Stop*.

She appeared on the group's 1995 album *Time* and was cajoled into joining the re-formed Fleetwood Mac for a sell-out tour in 1998. After that she returned to England, where she bought a house in the quiet Kent village of Wickhambreaux.

She released one last solo album, *In the Meantime* (2004), recorded in a converted barn at her Kent home, but while promoting the record she admitted that she no longer listened to pop. She initially declined to rejoin Fleetwood Mac, with former bandmate Lindsey Buckingham noting: "She wanted to reinvent herself. She seems to want to lead the antithesis of the life she led before."

There was an encore, however. McVie returned to the group in 2014, following what was thought to be a one-off appearance in London a year earlier. Having become a star in the Seventies, she remained one in her seventies.

Christine McVie, musician, was born on July 12, 1943. She died after a short illness on November 30, 2022, aged 79

LEONARD COHEN

———————•———————

Melancholic singer and songwriter who, along with Bob Dylan, was considered the most poetic and enigmatic lyricist of his era

The Times, November 11, 2016

For someone whose songs earned him the epithet "the godfather of gloom", Leonard Cohen had a highly developed and mischievous sense of humour. "I don't consider myself a pessimist," he noted. "I think of a pessimist as someone who is waiting for it to rain – and I feel soaked to the skin."

The subject of his songs over a career that spanned half a century was the human condition, which inevitably led him into some dark places. He suffered bouts of depression in his own life and his mournful voice and the fatalism of his lyrics led his songs to be adopted by the anguished, lovelorn and angst-ridden as a personal liturgy.

However, there were also what Cohen called "the cracks where the light gets in". Despite his image as a purveyor of gloom and doom, the inherent melancholia of his songs was nuanced not only by deep romanticism but by black humour.

A published poet and novelist who was in his thirties before he turned to music, Cohen was the most literate singer and songwriter of his age. With Bob Dylan he occupied the penthouse suite of what he called "the tower of song". Together Cohen and Dylan not only transformed the disposable, sentimental métier of popular music into something more poetic and profound but, for better or worse, made the pop lyric perhaps the defining form of latter 20th-century expression. In an era in which anyone who warbled about "the unicorns of my mind" was liable to be hailed as a poet, Cohen was the genuine article.

Many of his best-known songs *Suzanne, So Long, Marianne* and *Sisters of Mercy* were romantically inspired by the women in his life. In *Chelsea Hotel #2* , the theme of longing, love and loss turned to pure lust as he described a liaison with the singer Janis Joplin as she gave him "head on the unmade bed/While the limousines wait in the street".

The Story of Isaac and *The Butcher* touched on religious themes and war and death loomed large, particularly after his experiences during the 1973 Arab-Israeli war when he offered to fight for Israel and ended up performing for Jewish troops in a tank division that was under fire in the Sinai desert.

Depression and suicide also informed several songs, including *Seems So Long Ago, Nancy* and *Dress Rehearsal Rag*. This tendency to lapse into morbidity led one critic to wail, "Where does he get the neck to stand before an audience and groan out those monstrous anthems of amorous self-commiseration?" Yet if his writing had a philosophical stock-in-trade, it was more stoical perseverance than the abandonment of hope.

Many of his compositions shared a search for self and meaning and were driven by a restless quest for personal freedom, nowhere more so than on *Bird on the Wire*, which opened with probably his most quoted lines *"Like a bird on the wire/Like a drunk in a midnight choir/I have tried in my way to be free"*.

The song was covered by dozens of artists including Johnny Cash, Willie Nelson, Judy Collins and Joe Cocker and was once memorably described as a bohemian version of *My Way*, sans the braggadocio.

Even at his darkest, the prospect of redemption and perhaps even a glimmer of salvation was evident. He described *Hallelujah*, perhaps his best-known composition – and certainly his most covered, with some 300 versions performed or recorded by other artists – as an affirmation of his "faith in life, not in some formal religious way but with enthusiasm, with emotion".

The song took him years to write as he pared back 80 draft verses until each line felt right, as with the second verse: *"Your faith was strong but you needed proof/You saw her bathing on the roof/ Her beauty and the moonlight overthrew you/She tied you to a kitchen chair/She broke your throne, and she cut your hair/And from your lips she drew the hallelujah."*

It was characteristic of the meticulous way he worked to make every word count and led to a well-documented exchange with Bob Dylan, who expressed his admiration for the song: "He asked me how long it took to write, and I lied and said three or four years when actually it took five. Then we were talking about one of his songs, and he said it took him 15 minutes."

Unfailingly courteous and possessed of an unfashionably old-world charm, Cohen's intellectual coming of age predated the advent of rock'n'roll. His early cultural heroes were not Elvis Presley and Chuck Berry but the beat writer Jack Kerouac and the poet Lorca, after whom Cohen named his daughter. His artistic leanings were liberal and bohemian, but he was never a hippy. Dressed in dark, tailored suits and smart fedoras, he had an elegance that was perhaps the legacy of his Jewish father, who owned a clothing store. Sylvie Simmons, his biographer, reckoned he looked "like a Rat Pack rabbi, God's chosen mobster". He spoke in a sonorous voice that was full of a reassuring calm, and yet animated at the same time. If it was a great speaking voice, it was perhaps not a natural vehicle for a singer, although he developed his own idiosyncratic style to overcome its limitations, one which was compared by the critic Maurice Rosenbaum to a strangely appealing buzz-saw: "I knew I was no great shakes as a singer," Cohen said, "but I always thought I could tell the truth about a song. I liked those singers who would just lay out their predicament and tell their story, and I thought I could be one of those guys."

He was handsome in a rugged and swarthy way, and women found the combination of his physical attraction and the sensitivity of his poetic mind to be irresistible. In turn he described love as "the most challenging activity humans get into" and took up the gauntlet with prolific enthusiasm. "I don't think anyone masters the heart. It continues to cook like a shish kebab, bubbling and sizzling in everyone's breast," he said.

Yet whether love ever bought him true happiness is debatable, and in his 2006 poetry collection, *Book of Longing*, he mocked his reputation as a ladies' man as an ill-fitting joke that "caused me to laugh bitterly through the ten thousand nights I spent alone".

He never married but perhaps came closest to contentment with Marianne Ihlen, the inspiration behind several of his early songs and with whom he lived on the Greek island of Hydra in the 1960s.

Their relationship lasted a decade through numerous infidelities. He also had a long relationship with the artist and photographer Suzanne Elrod, with whom he had two children. His son, Adam Cohen, is a singer and songwriter who produced his father's 2016 album *You Want It Darker*. His daughter, Lorca, is a photographer, who gave birth to a surrogate daughter for the singer Rufus Wainwright and Jörn Weisbrodt, his partner.

For all his protests to the contrary, his love life was complicated, almost Byronic in its profligacy. As well as his assignations with Janis Joplin and Joni Mitchell, for example, he bedded the fashion photographer Dominique Issermann, the actress Rebecca De Mornay and the songwriter Anjani Thomas. Mitchell, who once said the only men to whom she was a groupie were Picasso and Cohen, celebrated their year-long relationship in several songs, including *A Case of You*, in which her lover declares himself to be as "constant as a northern star". He certainly was not, and yet she sang that he remains in her blood "like holy wine".

Summing up his lifelong serial inconstancy, his biographer, Simmons, wrote that Cohen's "romantic relationships tended to get in the way of the isolation and space, the distance and longing, that his writing required".

Yet he was as fixated on metaphysical matters as he was on carnal pleasures, and many of his best lyrics fused the erotic and the spiritual. In the 1990s his search for enlightenment resulted in him disappearing from public view for several years to live an ascetic life in a Zen Buddhist monastery on the snow-capped Mount Baldy in California. Although he remained a practising Jew, he was ordained as a Buddhist monk in 1996.

He came down from the mountain three years later and returned to civilian life, only to find that while he was sequestered he had been robbed by his long-time manager (and, perhaps inevitably, former lover), Kelley Lynch. He issued legal proceedings against her for misappropriating millions from his retirement fund and swindling him out of his publishing rights. Left with a huge tax bill and a relatively modest $150,000, he remortgaged his home. He was awarded $9 million by a Los Angeles court in 2006.

When Lynch – who was later jailed after violating a court order to keep away from Cohen – was unable to pay, he undertook his first concert tour in 15 years to replenish his funds. It was estimated by *Billboard* magazine that he earned almost $10 million from the 2009 leg of the tour alone. A golden period of late creativity followed. After releasing a parsimonious 11 studio albums in 45 years, he released three in four years between 2012 and 2016, including *Old Ideas*, which became the highest-charting album of his career, when he was 76.

Leonard Norman Cohen was born in Montreal in 1934, into a prosperous and middle-class Jewish family. His father was already approaching 50 when his son was born, and died when Cohen was nine years old, leaving him with a small trust fund income. His mother Masha was the daughter of a rabbi and brought him up steeped in Talmudic lore and the stories of the Old Testament. He later recalled a "Messianic" childhood.

In an era before rock'n'roll he was drawn to the folk and country music he heard on the radio. He learnt to play the guitar as a teenager "to impress girls" and formed a group called the Buckskin Boys. Women also loomed large in his adolescent life. After reading a book about hypnosis, he tried out the technique and persuaded the family's maid to disrobe. He was 13 at the time.

At the age of 15 he stumbled on a volume by the Spanish poet Federico García Lorca in a second-hand bookshop in Montreal. Inspired by Lorca's erotic themes, he decided to become a writer and adopted his lifelong credo that his creative muse was best served via the entanglement of heart and limbs.

At McGill University he chaired the debating society and won a prize for creative writing. His first book of verse, *Let Us Compare Mythologies*, appeared in 1956. A second volume, *The Spice-Box of Earth*, was published five years later and put him on the literary map. By then wanderlust had set in and he travelled widely, spending time in Castro's Cuba before buying a small house without electricity or running water on the Greek island of Hydra. There he wrote further books of verse and the novels *The Favourite Game* and *Beautiful Losers*, as well as conducting a decade-long romantic relationship with Ihlen.

His books were critically acclaimed and one enthusiastic reviewer gushingly likened *Beautiful Losers* to James Joyce. But good reviews don't put food on even Greek tables and his books initially sold fewer than 3,000 copies. In need of cash, he returned to North America in 1966, planning to try his luck as a singer and songwriter in Nashville.

"In retrospect, writing books seems the height of folly, but I liked the life," he recalled. "It's good to hit that desk every day. There's a lot of order to it that is very different from the life of a rock'n'roller. I turned to professional singing as a remedy for an economic collapse."

He never got as far as Nashville. After landing in New York, he was "ambushed" by the new music he heard all around him. "In Greece I'd been listening to Armed Forces Radio, which was mostly country music," he said. "But then I heard Dylan and Baez and Judy Collins, and I thought something was opening up, so I borrowed some money and moved into the Chelsea Hotel."

Collins became the first to record one of his songs and invited him to sing with her on stage. His first live performance caused him to flee with stage fright, but his shyness appealed to the audience who encouraged him back and set him on his new career as a troubadour. Already in his thirties, he was described by one critic as having "the stoop of an aged crop-picker and the face of a curious little boy".

His singing, too, provoked mixed reactions but John Hammond, the legendary Columbia A&R man who had already signed Bob Dylan to the label, was not one to be put off by an unconventional voice. "He took me to lunch and then we went back to the Chelsea," Cohen remembered. "I played a few songs and he gave me a contract."

He spent two years living in the Chelsea Hotel, fell in with Andy Warhol's set, became infatuated with the Velvet Underground's German chanteuse Nico and released his debut album. Sales in America were initially modest but the record found a cult following in Europe and Britain, where he was dubbed "the bard of the bedsits". Among his most memorable concerts from this time was his appearance at the Isle of Wight Festival in 1970. Unpromisingly he had to go on after an electrifying performance by Jimi Hendrix, yet instead of bringing down the mood he managed to win over the pumped-up 600,000-strong crowd by telling them gentle self-deprecating anecdotes in a hushed voice, in between his equally low-key numbers.

Although his early records sounded austere, centred around little more than his voice and a softly strummed guitar, in later years he expanded his musical palette, adding a full band and chorus of backing singers. Initially he appeared to be a literary aesthete, aloof from the hurly-burly of rock'n'roll, but by the mid-1970s his life was unravelling in a midlife crisis in which LSD experimentation featured. "I got into drugs and drinking and women and travel and feeling that I was part of a motorcycle gang or something," he admitted 20 years later.

His confusion led him to record with Phil Spector, whose production banished the simplicity of his earlier recordings in favour of melodramatic rock arrangements. One grotesque track, *Don't Go Home With Your Hard-On*, featured a drunken chorus of Cohen, Dylan and Allen Ginsberg repeating the title line over and over again.

Working with the volatile Spector was a fraught process. "I was flipped out at the time and he certainly was flipped out," Cohen recalled. "For me, the expression was withdrawal and melancholy, and for him, megalomania and insanity and a devotion to armaments that was really intolerable."

At one point during the sessions, Spector locked Cohen out of the studio, put an armed guard on the door and would not let him listen to the mixes. When Cohen protested, Spector threatened him with a gun and a crossbow.

The resulting album, *Death of a Ladies' Man* in 1977, was a career nadir that horrified his fan base, and he swiftly returned to something closer to his old style. When five years passed between the release of albums it appeared that his inspiration had dried up, a blockage that he later attributed to having become addicted to amphetamines. *Various Positions* in 1984 was a triumph and included *Hallelujah*. It sparked a revival both creatively and commercially as Cohen adopted the mode of a fashionable boulevardier.

With an increasingly sardonic humour he surveyed the wreckage of the modern world in songs such as *First We Take Manhattan*, *Democracy* and *Everybody Knows* and painted an apocalyptic picture of the world. It was a vision that struck a hellish chord with the film director Oliver Stone who included three of Cohen's songs from the period in his horrifyingly violent, dystopian movie *Natural Born Killers*. Shortly after the film's release, Cohen retreated to his Zen Buddhist monastery.

When he returned to recording and live performance after a decade-long break, he was treated more like a guru than a peddler of popular songs. Seated on a stool, guitar in hand, or cupping a microphone ("as Hamlet held Yorick's skull", one critic suggested), his concerts became acts of communion, with reverential audiences treating his every utterance as if it were holy writ.

Age seemed to suit him, uniquely emphasising his sagacity, while the advancing years simply made other fading rock stars appear irrelevant. Eschewing make-up, surgery and denial, he embraced getting old as "the only game in town". That he was still writing compelling songs and releasing records into his eighties was "the ash" that showed his life was still "burning well".

Despite continuing his recording career until his final months, Cohen stopped touring in 2013 and hinted at his preparedness for the end in the summer of 2016. After the death of Marianne (obituary, August 27), a letter from Cohen was released in which he said goodbye to his muse and former lover. "Our bodies are falling apart and I think I will follow you very soon," he wrote. "Know that I am so close behind you that if you stretch out your hand, I think you can reach mine."

Leonard Cohen, poet and songwriter, was born on September 21, 1934. His death, aged 82, was announced on November 10, 2016

JIMI HENDRIX

●

American singer and songwriter who expanded the range and vocabulary
of the electric guitar into areas no musician had ever ventured before

The Times, September 18, 1970

Jimi Hendrix, the pop musician, died in London yesterday. If Bob Dylan was the man who liberated pop music verbally, to the extent that after him it could deal with subjects other than teenage affection, then Jimi Hendrix was largely responsible for whatever musical metamorphosis it has undergone in the past three years.

Born in Seattle, Washington, he was part Negro, part Cherokee Indian, part Mexican, and gave his date of birth as November 27, 1945. He left school early, picked up the guitar, and hitchhiked around the southern States of America before arriving in New York, where he worked for a while with a vaudeville act before joining the Isley Brothers' backing band. He toured all over America with various singers, including Sam Cooke, Little Richard and Ike and Tina Turner, until in August, 1966, he wound up in Greenwich Village, New York, playing with his own band for $15 a night. It was there that he was heard by Chas Chandler, former bass guitarist with the Animals, who became his manager and persuaded him to travel to England.

Once in London he put together a trio with drummer Mitch Mitchell and bass guitarist Noel Redding, called the Jimi Hendrix Experience. The guitarist's wild clothes, long frizzy hair, and penchant for playing guitar solos with his teeth quickly made him a sensation.

His playing was rooted in the long-lined blues approach of BB King, but was brought up to date through the use of amplification as a musical device, and his solos were often composed of strings of feedback sound, looping above the free-flowing bass and drums. The whole sound of the group, loose and improvisational and awesomely loud, was quite revolutionary and made an immediate impact on his guitar-playing contemporaries. As a singer and composer he was one of the first Black musicians to come to terms with the electronic facilities offered by rock music, and his songs and voice, influenced considerably by Dylan, created perhaps the first successful fusion of blues and White pop.

After his phenomenal success in Britain he returned to America, where he was banned from a concert tour by the Daughters of the American Revolution, who considered his onstage physical contortions obscene. That served only to increase interest in him and he rapidly became one of the world's top rock attractions. Then, at the beginning of 1969 and at the height of his fame, he disappeared and spent more than a year in virtual seclusion, playing at home with a few friends. Early in 1970 he unveiled a new trio, the Band of Gipsies, and returned to Britain last month to play at the Isle of Wight festival.

In his last interview he was quoted as saying that he'd reached the end of the road with the trio format, and was planning to form a big band. In direct contrast to the violence and seeming anarchy of his music, Hendrix was a gentle, peaceful man whose only real concern was music. His final public appearance was when he sat in with War, an American band, at Ronnie Scott's club in London last Wednesday, and it was typical of the man that it was he who felt honoured by being allowed to play.

Jimi Hendrix, musician, was born on November 27, 1942. He died of barbiturate intoxication on September 18, 1970, aged 27

AMY WINEHOUSE

———————•———————

Singer and songwriter with an astonishing voice and talent, her career was tarnished by drugs, alcohol and scandal

The Times, July 25, 2011

Out of the chaos of a deeply troubled personal life and an unhealthy predilection for self-destruction, Amy Winehouse fashioned a rare artistry to become the most talented British female singer of her generation.

When she burst on to the scene in 2003, pop music was dominated by girl-next-door types such as Dido and Katie Melua. It was immediately evident that Winehouse came from a quite different tradition and her whisky-breathed, nicotine-stained bad-girl attitude, allied to a powerful and lived-in voice, revived the lusty, man-eating spirit of ball-busting but troubled divas of earlier eras such as Billie Holiday and Janis Joplin.

The image could have been contrived but sadly it was all too dangerously real. Almost from the outset, she cut a doomed figure who lived on the edge. Yet along with the impression that she was never far away from self-destruction came real talent. She was just 20 when she made her breakthrough but her artistic maturity was remarkable as she married a thrilling jazz-soul voice of compelling conviction to a precocious songwriting talent.

Success was almost instant. Within three years of her debut she had become the biggest female singer in Britain, showered with Ivor Novello and Brit awards and half a dozen Grammy awards for her two critically acclaimed multimillion-selling albums. But she was also living up to her bad-girl image and was regularly photographed by the paparazzi falling out of her high heels as she left clubs considerably the worse for wear in the early hours.

As it became increasingly obvious that she was finding it difficult to cope with fame, fears about her health spread. She shed her original, voluptuously full figure and became stick-insect thin, leading to much tabloid speculation. She later admitted that she was a manic depressive and suffered from eating disorders. Performances were abandoned when she appeared on stage intoxicated or concerts were cancelled at short notice with the singer pleading "exhaustion", although on at least one occasion when she should have been on stage, she was then photographed drinking in a bar.

Her notoriety was such that bookmakers began offering odds on whether she would turn up for her next gig. Instead of destroying her career, for a while her unreliability and much-publicised troubles only seemed to enhance her appeal. On her biggest hit *Rehab* she boasted of her refusal to seek help for her drinking. It appeared that much of her audience not only accepted her "unpredictability" as the by-product of a genuine artistry but indulgently admired her wildness as a not-unwelcome antidote to the cold calculation and manipulative spin of much of the rest of the pop world.

But as the years rolled by without any sign of her getting her act together, the patience of even her most dedicated fans began to wear thin. Her sporadic concerts were often booed when audiences realised she was too drunk to deliver a professional performance. Her record company grew increasingly frustrated by her failure to follow up her triumphant 2006 album *Back to Black*, which won six Grammy awards.

Amy Jade Winehouse was born in 1983 into a Jewish family in Southgate, north London. Her father Mitch was a taxi driver and her mother Janis a pharmacist, but there were several jazz musicians in the family and she grew up listening to such singers as Sarah Vaughan, Dinah Washington and Ella Fitzgerald, as well as to the pop music of the time. She also showed a precocious interest in performing herself.

At the age of ten she formed a rap duo with a schoolfriend called Sweet-n-Sour, in the style of the Black American female duo Salt-n-Pepa. She was Sour and her enthusiasm and precocious talent encouraged her parents to enrol her when she was 12 at the Sylvia Young Theatre School, where other famous former pupils include members of the Spice Girls and All Saints.

However, the rebellious streak that was to become a trademark of her career asserted itself immediately and within a year she had been expelled for "not applying herself" and for defying school rules by piercing her nose.

In 1997 she transferred to the Brit School in Croydon, another performing arts college but where a more relaxed attitude to the creative process prevailed. While there she took guitar lessons and began writing her own songs. By 1999 she was already singing professionally. After her friend Tyler James, the singer, circulated her demo tape to a number of contacts in the music business, she signed a deal with 19 Management, owned and run by Simon Fuller, whose other clients included the Spice Girls and who went on to launch the *Pop Idol* TV series.

He secured her a contract with Island Records, which in turn teamed her with the producer Salaam Remi to write and record her debut album, *Frank*. Released in October 2003, the album's combination of jazz, funk and R&B received enviable reviews and excited flattering comparisons with everyone from Nina Simone to Erykah Badu. Her husky vocals exuded a potent sexual charge and her lyrics were wantonly honest and risqué, no more so than on *I Heard Love Is Blind*. The song was about infidelity but found her professing no guilt as she explained: "*What do you expect?/ You left me here alone/ I drank so much and needed to touch/ Don't overreact/ I pretended he was you/ You wouldn't want me to be lonely* ."

Yet there was also warmth and a tongue-in-cheek wit alongside the feistiness and it seemed astonishing that she was only 20, for she sounded as if she had been singing the songs in jazz clubs every night for years.

Critical acclaim was swiftly translated into commercial success and in early 2004 the album broke into the British Top 20. She was also nominated for Brit awards as best female solo artist and best urban act. She won neither but later that same year she scooped the prestigious Ivor Novello award for best contemporary song for *Stronger Than Me*, the album's first single, which she co-wrote with Remi. *Frank* also made the shortlist for the 2004 Mercury Music prize. But despite such accolades, Winehouse later said that she was "only 80 per cent" behind the album and complained that her record label had interfered by demanding the inclusion of certain songs and mixes she disliked.

Back to Black, her second album, appeared in October 2006, exactly three years after her debut. It swiftly dwarfed the success of that earlier record, topping the British album charts and reaching No 7 in the US, at the time the highest debut entry for an album by a British female solo artist (a record soon to be snatched away by Joss Stone, who debuted at No 2 with her first album, *Introducing Joss Stone*).

This time Remi shared the production credits with the New York-based Mark Ronson, while Winehouse's jazz leanings were augmented by a new set of influences derived from a love of the classic "girl groups" of the 1950s and early 1960s. Among the album's most potent songs was *Rehab*, a real-life drama about her own refusal to attend an alcohol rehabilitation centre, and which gave her a Top 10 single in both Britain and America. The song was written in response to her management's attempt to force her to attend a clinic and she fired them in protest.

That she had an alcohol problem, though, was all too obvious. While promoting *Back to Black* she appeared intoxicated on Charlotte Church's TV show and on *Never Mind the Buzzcocks* and garnered further lurid tabloid headlines when she drunkenly heckled a speech by Bono at the Q awards. She also got into a fight at her album launch party and later confessed that when she drank she became "an ugly dickhead". Around the time of the release of *Back to Black* she also revealed that she was bipolar but refused to take any medication for the condition.

She further confirmed rumours that she suffered from eating disorders, confessing to "a little bit of anorexia and a little bit of bulimia". Photographs of her with scars on her arm, some old and some apparently freshly inflicted, also led to speculation that she was subject to bouts of self-harm.

None of this hindered her success or harmed her record sales. In February 2007 she won a Brit award as best female artist and three months later *Rehab* won her a second Ivor Novello award. Her growing celebrity, however, only appeared to amplify her problems. During early 2007, she began cancelling concerts at short notice and with increasing regularity. On the day of one cancelled appearance she was photographed buying drink in her local supermarket in the morning and boozing in a Camden bar that night. In Australia, a performance was halted after one song when she vomited on stage.

Part of her unhappiness was attributed to her estrangement from her boyfriend Blake Fielder-Civil, but after a year apart they were reconciled and married in Miami in May 2007. Yet marriage did nothing to stem the chaos and the cancelled shows. Both were drug addicts and their relationship remained turbulent.

"I'll beat up Blake when I'm drunk," she told a TV interviewer a month after they had wed. "I don't think I have ever bruised him, but I do have my way. If he says one thing I don't like, then I'll chin him." They were eventually divorced in 2009.

During the last five years of her life there was plenty of tabloid notoriety, legal troubles and numerous paparazzi pictures of her in various states of dishevelment and distress. But there was little new music. A cover of a Sam Cooke song appeared on a charity album and a version of *It's My Party* was recorded for a Quincy Jones tribute. But despite repeated claims that she was starting work on the follow-up to 2006's *Back to Black*, nothing appeared. She even announced she was setting up her own record label, Lioness Records, but all that emerged was an album by Dionne Bromfield, Winehouse's 13-year-old goddaughter, on which she sang some backing vocals.

Despite the defiance of the lyrics of her hit song, there were several attempts at rehab, the most recent of them only a few weeks before her death. Her short stay in a clinic was prompted by her need to get in shape for a European tour. In the event, the attempted return to the stage was a disaster; after being booed when she appeared too drunk to sing on the opening night in Belgrade, the remaining dates were cancelled.

Amy Winehouse, singer, was born on September 14, 1983. She was found dead on July 23, 2011, aged 27

GEORGE MICHAEL

━━━━━━━━●━━━━━━━━

Pop superstar who enjoyed huge success – with Wham! then as a solo artist – but whose demons almost came to eclipse his prodigious musical talents

The Times, December 27, 2016

George Michael's turbulent career embraced pop exuberance as a teenage pin-up in Wham! and a reinvention as a serious and brooding solo artist. In the course of it, he made some memorable music, sold an estimated 100 million records and became a superstar. In later years, however, he fell into disenchantment with his celebrity and hit the headlines for a disastrous lawsuit against his record company – one that cost him millions – and a conviction for lewd behaviour in a public lavatory.

It was this latter indiscretion that encouraged him to dispel an impression he had been cultivating for years, namely that his companionable ways were appreciated by women more than men.

In fact, as he then felt obliged to disclose, he was gay and hadn't slept with a woman in ten years.

He attempted to rebuild his career after these difficulties in his private life, but struggled to replicate his earlier commercial success. In 2005 he went so far as to announce his farewell to the world of pop music, declaring the genre "dead".

Although Michael was a curious mixture of restlessness, angst and self-possession, he was capable of laughing at his own absurdities. In 2007, not long after one of his periodic arrests for possession of drugs, he agreed to a cameo in Ricky Gervais's *Extras* – a self-parodic scene in which he "cottaged" on Hampstead Heath, while eating a kebab and smoking a joint.

"I want to apologise to my fans for screwing up again," he said the next time he was arrested. "I want to promise them I'll sort myself out. And to say sorry to everybody else, just for boring them." There was another self-parody, this time for *Comic Relief* in 2011. He was seen sharing a car with Smithy, the character played by James Corden in *Gavin and Stacey*. Michael sulks when Smithy tells him he can't take part in a charity event because he's become too much of "a joke".

He was born Georgios Kyriacos Panayiotou in 1963, in Finchley, north London. His father was a Greek-Cypriot restaurant-owner, his mother an English dancer. When he was 11, on his first day at Bushey Meads School, he met Andrew Ridgeley. Initially Michael was the less confident figure, an odd-looking, overweight youth with an ungainly and self-conscious demeanour. Yet the two became firm friends and a shared love of pop music led them in 1979 to form their first group, the Executive, inspired by the ska revival of the time, led by the Specials and Madness. The group lasted only 18 months, but afforded Michael the opportunity to both shed his awkwardness and hone his songwriting skills.

By 1981, he and Ridgeley, now performing as Wham!, had written several of the songs that were to define their career, including *Club Tropicana* and *Careless Whisper*. They had also written a number called *Wham Rap! (Enjoy What You Do)*, which exploited the name the pair had decided to give their new group and which was taken – or so it was claimed subsequently, and perhaps not totally reliably – from a Roy Lichtenstein painting. After hiring portable equipment to record the songs in the front room of Ridgeley's parents' house, they hawked the tape around all of the big record companies, receiving countless rejections, until a tiny dance-based label, Innervision, showed an interest in early 1982.

Success was not instant, but by the end of that year the duo's second single, *Young Guns (Go for It)*, had risen to No 3 in the British charts, helped by a sensational dance routine on *Top of the Pops* and the smouldering good looks of Michael, now transformed into a perma-tanned, blow-dried, bare-chested Adonis in a sleeveless leather jacket.

The next year brought them further Top 10 singles, with a reissue of *Wham Rap!* and *Bad Boys*. As Michael assumed full control of the band's music and teen-orientated lyrics, Ridgeley concentrated on style, image and visuals, including a video of the pair cavorting on stage in their shorts, complete with strategically placed shuttlecocks. The combination helped Wham!'s debut album, *Fantastic*, to reach No 1 in the British charts in 1983.

After a legal battle with Innervision, the duo signed to Epic Records and hit gold immediately when the first single for the new label, *Wake Me Up Before You Go-Go*, topped the charts in Britain and America. This catchy song was followed to the No 1 spot by *Careless Whisper*. A smooching ballad quite different from Wham!'s up-tempo style, it was released as a solo effort by Michael, who dedicated it to his parents and declared it was "five minutes in return for 21 years".

With Michael increasingly the dominant character, Wham!'s second album, *Make It Big*, also topped charts on both sides of the Atlantic in 1984, confirming them as the world's leading teen-pop sensation of the Eighties and paving the way for the plethora of boy bands that would follow in the Nineties.

By now it seemed that commercially Wham!, and Michael in particular, could do no wrong. The singer was featured on Band Aid's all-star charity release, *Do They Know It's Christmas?*, which ironically kept Wham!'s own rather charming seasonal offering, *Last Christmas*, from the No 1 spot in December 1984.

The duo's *annus mirabilis* came in 1985, when they won the British group award at the Brits, became the first western group to tour China, and released the chart-topping single *I'm Your Man*. Michael also won an Ivor Novello for his songwriting. Yet by the end of the year, he and Ridgeley had decided that they would go their own ways.

Michael had already released his second solo single, the stark and introspective *A Different Corner*, which again went to No 1. It made him one of the hottest properties in the market as he embarked on a solo career and, in a move that would have serious repercussions, Sony/Epic extended his contract for five further albums.

Although still only 23, Michael was anxious to shed the teenage heart-throb image and to establish himself as a grown-up singer and songwriter. His desire for critical acclaim as a serious artist was evident when one of his first post-Wham! releases was a duet with Aretha Franklin, the much-revered "queen of soul", on *I Knew You Were Waiting (For Me)*. The single topped the charts in Britain and America and went on to win a Grammy. Less happily, it was followed by the facile solo single, *I Want Your Sex*, which peaked at No 2 in America and No 3 in Britain. Michael believed the song was kept from the top spot by the fact that a number of radio stations banned it. The more honest explanation was that it was not his finest hour musically.

Nevertheless, its parent album, *Faith*, which he wrote, arranged and produced, restored him to the No 1 spot in both Britain and America in late 1987. Packed with power ballads and sleek pop-soul numbers, it won him another Grammy award and sold more than 20 million copies.

Yet he was feeling increasingly trapped by the pressures of stardom, a fact that was reflected on his second solo album, *Listen Without Prejudice Vol. 1*, released in 1990. Full of soul-searching songs that signalled his disenchantment, its release was followed by the publication of his autobiography, *Bare*, and a declaration that he was rejecting the rock-star lifestyle and eschewing pop videos and stadium tours to concentrate on his songwriting. His growing subtlety was demonstrated by *Cowboys and Angels*, a song with descending minor chords written in a waltz time and with a haunting saxophone solo by Andy Hamilton.

Michael could certainly afford to turn his back on the promotion side of things, for by then he was comfortably ensconced on *The Sunday Times* Rich List. His bulging bank balance was swelled further when the album rode high in the charts on both sides of the Atlantic and produced the hit singles *Praying for Time* and, surely his most powerfully soulful and funky song, *Freedom! '90*. The latter, despite his earlier protestations, was accompanied by a video featuring a gaggle of lip-syncing supermodels, including Naomi Campbell and Cindy Crawford.

Listen Without Prejudice Vol. 1 was to be his last album for almost six years, during which his attention was engaged elsewhere. *Don't Let the Sun Go Down on Me*, an overblown duet with Elton John released in 1991, gave him a No 1 in Britain and America and he donated half a million dollars from his royalties to AIDS charities, a subject that, for reasons not apparent at the time, was becoming of increasing concern to him.

He was equally exercised by what he regarded as the rapaciousness of his record company and its failure to market him properly. In October 1992 he launched an unprecedented restraint of trade action against Sony Music, seeking to nullify his contract with the label. After a lengthy High Court hearing, judgment was delivered two years later in a 273-page ruling in favour of Sony, which declared that his deal with it was "reasonable and fair". Michael was ordered to pay £3 million in costs. The acrimony meant he could never work for the company again, and in 1995 Sony announced that he was free to leave.

Yet it was at a price. Signing to DreamWorks in America and Virgin for the rest of the world, his two new record companies had to pay Sony an estimated £25 million plus a percentage of the sale of his next two albums. To his chagrin, his former label kept the rights to his back catalogue.

Older, his first album under his new deal, appeared in 1996 to lukewarm reviews. Certainly it was a melancholy and at times po-faced collection, but it still topped charts all over the world. When his mother died of cancer the next year, he was inconsolable and sank into depression. Later he admitted he felt so "worthless" he had contemplated suicide.

If the court case against Sony had been traumatic enough, worse was to follow. In 1998, he was arrested and charged with lewd behaviour in a public lavatory in Beverly Hills. Three days later he gave an interview revealing for the first time that he was gay. It also emerged that his Brazilian boyfriend, Anselmo Feleppa, had died from an AIDS-related illness in 1993 at the height of Michael's battle with Sony. As a result of his arrest, he was sentenced to community service. He also had to endure the criticisms of those who felt he should have revealed his sexuality sooner. "I find him very frustrating," his friend Sir Elton John said. "To be busted in the toilet is not the best way to come out of the closet, is it?"

The revelations about his private life did little to diminish his popularity in Britain, where the album *Ladies & Gentleman: The Best of George Michael* topped the charts and the single *Outside*, about alfresco sex, made No 2. It was supported by a video that mischievously hinted at the events surrounding his arrest, featuring urinals, kissing policemen and silver disco balls.

Yet in America the backlash was considerable and the album struggled to No 24, a poor showing for an artist whose previous album had featured a record-breaking six Top 5 singles.

He excited further controversy in 2002 with the satirical anti-Iraq War single *Shoot the Dog*, which was accompanied by a cartoon video depicting George W Bush in bed with Tony Blair and his wife.

His album *Patience* appeared in 2004. Only his fourth solo album of new material since Wham! had split up 18 years earlier, the title was apt enough. But it was savaged by most critics, a reaction that surely influenced his decision in early 2005 to announce the end of his pop career in a candid film documentary called *George Michael: A Different Story*. One of those critics was his now former friend, Sir Elton John, who declared the album "disappointing" and added that Michael appeared to be in a "strange place", smoked too much marijuana and had a "deep-rooted unhappiness in his life". Michael retaliated with the words: "Most of what Elton knows about my life is limited to the gossip he hears on the gay grapevine." It emerged that the two had been engaged in a feud for about five years (and another five would pass before the napkins of peace were billowed between them over the dinner table).

Michael returned to live performance, embarking on a mammoth tour that began in Barcelona in September 2006 and finished in Abu Dhabi in December 2008. He also became the first artist to appear at the reopened Wembley Stadium, recorded three new songs and a duet with Sir Paul McCartney, and took part in a second edition of the *South Bank Show* dedicated to his work.

He toured Australia in 2010, but the year was dominated by his conviction and subsequent prison sentence for driving under the influence of drugs. He was arrested in July for crashing his Range Rover into a Snappy Snaps photo store in Hampstead and in September was sentenced to eight weeks in prison and banned from driving for five years. He served half of the sentence and said later: "Remarkably enough – I know people must think it was a really horrific experience – it's so much easier to take any form of punishment if you believe you actually deserve it, and I did."

In May 2011 Michael announced another long and grandiose tour, this time with a 41-piece orchestra and playing some venues more usually associated with classical music. It was during an opening-night performance in Prague that he revealed that he had split up from his long-term partner, the Texan art dealer Kenny Goss, two years earlier, although their relationship, which was "no strings attached", had been the subject of considerable debate before this confirmation. Michael explained in detail that seemed a little overgenerous that although they often had sex with other men they were "emotionally monogamous" to one another.

The tour came to an abrupt end in Vienna when Michael was admitted to hospital suffering from pneumonia. The rest of the dates, including his return to the stage in the UK, were cancelled. After treatment in hospital, he made a tearful appearance outside his London home and said it had been "touch and go" whether he would live.

Earlier this month it was announced that the producer and songwriter Naughty Boy was working with Michael on a new album, and the tabloids reported that he and Goss might have rekindled their relationship. The news stories, it seems, followed him like pecking birds to the very end of his life.

George Michael, singer and songwriter, was born on June 25, 1963. He died of heart failure on December 25, 2016, aged 53

JOHN LENNON

———————•———————

*Innovative and influential singer, songwriter and musician who played
a dominant role in a pop music revolution*

The Times, December 10, 1980

John Lennon who, as a dominating member of the Beatles,
played an important part in a pop music success extraordinary even
by the standards of that extraordinary genre, died after being shot
outside his New York home on December 8. He was 40.

The Beatles dominated the pop music of the 1960s, creating in
the "Beatlemania" which struck their audiences and young followers
wherever they went paroxysms of enthusiasm which rivalled and
even surpassed anything that had gone before them in the short
history of rock'n' roll.

Hairstyles, styles of dress, even styles of speaking – for the first
time a transatlantic twang ceased to be a sine qua non for pop
performers – followed in their wake. Indeed, not only were they an
astonishing success in America but they completely wrested the palm
from the country where rock'n'roll had been born and bred, and
which in those days seemed to have a prescriptive right to adjudicate
on what was feasible and what was not in pop music. After the
Beatles it was never again possible for British groups to think of
themselves as the poor relations in pop music.

The Beatles paved the way for the American successes of the
Rolling Stones and many others. They encompassed the change of
heart which could lead an American rock writer to remark in the
later 1960s, "Everyone's just wild to see an English rock band." But
this success was not merely a matter of finding a new formula to
succeed the languorous balladeering into which rock'n'roll seemed
largely to have sunk after the initial drive of Bill Haley, Elvis Presley
and Buddy Holly ran into the sands in the early 1960s.

The Beatles brought a new musicality to pop music, which
succeeded in giving it a much wider appeal than it had had previously.

In their genial, at any rate seldom less than pleasing, melodies and enticing, attractive harmonies, they somehow gave an impression of being more musically literate than any of their predecessors, though in fact none of the four could either read or write music. And this impression coupled with their "clean-looking" appearance, gave pop music a sudden entree into quarters where it had previously been virtually a proscribed subject. The mothers of their besotted fans liked the Beatles too – could contemplate in them, perhaps, future sons-in-law – while in the most severely critical musicological circles immoderate rhapsodies were to be heard on their musicianly attainments.

With the pronouncement from one distinguished critic that the Beatles were the "greatest songwriters since Schubert" they appeared as ambassadors for pop music to have secured an accolade for their genre that would have seemed impossible a few years previously. Of this success John Lennon was an important – perhaps the most important – component. It was he who had started the group. With Paul McCartney he composed the songs which first projected the Beatles to fame. His caustic wit, his intellectual sharpness and perhaps his sense of what was likely to be good for the mental health of a group of young men caught up in the kind of success which overtook the Beatles were formative influences on the way the Beatles behaved.

It was he who in particular disliked the fact that the Beatles appeared to have become the property of their more respectable fans. And when first the distancing from, and then the alienation of, those fans began with the retreat into kaftans, joss sticks and drugs it bore the hallmarks of Lennon's cast of mind and intellectual preoccupations.

John Winston Lennon was born in Liverpool in 1940. His father, Fred Lennon, a ship's steward, and his mother, Julia separated when he was a small child and John was brought up by his aunt Mimi. He was educated at Dovedale Primary School, Quarry Bank High School and the Liverpool College of Art. A rebel in an era before child rebellion was officially subsidised by adult indulgence, he took little interest in the formal side of his schooling and in consequence made little formal progress. However his headmaster at Quarry

Bank did take an interest and it was this interest which enabled him to get into Liverpool College of Art in spite of the fact that he had none of the necessary certificates. At art college he followed the prevailing mode of dress and behaviour, that of the Teddy boy, and under the tutelage of his mother, who had reappeared in his life when he was in his early teens, learnt the banjo.

The skiffle craze was then sweeping through Britain and this species of music which required little or no formal musical knowledge was enabling thousands of teenagers to participate in music making. In particular hundreds of groups sprang up all over Liverpool, among them the Quarrymen, the group Lennon had formed at school. This group was joined in 1956 by a boy from another Liverpool school, Paul McCartney. George Harrison joined in the following year, and later, Ringo Starr replaced Pete Best as the drummer, to give the group the final form in which it was to take the world by storm.

Lennon's mother died in a road accident in 1958, an event which affected him deeply. Between 1956 and 1960, the name of Lennon's group was to undergo several metamorphoses – from the Quarrymen it was successively the Moondogs, Rainbows, Silver Beatles and finally Beatles. None of these transformations brought much success however; the group came close to being discovered at talent shows and auditions on a couple of occasions, but a full career launch evaded it.

For several years the group played, in common with its many rivals, the round of coffee bars, parties, small teenage clubs and dances, often for slender remuneration. Lennon had however found that his meeting with McCartney enabled him to compose songs and the confidence this gave both men enabled them to persist. As these songs and their performance took on a more distinctive quality they began to become known especially in the Cavern Club in Liverpool, one of the foci of the new Merseyside sound.

From 1960 onwards they also played at a nightclub in Hamburg's Reeperbahn – their first formal professional engagement to that date and one which had an important effect on their development. In the next two years they were to play at this and other Hamburg nightclubs, and it was a song recorded in Germany which brought them to the attention of Brian Epstein, who was then running a record department in Liverpool. More discouragement was to follow – they were turned down by almost every major recording company in Britain– but it was Epstein's persistence which finally saw them to a recording contract with Parlophone in 1962.

Their first single, *Love Me Do*, was released in October of that year and entered the charts, drawing considerable attention; *Please Please Me* was at No 1 in the January of 1963. These records were merely the first of a stream of singles which had by the summer of 1963 established a rhythmical style which took the music business and the young by storm.

Twist and Shout, She Loves You, I Want to Hold Your Hand – these and countless others invaded the dancefloors and discotheques with their fresh, insistent rhythms and boisterous, almost healthy message, and drove the outmoded sentiment of the earlier 1960s before them. This was the zenith of Beatlemania. On tour in this country they were mobbed wherever they went. America succumbed, audiences even outdoing the scenes of frenzy registered in Britain.

With their triumphant return from the United States the Beatles seemed almost to become a piece of national property. They appeared to advertise abroad an English way of life – dynamic, creative, progressive, forward-looking – that was pleasantly at odds with the received image of a country suffering economic, political and foreign policy problems, with only a past to find pleasure in.

And in 1966, the group's joint appointment as Members of the Order of the British Empire echoed a general feeling that the Beatles had been at the spearhead of – the formation of a new role for – Britain in the world.

The Swinging Sixties were suddenly launched. The lead in progressive music had been plucked from America's grasp; that in fashion was wrested from Paris. In design, architecture, motor engineering and lifestyle, the national mood was suddenly buoyant and the Beatles seemed to be the apostles of this buoyancy. Lennon himself had, in fact, had to acquiesce somewhat reluctantly in this species of popularity.

It was not in his iconoclastic nature to relish, for example, an invitation to a formal banquet from a grateful local council. Journalists, too, found that his barbed ripostes went some way beyond the characteristic Beatles jollity and candour. This individuality became more and more marked after 1966, when the group had ceased to tour and largely lived as individuals, coming together for recording sessions. Lennon embraced transcendental meditation, drugs and religion, especially that of a mystical kind.

This did not stop the production of music. A flow of albums continued, culminating in the brilliant *Sgt Pepper's*; but Lennon now composed his own songs instead of working jointly with McCartney. Lennon's own contribution to these became, too, more surreal and enigmatic, with songs such as *Lucy in the Sky with Diamonds* and *Strawberry Fields Forever.*

In 1968, too, he divorced his first wife Cynthia, whom he had married in Liverpool in 1962, and became associated with the Japanese film producer Yoko Ono, who later became his wife. This seemed to increase his distance not only from the other Beatles but from the rest of the world. His returning the insignia of MBE in what he described as a protest against British involvement in Vietnam, Biafra and Nigeria, appeared to signal his final renunciation of what the Beatles had stood for in their early days.

The end of the Beatles eventually came in 1971 when the partnership was finally wound up in the High Court. The Beatles Fan Club was disbanded in the following year and it was left to the millions of followers merely to dream of that chimerical event, a reunion in the recording studio of the four members of the group.

Lennon then began a long seclusion with his wife, Yoko Ono, surfacing only occasionally to make headlines with news that he was struggling against drugs, was resisting the attempts of the United States authorities to deport him, or that he had exchanged roles with his wife and was now devoting his entire energies to bringing up the son from their marriage. Only recently had he shown signs of ending this seclusion. A new single, *Starting Over*, recently released, seemed to mark the end of a virtual five-year retirement and this record was merely a precursor to a new album, *Double Fantasy*.

At the time of his death Lennon's fortune was estimated at £100 million. Lennon had a son, Julian, of his first marriage and a son, Sean, of his second.

John Lennon, musician, was born on October 9, 1940. He died on December 8, 1980, aged 40

TINA TURNER

Singer and ultimate diva, whose rising and falling and rising again backstory was stranger than fiction

The Times, May 25, 2023

One day in 1976, a distraught Tina Turner turned up at the Ramada Inn in Dallas wearing a blood-stained white suit and with 36 cents in her purse. She had finally left her abusive husband Ike Turner after one beating too many.

The duo were meant to be playing a concert in Dallas that night but, with her face "all beat up and battered and one eye swollen shut", she had reached the end of the road. The hotel manager gave her a room and posted a security guard at her door, in case Ike should discover where she was.

By the time their divorce was finalised two years later, Turner and her children were living on food stamps. Seldom had any chart-topping star fallen so low.

With no recording contract, she was reduced to playing low-rent cocktail lounges in an attempt to pay off the $500,000 of debts with which the split had saddled her. Even her name was not her own, for Ike had copyrighted it. As part of the settlement she got to keep her name but in return Ike loaded on to her the entirety of a vast tax bill that the couple owed on their musical earnings.

Yet her pride and self-respect were intact and she gradually began not only to rebuild her life but to stage one of the most extraordinary comebacks in showbusiness history.

With an ambitious young Australian promoter named Roger Davies installed as her new manager, she determined to break out of the cabaret circuit and refashion herself as rock's ultimate diva. Her first step was to call on the help of some heavyweight celebrity fans. The Rolling Stones and Rod Stewart were persuaded to book her as their support act and David Bowie intervened to get her a recording contract, telling executives at his label, EMI, that she was his "all-time favourite singer".

To please their biggest star they signed her as Bowie's vanity project but what happened next took everyone by surprise. When Turner's 1984 single *What's Love Got to Do With It* went to No 1, the label was caught totally unprepared. It had been five years since her previous album and EMI had not thought to record another one.

She was rushed into the studio and two weeks later emerged with *Private Dancer*, which included a cover of Bowie's song *1984* as a thank you. The album went on to sell 14 million copies and won Turner three Grammy awards. She had gone almost overnight from living on food stamps to rivalling Michael Jackson and Madonna as the biggest-selling solo star of the decade.

Turner's second coming continued with a film role in 1985's *Mad Max: Beyond Thunderdome*, alongside Mel Gibson. The film gave her another hit single with its theme song, *We Don't Need Another Hero*. That same year there followed a raunchy duet with Mick Jagger, which was one of the highlights of Live Aid, and there were further multimillion-selling albums with *Break Every Rule* (1986) and *Foreign Affair* (1989). Each new release was accompanied by a spectacular world tour and a 1988 concert in Rio de Janeiro, attended by 180,000 fans, earned Turner a place in the *Guinness World Records*.

Such a triumphal tale of resilience in the face of adversity was tailor-made for Hollywood, and her autobiography, *I, Tina,* was turned into the 1993 biopic *What's Love Got to Do With It,* starring Angela Bassett as Tina and Laurence Fishburne as a particularly unpleasant Ike.

After a decade and a half back at the top, she announced she was signing out in 2000 with a farewell world tour. Despite being in her sixties she continued to wear her trademark miniskirts, displaying the legs which President George W Bush had called "the most famous in showbusiness". Her explanation for her skimpy costumes was simple. "You can't dance in a long dress," she said with a logic that was incontrovertible.

She stayed retired until she was persuaded back for one last hurrah in 2008, to undertake what was billed as her 50th anniversary tour. Still not quite done, in 2013 she appeared on the cover of *Vogue.* At 73, she was by some way the oldest pin-up in the business.

The fairytale extravaganza of the second half of her career made it easy to overlook her earlier successes as an R&B singer with her husband, particularly as she insisted that *Private Dancer* should not be called her comeback album. "It was Tina's debut," she said, having become one of the tiny handful of stars who are identifiable solely by their first name.

Yet the first phase of her career with Ike, in which the duo had topped the charts with Phil Spector's *River Deep – Mountain High,* had in its way been every bit as momentous as her solo success, if considerably more troubled.

Born Anna Mae Bullock in 1938 in Nutbush, near Brownsville, Tennessee, she memorably described the rural poverty of her upbringing in the 1973 hit single *Nutbush City Limits.* Her home town consisted of little more than "church house, gin house, school house, out-house" and it was in the choir of her local Baptist church that she took her first steps to becoming a singer.

Her father, Floyd Bullock, was a sharecropper and she recalled picking cotton as a child. Her mother, Zelma (née Currie), already had two daughters and did not want another, so "little Annie" was passed around the family.

Her early years were spent living with her paternal grandparents before she was briefly reunited with her parents. When she was 11 her mother ran off to escape the abuse of her husband and she was sent to live with her maternal grandmother. The relationship with her mother remained strained all her life. "Mom was not kind," Turner later said. "When I became a star she was happy because I bought her a house, but she still didn't like me."

At school she was a cheerleader and played in the girls' basketball team, and a high-school yearbook found her confidently predicting that she was going to be an "entertainer". When her grandmother died in 1954, she was sent with her older sister Alline to live once again with their mother in St Louis, Missouri.

She took a job as a hospital orderly and by night frequented the local R&B clubs with her sister. One evening at the Club Manhattan, where Ike Turner was playing, she asked if she could get up and sing with his band, the Kings of Rhythm.

Ike was already a formidable music industry figure as a guitarist, session musician, producer, talent scout, disc jockey and songwriter and had been the man behind Jackie Brenston's 1951 recording *Rocket 88*, frequently cited as the first rock'n'roll record.

She was just 17 and Ike dismissively refused her request. A few nights later she was back and during the band's intermission grabbed the microphone and started belting out a BB King song.

Her impromptu performance tore the house down and Turner made her a part of his revue, initially billing her as "Little Ann", before he changed her name to Tina and ordered her to develop a "wild" stage persona based on *Sheena, Queen of the Jungle*, a popular television series.

At 18 she fell pregnant by the band's saxophonist, Raymond Hill, who disappeared before her son Craig was born, leaving her to bring him up as a single mother. Ike invited her to move into his house, promising that the arrangement was platonic and purely for practical purposes. Inevitably, though, it led to the arrival of another son, Ronnie, in 1960. "I didn't know how to say no because I would have been lost without him at that point because I needed the work," she said. "I mean, I could do two things – work in a hospital or sing in Ike's band. I didn't know anything else."

They married in Tijuana, Mexico, in 1962 and she adopted Turner's two sons from his previous marriage. Her son Craig committed suicide in 2018.

The relationship with Ike was abusive from the outset. On stage, Tina was an indomitable force of nature. Off stage, she was enslaved. She was heavily pregnant with their son, Ronnie, when Ike administered the first beating because she disagreed with the travel arrangements he had made for the band. "Busted lips, black eyes, dislocated joints, broken bones and psychological torment became a part of everyday life," she wrote in her autobiography. She attempted to conceal the bruises he inflicted with layers of make-up and once sang on stage with a broken jaw.

She also revealed that his cruelty had led her to attempt suicide when she took an overdose of sleeping pills before a concert in 1968. The backstage crew rushed her to hospital, where her life was saved with a stomach pump.

Ike went to his grave in 2007 insisting that the stories of his abuse were exaggerated. "Sure, I've slapped Tina. There have been times when I punched her to the ground. But I never beat her," he said. The distinction was lost on all but him.

One of the things that got her through was that she did not turn to drugs as an escape. "When Ike started to do drugs, I realised he had no control, and I felt I needed all the control I could get, living in that environment," she noted.

Instead, in 1973 she became a Buddhist. She practised chanting and meditation but still found forgiveness hard. "Ike was not the sort of person it was easy to forgive," she said. On his death in 2007 she issued a terse statement saying she hadn't had any contact with him for 30 years and would not be making any further comment. She did not attend his funeral but subsequently said she "realised he was a sick person, an ill person at the soul".

Yet there is no denying that it was Ike who made Tina Turner a star, first time around, and that without him Anna Mae Bullock would in all probability have remained unknown. Her first hit with Ike came in 1960 by chance. He had booked a male vocalist to record a song called *A Fool In Love* and when he failed to show up and with the studio time paid for, Ike asked Tina to step in.

The song made No 2 on the R&B chart and crossed over to the mainstream pop chart, pushing her to the forefront of the group and prompting a name change to the Ike & Tina Turner Revue. "She really was young. She had no ambition to be a superstar," said Jimmy Thomas, who sang background vocals for the revue. "But when she sang, she just had it. And Ike exploited it."

A string of further hits followed as the revue became one of the most dynamic live shows on the circuit, with Tina's short-skirted gyrating complemented by an equally leggy group of backing singers called the Ikettes.

As pop fashion and musical tastes changed, by the mid-1960s the hits had dried up, until in late 1965 Phil Spector came calling. After making some pioneering pop records earlier in the decade with girl groups such as the Crystals and the Ronettes, Spector's own star was also in decline, his sound having been eclipsed by the more advanced pop productions of the Beatles and the Beach Boys.

He saw the big, dramatic voice of Tina Turner as the perfect vehicle for his own renaissance on a song written with Jeff Barry and Ellie Greenwich and titled *River Deep – Mountain High*. With a bombastic and magnificently over the top symphonic backing, the song was Spector's masterpiece as he laid Tina's vocals on top of his "wall of sound" to create a track so thrilling that half a century later she claimed "it still gives me shivers". Released in Britain in 1966, the record made the Top 3 but in America it flopped, a failure that left Spector so disillusioned that he retired from record production.

Tina enjoyed working with Spector – or more specifically she enjoyed working without her husband. "Ike would always have me screaming and shouting on his songs to sell them," she said. "Phil Spector just asked me to stick to the melody and to use my voice to tell the story."

That there were no more records with Spector was a relief to Ike. Both men were control freaks and Spector reportedly paid him $20,000 to stay out of the studio while Tina recorded. As soon as Ike was back in charge, he returned to cheapskate, low-budget recordings for small, independent labels and the hits dried up once more.

The duo's fortunes revived when the Rolling Stones asked them on the road in 1969 as their opening act, an invitation largely down to Mick Jagger's unrequited lust for Tina.

Astutely adjusting their sound to appeal to White rock audiences, the change of style returned Ike and Tina to the charts with covers of the Beatles' *Come Together* and Credence Clearwater Revival's *Proud Mary*, the latter giving the duo their first American Top 10 hit in 1971.

However, their partnership was fraying badly as an increasingly assertive Tina tired of Ike's violent behaviour. Their final hit as a duo came with 1973's *Nutbush City Limits*. Away from Ike she played the Acid Queen in Ken Russell's 1975 film of The Who's rock opera, *Tommy*, and to the surprise of no one, she left her husband for good the following year.

Asked why she had put up with his violence for so long, she replied, "Maybe I was brainwashed. I was afraid of him, and I knew that if I left, there was no one to sing." Like many victims of domestic abuse, she blamed herself and said she had felt "ashamed". Ike begged her to complete a scheduled tour with him to prevent the promoter suing for loss of earnings but she knew she had to make a clean break and refused.

As she rebuilt her career away from Ike, she also found personal contentment. "I have not received love almost ever in my life. I did not have it with my mother and my father from the beginning of birth, and I survived," she said in her 1986 memoir *I, Tina*. "Why did I get so far without love? I have had not one love affair that was genuine and sustained itself. Not one."

Straight after the book was published she met Erwin Bach, a German music executive 16 years her junior, who had been sent by her European record label to meet her at Düsseldorf Airport.

"He was just so different," she said. "So laid back, so comfortable, so unpretentious, and I needed love." They set up home together in Zurich although they did not formally marry until 2013, when Turner also took Swiss citizenship. In addition to her main lakeside home, Château Algonquin, she also had homes in Cologne, London and Los Angeles, and a villa on the French Riviera.

Her later years were dogged by ill health. Shortly after her wedding she suffered a stroke and had to learn to walk and talk again. Three years later she was diagnosed with intestinal cancer. Kidney failure followed and she considered assisted suicide until Bach offered to donate one of his kidneys. She underwent a transplant in 2017 and her resilience in the face of adversity had won out yet again.

"People think my life has been tough, but I think it has been a wonderful journey," she said. "The older you get, the more you realise it's not what happens, but how you deal with it."

Tina Turner, the queen of rock'n'roll, was born on November 26, 1939. She died after a long illness on May 24, 2023, aged 83

ROBIN GIBB

———●———

*Singer and songwriter with the Bee Gees, whose angelic vibrato voice
provided high harmonies for the band's memorable disco hits*

The Times, May 21, 2012

Robin Gibb's distinctive vibrato voice was at the heart of the rich three-part harmonies which over more than 40 years of hit-making made the Bee Gees the world's second-biggest-selling group, behind only the Beatles.

If he was the least photogenic of the three singing brothers, there was no doubting that he could sing like an angel. In the early years of the Bee Gees, he took the lead vocal on most of their hits, including *Massachusetts, I've Gotta Get a Message to You* and *I Started a Joke*. But his older brother Barry was always a rival for lead vocal duties, and the competition between them grew so intense that for a while in the late 1960s Robin left the group and launched a solo career.

Within a year the three brothers were back together as the Bee Gees, although the early 1970s found them struggling to recreate their earlier success – even to the point of being "washed up", as Robin admitted to one interviewer. But in 1975 the group embraced disco music and with Barry Gibb's falsetto now taking most of the lead vocal duties, ably backed by Robin's high harmonies, the group enjoyed a spectacular string of hits, including *How Deep Is Your Love, Stayin' Alive* and *Night Fever*. When they followed with *Too Much Heaven, Tragedy* and *Love You Inside Out*, it meant that they had scored a record-breaking six successive No 1s in 18 months.

The collapse of the disco music phenomenon put the Bee Gees back in the shade during the 1980s, but Robin, his twin brother Maurice and Barry continued to have a major presence in the charts as songwriters, penning hits for Barbra Streisand, Dolly Parton and Kenny Rogers, Dionne Warwick, Diana Ross and others. The brothers had always written their own material from the outset of their recording career and an informed estimate suggests that more than 2,500 artists have since covered their songs.

Over the years, Robin released half a dozen solo albums, without ever repeating the commercial success enjoyed with his siblings as the Bee Gees. But then who could? By 2011, it was estimated that the group had sold more than 220 million records, a figure topped only by the Beatles among other groups and by Elvis Presley, Garth Brooks, Michael Jackson and Paul McCartney among solo artists.

After Maurice Gibb died in 2003, the two surviving Gibbs announced that the group would continue. But without the third brother who had sung with them for more than 40 years, their hearts were no longer in it and a decision was soon taken to retire the name. Robin and Barry made several joint appearances after Maurice's death, but refused to be billed as the Bee Gees. Rumours that they would re-form came to nothing, although it emerged in 2010 that they were planning to work with Steven Spielberg on a film to tell the group's story.

Robin was appointed CBE in 2002 along with his brothers Maurice and Barry. After rumours of drug problems early in his career, in later life he became a health obsessive and was teetotal and an ardent vegan.

Robin Hugh Gibb was born in 1949 in Douglas on the Isle of Man. He arrived into the world 35 minutes after his twin brother Maurice, and was preceded by a sister, Lesley, and Barry, born in 1946. In the early 1950s the family moved to Chorlton-cum-Hardy, Manchester, where they lived until 1958, when the Gibb clan emigrated to Brisbane after the birth of a fifth child, Andy.

Almost as soon as they arrived in Australia, the three older brothers formed a singing group, calling themselves first the Rattlesnakes and then Wee Johnny Hayes and the Blue Cats, before a Brisbane DJ, Bill Gates, named them the Bee Gees.

By 1960 the youthful Bee Gees were appearing on local TV talent shows and in 1963 they signed with Leedon Records. With older brother Barry writing the songs, they recorded a succession of unsuccessful singles plus an LP, *The Bee Gees Sing and Play 14 Barry*

Gibb Songs, which appeared in 1965. Moving to Spin Records, they scored their first Australian hit in late 1966 with *Spicks and Specks*.

By then, though, the three Gibb brothers had embarked on the sea voyage that would take them back to England, encouraged by the positive response of the Beatles' manager Brian Epstein, to whom the brothers' father had sent a demo tape. Epstein handed the tape to the entrepreneur Robert Stigwood, who auditioned the group on their arrival in early 1967 and immediately secured them a five-year recording deal with Polydor Records.

With Robin as lead singer, the rest of the band by now consisted of Barry on rhythm guitar, Maurice on bass, Vince Melouney on lead guitar and Colin Petersen on drums. Success was instant. *New York Mining Disaster 1941*, featuring a plaintive lead vocal from Robin as the voice of a miner trapped deep underground, climbed into the Top 20 in 1967 and was followed by *To Love Somebody*, written by Barry and Robin in the style of an Otis Redding soul ballad. By the end of the year, the Bee Gees had their first British No 1 with *Massachusetts* and in 1968 they had further hits with *Words*, *I've Gotta Get a Message to You* (their second No 1, with lyrics by Robin, about a man awaiting execution in the electric chair) and *I Started a Joke*.

But by 1969 the sibling rivalry between Robin and Barry was threatening to split the group. The younger man felt that Stigwood was favouring his older brother as the group's frontman and after recording the double album *Odessa* – the group's most determined effort to move away from being a singles-orientated act and become serious-minded "album artists" – he announced that he was leaving for a solo career.

Still not yet 20, his first single, *Saved by the Bell* made No 2 in the British charts in 1969, but the accompanying album, *Robin's Reign*, fared less well. Within a year the three brothers were back together, but without Melouney and Petersen, who had never really been more than hired hands in any case. *How Can You Mend a Broken Heart* gave the group a No 1 in America in 1971 and the singles *My World* and *Run to Me* made the British Top 20. But they were rare beacons in a mostly dispiriting period and by 1975 the Bee Gees had gone for three years without a chart hit.

What turned their fortunes around was disco. At Eric Clapton's suggestion, the three Gibb brothers flew to Miami, Florida, in early 1975, to record with the veteran soul producer Arif Mardin – and to reinvent themselves. The result was the album *Main Course* and a set of highly rhythmic dance songs, including *Jive Talkin'*, a US No 1 in 1975, and *Nights on Broadway*, the latter unveiling Barry Gibb's first lead as a falsetto and some similarly high backing vocals from Robin.

The follow-up album, *Children of the World* (1976), developed the tight-trousered falsetto sound further on hits such as *You Should Be Dancing*, *Love So Right* and *Boogie Child*. But with discomania by now in full swing, bigger and better was to come when the Bee Gees were commissioned to write songs for the dance film starring John Travolta, *Saturday Night Fever* (1977).

Three Bee Gees singles from the film – *How Deep Is Your Love*, *Stayin' Alive* and *Night Fever* – topped the charts around the world over the winter of 1978–79, while the soundtrack album went on to sell 40 million copies. More than 30 years on, it still holds a place in the list of the bestselling albums.

As songwriters too, the brothers had hit a rich vein and Robin co-wrote two further No 1s before the decade was out, *If I Can't Have You* for Yvonne Elliman and *Shadow Dancing* for his younger brother Andy.

Yet not quite everything the Gibbs touched turned to gold. An appearance by the trio with Peter Frampton in the 1978 film *Sgt Pepper's Lonely Hearts Club Band* was a flop, although Robin's cover of the Paul McCartney song *Oh! Darling* from the film made the American Top 20. More successful was the 1978 single *Too Much Heaven* which reached No 1. The brothers donated the royalties from the song to UNICEF and over the years it earned an estimated £7 million for the organisation.

They returned to Criterion Studios in Miami to record the 1979 album *Spirits Having Flown*, which gave them three more chart-topping singles in *Too Much Heaven*, *Tragedy* and *Love You Inside Out*. But the disco boom was not only coming to an end; there was a growing backlash against its hedonistic sound.

The 1980s consequently found the Bee Gees out of fashion – and out of the charts. The trio's only hits of the decade under their own name were *You Win Again*, a British No 1 in 1987, and *One*, which made the American Top Ten in 1989. Their commercial decline was not assisted by their refusal to tour during this period.

That they were still master songwriters was undisputed, though, and Robin co-wrote numerous 1980s hits for others, including Barbra Streisand's *Woman in Love* (1980), Dionne Warwick's *Heartbreaker* (1982), *Islands in the Stream* (1983) sung by Dolly Parton and Kenny Rogers and Diana Ross's *Chain Reaction* (1986).

Towards the end of the decade, the three brothers decided to take to the stage again and intended to add their younger brother Andy to the line-up, a plan that was scotched by his death from heart disease at the age of 30 in 1988. The three remaining brothers eventually returned to the stage in 1991, after the release of the album *High Civilization*, which contained the hit single *Secret Love*.

The group's final album of new material, *This Is Where I Came In*, was released in 2001 and included each member writing individually rather than as a team, with Robin contributing and singing lead on *Déjà Vu*, *Promise the Earth* and *Embrace*. All further group activity was ended by Maurice's death from a heart attack at the age of 53 in 2003.

After that Robin and Barry made various charitable and TV appearances together but never appeared again as the Bee Gees.

Robin was married twice and is survived by his second wife, Dwina, and by a son and a daughter from his first marriage and a son from his second.

Robin Gibb, CBE, singer with the Bee Gees, was born on December 22, 1949. He died of cancer on May 20, 2012, aged 62

Robin Gibb (far right) with brothers and bandmates Barry and Maurice Gibb

JET BLACK

Drummer of the Stranglers, the punk band that ranked alongside the Sex Pistols but let the side down by winning an Ivor Novello award

Jet Black (second from left) with bandmates Hugh Cornwell, Dave Greenfield and Jean-Jacques Burnel

The Times, December 13, 2022

To almost everyone but Jet Black, the Stranglers were one of the most ferocious of all punk bands, with a reputation to rival the infamy of the Sex Pistols and the Clash.

The Stranglers' drummer and founder disagreed. "We were never a punk band," he insisted. "We could play our instruments, that's the difference. Punk was a flash in the pan; here today, gone tomorrow. We were the real thing."

Certainly the Stranglers endured long after most of their rivals had faded away and in a career that spanned more than 40 years the band scored 23 Top 40 singles and 17 entries in the albums chart.

Despite Black's protestations, the Stranglers' early posturing was pure punk and he played his part in creating the band's tough, aggressive persona. His bandmates Hugh Cornwell on vocals and guitar, bassist Jean-Jacques Burnel and keyboard player Dave Greenfield called him "The Hoover". The nickname didn't come from his fondness for housework and his vaguely menacing aura drove the message home.

A string of Top 10 hits with risqué and sometimes crude lyrics such as *Peaches*, which was banned by radio for using the word "clitoris", and *Nice 'n' Sleazy* reinforced the Stranglers' image as transgressive iconoclasts.

Yet Black had a point in his dislike for the "P" word, for beneath the carefully cultivated yobbish veneer lurked a band with serious musical aspirations and whose songs had a sophistication that transcended the primitive three-chord thrash of so many of the punk hordes. As punk faded and gave way to "new wave", the Stranglers emerged as sophisticated master pop craftsmen on radio-friendly hits such as *Strange Little Girl*, *European Female* and, most notably of all, the baroque-sounding *Golden Brown*, which featured a harpsichord and won the band an Ivor Novello award. George Melly, who sang on the track *Old Codger* on their 1978 album *Black and White*, called them "punk's dada surrealists". Later came a concept album about religion and extraterrestrials, and synthesisers were added to the sound.

Whether Black liked it or not, he earned his spurs as "the oldest punk rocker in town" for by the time the Stranglers scored their first Top Ten hit in 1977 he was already in his 40th year. Punk's target audience was half his age, largely made up of spotty teenagers who had rejected the prog-rock pretensions favoured by their older brothers and sisters in favour of something more basic and visceral.

Without Black, the Stranglers would never have existed and it was his funding that got the band off the ground. Prior to the band's formation, he had been a successful businessman who owned an off-licence in Guildford, where he brewed his own beer and sold home brewing equipment. Called The Jackpot, it became the Stranglers' HQ. He also operated a fleet of ice-cream vans which he sold when the band started, although he kept one which served as the Stranglers' transport to gigs for several years. "We had a special way of arranging the speakers and equipment so they'd all fit in," he recalled.

Band members lay awkwardly on top of the gear but it was too uncomfortable for sleep. Driving home from a gig at the other end of the country, on more than one occasion Black parked the van on a grass verge and the band slept in a nearby field. One morning, the group awoke to the sound of a lawnmower. They had slept on a cricket pitch and were disturbed by the groundsman's preparation for the next match.

Early gigs were not always well received. Booked to play at a Young Conservatives dance, Black recalled that the Stranglers managed to empty a hall of 300 people before they had finished their first song. Things picked up when they supported the Ramones on the New York band's first visit to Britain in 1976 and as the punk phenomenon exploded, notoriety began to follow the Stranglers wherever they went.

There was a fist fight with members of the Clash and the Sex Pistols in a north London club and a journalist who had given them a bad review was "sorted out" with a beating. Their "punk and disorderly" flair for controversy boiled over in 1980 when the group spent a week in a French jail for inciting a riot at a concert in Nice, where they left a trail of destruction. They were eventually fined the equivalent of £10,000 but Black judged that it had been worth it. "We laughed all the way to the bank. Before that, we were unknown in Europe. From then on, we played to packed houses," he said.

They were arrested again in Australia for swearing on primetime television and thrown out of Sweden after a running battle with a local gang who attempted to take them hostage in their dressing room. The Stranglers responded by making petrol bombs and lobbing them at their assailants.

They were expelled from Sweden a second time after Black got into a fight with staff at the band's hotel. "I kicked up a fracas because I couldn't get served any food and they called the police, who turned up with machineguns to escort us on to the next plane," he recalled.

On another occasion a hotel night porter who refused to serve them more drinks was locked in a broom cupboard, where he was found the following morning by the receptionist.

Black was unapologetic about such behaviour. "We've always had to respond to circumstances and you've got to defend yourself," he said.

Over the years the band mellowed and when Cornwell left in 1990 it was Black who persuaded his colleagues to carry on. Despite being diagnosed with a heart condition in 2007 that caused him to miss several gigs, he continued touring with the Stranglers until 2015, when ill health eventually caused his retirement at the age of 77.

He is survived by his wife Ava and his two children Charlotte and Anthony. From his home in north Wales, he continued to support his former bandmates from the sidelines, telling them, "Don't stop! Don't get sloppy!" They called him their "talisman".

Jet Black was born Brian John Duffy in 1938 in Ilford, Essex. His father was a schoolteacher and as a child he took piano lessons, an experience he likened to "being in a prison and forced to sew mailbags".

Sickly with chronic asthma, he was sent to board at a Catholic prep school in Broadstairs on the grounds that the sea air would do him good. There he switched to violin lessons, which also soon fell by the wayside.

He later described his education as a "disaster", which he claimed had left him "almost illiterate", although in truth in adulthood he was erudite and well informed with a wide hinterland of interests. By his early teens he had discovered jazz, bought a second-hand drum kit and was soon playing at weddings and in local pubs. On leaving school in 1953 he signed on for a seven-year apprenticeship as a joiner and cabinet-maker, a trade he abandoned as soon as he was qualified in favour of drifting through a variety of odd jobs.

By the mid-1960s he had acquired his first ice-cream van and there was no time to pursue his musical ambitions.

When he bought a new drum kit in the early 1970s and began answering small ads in *Melody Maker*, he had not wielded a drumstick in a decade.

By 1974 he had hooked up with Cornwell, whose band Johnny Sox was falling apart. Black invited the guitarist to stay at the off-licence and the pair set about reconstructing the band as the Guildford Stranglers, as they were initially known.

What persuaded him to wind up a successful business and risk his capital in the uncertain enterprise of starting a band he was never fully able to articulate. It was simply something that he felt he had to do regardless of the consequences, which included the end of his marriage to his wife Helena. According to Cornwell, the final straw that resulted in her walking out was the noise of the band rehearsing in the family home.

As they slogged around the circuit of pubs and college gigs, the Stranglers were turned down by no fewer than 24 record companies. They were eventually signed by United Artists in 1977, punk's annus mirabilis, as label executives rushed to jump on a rapidly growing bandwagon which they had initially tried so hard to resist.

Black didn't write the Stranglers' songs and nor did he sing them, but he was in many ways the band's heartbeat. "He was a force of nature and an inspiration," said Burnel, who continues to lead the band as its only original remaining member. "The Stranglers would not have been if it wasn't for him."

Jet Black, drummer, was born on August 26, 1938. He died after a long illness on December 6, 2022, aged 84

WHITNEY HOUSTON

———————•———————

One of the most successful female singers whose wholesome image as an American icon was later tarnished by alcohol and drug dependency

The Times, February 13, 2012

In any era, Whitney Houston's remarkable voice would have ensured her a highly successful career as a singer. In earlier decades that would perhaps have been all, as it was for Black female singers from Billie Holiday to Aretha Franklin, whose celebrity was considerable, but remained largely confined to the musical arena. Houston was far more, an American icon with a universal appeal that spanned both White middle America and a Black urban audience, fêted from the inner-city ghetto to the White House.

Hits such as *Saving All My Love for You*, *Greatest Love of All*, *I Wanna Dance with Somebody (Who Loves Me)*, *Didn't We Almost Have It All* and *I Will Always Love You* helped her to worldwide record sales estimated to be close to 200 million. There were six Grammys and countless other awards. But the breadth of her appeal allowed her to become not only one of the most successful female singers in recorded history, but also a successful film actress and an all-round patriotic American entertainer. She sang the American national anthem at major national sporting events, performed at the White House for the visit of Nelson Mandela and was selected to headline the "welcome home" concert for American troops returning from the Gulf War. Only Diana Ross among Black female performers had previously come near achieving such recognition.

But the wholesome image of her early career became seriously tarnished in later years. A disastrous and abusive marriage to the singer Bobby Brown was followed by her descent into alcohol and drug dependency. She became unreliable and missed shows, and when she did appear, her performances were often erratic. She later confessed in a televised interview with Oprah Winfrey that drugs had been "an everyday thing" in her life for many years.

She divorced Brown in 2007 and staged a commercially successful comeback, when 2009's *I Look to You* became her first No 1 album in more than a decade. Sadly, though, the abuse had taken its toll on her once mighty voice. While the skills of a studio producer could conceal this decline on record, on stage she was exposed and a world tour to support the album received negative reviews and left many fans bitterly disappointed.

Houston opened the doors for the success of other Black female singers such as Beyoncé Knowles and Alicia Keys, and her dramatic vocal style was also a role model for such would-be divas as Mariah Carey and Christina Aguilera. Certainly, many of the doors she opened had been closed to her mother, the singer Cissy Houston, and her cousin Dionne Warwick, who had both emerged as talented soul singers in the 1960s. From an early age she followed in their musical footsteps by singing gospel music in church. By the age of eight she had recorded *Guide Me O Thou Great Jehovah* with the New Hope Baptist Junior Choir and by the time she was in her teens she was in demand as a backing singer for the likes of Chaka Khan and Lou Rawls. She also worked as a teenage model and appeared in minor roles in various television shows, including *Give Me a Break*.

Her own break came when she was signed to Arista Records in 1983 by Clive Davis, a near-legendary figure in the music industry who had been associated with the development of several big stars, including Santana, Janis Joplin and Sly and the Family Stone. Davis's first move was to pair her with Teddy Pendergrass on the hit duet *Hold Me*. He then moulded and coached her carefully, taking his time to choose the right songwriters, producers and material for her solo debut. As a result, her painstakingly prepared self-titled first album did not appear until early 1985.

Commercial success was not instant, but by the end of the year *Saving All My Love for You* had given her a chart-topping single around the world. It won her the first of her seven subsequent Grammy awards and belatedly ignited interest in her album, which eventually topped the American charts almost a year to the day after its release. Two further singles from the album, *How Will I Know* and *The Greatest Love of All*, kept her in the charts for most of 1986.

The run of hit singles continued the following year with *I Wanna Dance with Somebody (Who Loves Me)*. The song topped the charts on both sides of the Atlantic and was a taster for her second album, *Whitney*, for which Davis was again the executive producer. It became the first album by a female artist to enter the American charts at No 1 in its week of release. It stayed there for three months and repeated the feat in Britain.

A duet with her mother Cissy on *I Know Him So Well* became another chart-topping American single. When *Didn't We Almost Have It All, So Emotional* and *Where Do Broken Hearts Go* followed in quick succession, she had by 1988 broken an American record, previously shared by the Beatles and the Bee Gees, for the most consecutive No 1 singles.

The sequence was broken finally in autumn 1988 by *Love Will Save the Day*, which stalled at No 9 in the American charts and No 10 in Britain. The record's sales may have been damaged by the controversy that surrounded her appearance at the 70th birthday tribute concert staged for Nelson Mandela at Wembley in June of that year. She was widely accused of behaving like a prima donna and making unreasonable demands at odds with the philanthropic spirit of the event. But any dent in her popularity was short-lived and *One Moment in Time*, her 1988 Olympics tribute, swiftly restored her to favour.

She appeared at the White House for a National Children's Day celebration and when she sang *The Star-Spangled Banner* at the Super Bowl in March 1991 during the Gulf War crisis, she became a symbol of American patriotism. Demand for the performance resulted in the rush-release of a video and single, and 750,000 copies were sold in a week, with all proceeds going to the Gulf Crisis Fund.

Her biggest success was still to come with her appearance in the film *The Bodyguard* in 1992. Having reportedly turned down offers to star in films opposite Robert De Niro and Eddie Murphy, *The Bodyguard*, in which Kevin Costner was her male lead, earned poor reviews from the critics.

But the bad notices failed to dent the huge box office returns or the multi-million sales for the soundtrack album, which gave her one of the biggest singles in chart history with her version of Dolly Parton's *I Will Always Love You.*

Around the same time, rumours of serious drug problems began to surface. In July 1992 she married the singer Bobby Brown, who had a track record of substance abuse. They had a daughter the following year but it was to prove to be a tempestuous relationship. Houston was said to have been admitted to hospital in June 1993 after overdosing on diet pills. She denied the story and sued. But three months later, nine drug officers acting on a tip-off stopped and searched her and Brown in a limousine on the way to JFK Airport. The rumours did not prevent her performing at the White House in 1994, following a state dinner for Nelson Mandela.

Yet the gossip about her personal life would not abate. In 1997 she received stitches for a two-inch gash in her face while on holiday with Brown. Several appearances cancelled at short notice during the same year further fuelled the drug allegations.

By now her problems were multiplying as her music was also attracting criticism. While none doubted her technical ability as a singer, many critics felt that her recordings lacked a cutting edge.

In January 2000, she was arrested in Hawaii and charged with possession of marijuana and the drug rumours grew ever louder when she was unable to sing at the Oscars that year and failed to show at a Rock & Roll Hall of Fame ceremony.

In September 2001, following another no-show at a Michael Jackson tribute concert in New York, rumours circulated that she had died of a drug overdose. The story was false but pictures at the time showed her looking gaunt and ill. Her problems did not prevent her from signing one of the biggest record deals in history in 2001 when she signed a deal with Arista/BMG for six new albums. She only ever delivered three of them.

A six-year gap followed before 2009's *I Look to You,* while she attempted to sort out her turbulent personal life. Her ill-advised appearance in the 2005 reality TV series, *Being Bobby Brown,* exposed many of her problems and it was no surprise when the couple separated the following year. An unseemly court battle followed for custody of their daughter, which she won.

When she returned to the stage in 2010 for her first world tour in a decade, the decline in her voice was sad to hear.

Whitney Houston, singer, was born on August 9, 1963. She was found dead on February 11, 2012, aged 48

JERRY LEE LEWIS

———•———

Notorious rock'n'roll star whose hit Great Balls of Fire *became a landmark*

The Times, October 28, 2022

Jerry Lee Lewis never wanted to record the song that became his signature tune. Raised in a devout Christian family and educated at a Bible school, halfway through recording *Great Balls of Fire* at the Sun studio in Memphis in 1957, he decided that the song was "sinful" and the Lord did not want him to sing its suggestive lyrics.

With the tape still rolling, Lewis's moment of moral crisis was captured for posterity as he argued with the Sun Records owner Sam Phillips.

"You can save souls!" Phillips told Lewis. "No, no, no, no! How can the Devil save souls?" he replied in anguished tones. "I got the Devil in me."

Lewis lost the battle with Phillips and with his conscience and his recording of *Great Balls of Fire* went on to become a million-seller and a rock'n'roll landmark. The moment defined Lewis's career in more ways than simply cementing his commercial success. He feared hellfire and damnation, yet he could not resist the lure of the "Devil's music" and once famously asked Elvis Presley if he believed a rock'n'roller could go to Heaven.

The conflict between singing gospel hymns to his God and celebrating carnality in his rock'n'roll hits was a leitmotif that was to run through his work and his life.

Lewis was rock's first wild man and original hell-raiser. Known as "the Killer", on stage he performed like a man possessed. His rabble-rousing singing ranged from a rebel yell to a bull-like roar. His boogie-woogie piano playing was crude but effective and consisted mostly of flashy glissandos and pounding the instrument as hard as he could, with his hands, elbows and feet, sometimes all at the same time.

Early records were credited to "Jerry Lee Lewis And His Pumping Piano". In his prime the climax of a show found him climbing on top of the piano in an outlandish display of feral energy that made Elton John, even at his most flamboyant, seem tame in comparison.

Nobody topped Jerry Lee Lewis, and those who tried usually came off worse. On one occasion when Chuck Berry was due to close a show they were playing together, at the end of his final number Lewis set fire to the piano and left the stage with the parting shot, "I'd like to see any sonofabitch follow that!"

His personal life was every bit as tempestuous as his stage performances. There were addictions to alcohol and pills and a string of stormy and often violent relationships. A bigamist before he was out of his teens, he was eventually married seven times.

His first marriage in 1952 to the 14-year-old Dorothy Barton, the daughter of a travelling preacher, lasted a year and a half. Before the divorce was finalised he had married again, to the 17-year-old Jane Mitchum. She threw a claw-hammer through his car windscreen, but he admitted that he had "deserved it".

By the time their volatile union was annulled in 1957 he had already married Myra Gale Brown, a premature jumping of the broomstick that forced a second ceremony. However, bigamy was the least controversial aspect of their union. Brown was 13 years old at the time and was also Lewis's first cousin.

When he arrived in Britain for a sell-out tour in 1958, a reporter noticed his young female companion and asked how old she was. Moral outrage followed. The word "paedophile" was not in widespread use at the time but Lewis was demonised in lurid headlines as a "cradle snatcher".

After initially lying that Myra was 15, the scandal escalated further when her real age emerged. Lewis's attempts to explain that it wasn't unusual for girls of 13 to marry in Mississippi only provoked further disgust.

The police interviewed the couple (Myra was reportedly watching children's TV in their hotel room when they arrived) and the Home Office minister Iain Macleod was called upon to answer questions in the House of Commons.

Hotels refused to accommodate Lewis and Myra, and jeers, catcalls and boycotts greeted his concerts. After completing just three of 37 scheduled shows, the tour was cancelled and Lewis and his child bride were put on a plane back to America, where nine months later she gave birth to a son.

The following year Elvis Presley took up with the 14-year-old Priscilla Beaulieu. Mindful of Lewis's experience, Presley's manager, Colonel Tom Parker, worked overtime to keep the relationship secret.

For Lewis, though, it was too late and his career never fully recovered. His booking fees fell from $10,000 a night to $100 a night. Disc jockeys around the world refused to play his music and record sales plunged.

Myra divorced him in 1970 after 12 years of marriage. Still only 25, she became an estate agent and wrote an autobiography, *Great Balls of Fire!*, which was filmed in 1989 with Dennis Quaid as Jerry Lee and Winona Ryder as Myra.

The hits may have dried up for Lewis, but the wives kept on coming. In 1971 he married Jaren Pate, who was found at the bottom of a swimming pool in 1982 as a divorce settlement was about to be finalised.

Lewis's fifth wife, Shawn Stevens, died of a drug overdose in 1983, after 77 days of marriage. Her body was bruised and battered and Lewis admitted they had been fighting that night, as they did most nights, but a jury cleared him of culpability. His marriage to Kerrie McCarver in 1984 fared better and lasted 21 years. He married for a seventh time in 2012 to Judith Brown. Yet nothing was ever simple in Lewis's relationships: she had previously been married to the brother of his under-age bride Myra.

His multiple marriages produced six children, two of whom predeceased him. Jerry Lee Lewis Jr, his first son, died in a car crash at the age of 19 in 1973. Steve Allen Lewis, to whom Myra gave birth in 1959, drowned in a swimming pool accident at the age of three.

He is survived by Ronnie Guy Lewis from his second marriage, by Phoebe Allen Lewis from his third marriage, by Lori Lee Lewis from his fourth and from his sixth by Jerry Lee Lewis III, who works at a club owned by his father.

The conflict between his wild side and his God-fearing faith was a source of constant torment. His uncle, Lee Calhoun, after whom Lewis took his middle name, was an influential member of the Assembly of God, a strict Pentecostal sect, of which Lewis remained a member all his life. The TV evangelist Jimmy Lee Swaggart, another conflicted soul who was defrocked for consorting with prostitutes, was a cousin who as a boy had learnt to play on the Lewis family piano. As a teenager, Lewis studied at the Southwestern Bible Institute in Waxahachie, Texas, before he was thrown out for playing a boogie-woogie version of *My God Is Real* at a church assembly.

He served as a youthful lay preacher, forbade swearing in his presence and throughout his life made his backing musicians pray before going on stage. As if to assuage for playing "the Devil's music" his discography included albums of gospel songs alongside the rock'n'roll records.

"I was a good preacher and I know my Bible," he insisted. But he admitted that he found himself "falling short of the glory of God" and was convinced that damnation awaited him.

"I was always worried whether I was going to Heaven or Hell," he said in an interview to mark his 80th birthday. "I still do. It's a very serious situation. When you breathe your last breath, where are you going to go?"

Jerry Lee Lewis was born in 1935 in Ferriday, a small Louisiana town near the Mississippi River. He was the second child of Elmo Lewis, a sharecropping farmer, carpenter and convicted bootlegger, and Mary (née Herron), known as Mamie. His older brother, Elmo Jr, died after being hit by a car. Lewis was three at the time.

When he was seven his father mortgaged the family home for $250 to buy his surviving son a piano. It was an investment as much as an act of generosity, for Elmo recovered the outlay by loading the piano on to the back of a wagon and travelling from town to town to show off his prodigiously talented son for money.

In Ferriday, a predominantly Black town, Lewis would sneak into the local juke joint, the only White youngster in the building, hiding under tables to listen to the blues musicians of the day.

He earned the nickname "Killer" at school when he tried to strangle a teacher by his tie. "I was swinging on it and he was weakening and losing his breath," he recalled.

After being expelled from seminary school, he became a sewing machine salesman, working a scam in which he told his customers they had won the machines and all they needed to pay was $10 in tax.

At 20, he pitched up at Sun Records in Memphis, and refused to leave until Sam Phillips, who already had Elvis Presley on his books, granted him an audition. Lewis's debut single, *Crazy Arms*, sold 300,000 on its release in 1956. At about the same time, Phillips recorded a jam session in the Sun studio with Lewis, Presley, Johnny Cash and Carl Perkins, later released under the title *The Million Dollar Quartet*.

Within a year he had become an international star with *Whole Lotta Shakin' Goin' On* and *Great Balls of Fire*. Both records were banned by conservative radio stations, but the greater the condemnation, the more records Lewis sold. Teenage rebellion had arrived as a lucrative marketing strategy. More hits followed with *Breathless* and *High School Confidential* and, with Presley away serving with the US army in Germany, Lewis was in pole position. Then came the child bride furore.

Disgraced and made to sound outdated by the advent of the Beatles, the 1960s were a lean period. By the end of the decade he had changed tack to find some success on the country charts.

Plagued by drink and drug problems, the old volatility remained and he became notorious for his violent outbursts. In 1976 he shot his bass player Butch Owens twice in the chest with a revolver. Miraculously, Owens survived and although Lewis was arrested, he escaped a prison sentence by claiming he did not know the gun was loaded.

A few weeks later, high on drink and drugs, he was arrested again outside the gates of Elvis Presley's Graceland residence, brandishing a gun and demanding an audience. Presley, who was reportedly watching on CCTV, told his security guards not to let him in and to call the police.

He found a more sympathetic reception when John Lennon turned up at one of his concerts. The former Beatle, who in his early days had covered many of Lewis's songs, knelt down and kissed his feet. The Killer was unimpressed. "I never did care for the Beatles all that much, to tell the truth," he remarked.

There were spells in rehab for his addictions and in hospital for a burst stomach ulcer that almost cost him his life. At one point he declared himself bankrupt and during the 1990s he left America to live in Dublin, on the run from a tax investigation.

Despite such tribulations, he kept enough of his cash to enjoy an opulent lifestyle, returning to America to live on a large ranch near Memphis with a piano-shaped swimming pool, a white, chauffeur-driven Rolls-Royce and a Harley-Davidson motorcycle which he reportedly insisted on parking in the living room.

Bouts of religious panic aside, he retained a self-belief that rivalled that of Muhammad Ali. "You can look at Elvis Presley, you can look at the Beatles and the Rolling Stones, but when it comes down to it, it's Jerry Lee Lewis," he said. "I could never find anybody that was better than me."

Jerry Lee Lewis, rock'n'roll star, was born on September 29, 1935. He died on October 28, 2022, aged 87

FREDDIE MERCURY

———————— • ————————

Flamboyant singer and songwriter who achieved worldwide fame
as the lead vocalist and pianist for the rock band Queen

The Times, November 26, 1991

To mark the occasion of his 41st birthday in 1987, Freddie Mercury hired a DC9 and flew 80 of his friends to Ibiza. There he took over Pikes, one of the island's most exclusive hotels, and threw an outrageously lavish party complete with flamenco dancers, a fireworks display flashing his name in lights across the sky and a 20-foot long birthday cake carried in by six Spaniards dressed in white and gold.

The affair was typical of a life lived, until the last two or three reclusive years, to the hilt in an unashamedly extrovert, over-the-top fashion. "I always knew I was a star," he declared after the first flush of success, "and now the rest of the world seems to agree with me."

Be that as it may, Mercury was also a remarkably private man when out of the limelight, granting few interviews and giving little away about his family background.

The son of Bomi and Jer Bulsara, he was born in Zanzibar, Africa; his father was of Persian descent. Part of his childhood was spent in comfortable surroundings in India, where he went to boarding school, before his family moved to Feltham, Middlesex, in 1959. There Mercury's early interest in music took him into the ranks of a local blues-based band called Wreckage.

For a while he studied design and ran a clothes stall in Kensington market. He was helped by a friend, Roger Taylor, who was a student at London University and the drummer in a group called Smile. Mercury would go along to see Smile perform on the local college circuit. "Why are you wasting your time doing this?" he would exclaim to Taylor and the group's guitarist, Brian May, also a London University student. "You should be more demonstrative."

When Smile split up in 1970, Mercury invited Taylor and May to start a new group featuring himself as lead vocalist. He also suggested the name Queen, a deliberately camp, attention-grabbing title which he was well equipped to embody. They recruited bassist John Deacon from the small ads, and played their debut performance at the London College of Estate Management in February 1971.

In the years that followed the group forged a unique combination of heavy metal thunder, complex vocal harmonies and a preposterous glam-rock image, woven into a package of dramatic excess. Mercury made a pivotal contribution not only as singer, pianist and one of the group's principal songwriters, but also in defining the group's image thanks to his flamboyant persona and ambiguous sexual appeal.

It was Mercury who wrote the group's best known hit, *Bohemian Rhapsody*, a long, elaborate piece which incorporated a cod-operatic sequence followed by a bludgeoning heavy-metal finale. The single stayed at No 1 in Britain for nine weeks in 1975 and its host album, *A Night at the Opera*, also sailed to the top of the chart. Such was the group's popularity at the start of 1976 that all four of their albums released to that date appeared simultaneously in the Top 30.

In keeping with the grandiose splendour of their music, Queen's live shows became ever more spectacular events, employing vast sets and lighting rigs. Deacon and May were both naturally retiring types and Taylor was stuck behind his drums, so the group depended heavily on Mercury's commanding stage presence. Prancing down multi-layered catwalks in a sequined, skin-tight jump suit and ballet slippers, preening his way through a myriad of costume changes, and singing in his majestic, slightly frayed tenor voice, Mercury always matched up to the demands of projecting the group's music and image to the four corners of the world's biggest stadiums.

The group's popularity continued unabated into the Eighties. *The Game* (1980), *Greatest Hits* (1981), *A Kind of Magic* (1986) and *The Miracle* (1989) all topped the UK chart. At the Live Aid concert in 1985 they turned in arguably the most resounding performance of that remarkable event, and their *Greatest Hits* album was rarely out of the UK chart for the following two years.

Mercury embarked on a sporadic solo career, which he slotted into breaks in Queen's schedule. His debut album, *Mr Bad Guy*, reached No 6 in 1985, while his greatest success with a single was his cover version of the Platters' 1956 hit *The Great Pretender*, a typically overwrought performance which he took to No 4 in 1987.

Also in 1987 he teamed up with Montserrat Caballe to record *Barcelona*, a mock-operatic folly composed by Mercury which was then mooted as the official anthem of the 1992 Olympics. It is still in contention for that accolade. In 1986 he contributed three songs, including the title track, to the cast recording of Dave Clark's stage musical *Time*, but despite his various outside activities his first commitment was always to Queen, whose personnel remained unchanged to the end.

The group's last tour, which included two shows at Wembley Stadium and a pioneering appearance in front of 80,000 Hungarian fans at Budapest's Nepstadioné, ended with a date at the Knebworth Festival on August 9, 1986. Mercury's renowned bisexual proclivities made him the target of sustained speculation when the AIDS epidemic began to take its toll. "Yes, I did have an AIDS test and I'm fine," he told *Woman's Own* magazine in November 1987, but rumours persisted that he had tested HIV-positive.

In February 1990, after Queen pulled out at the last minute from an appearance at the Brit awards, photographs of a very sick-looking Mercury were circulated. But by the autumn of 1990 he was back in the studio with Queen, recording what was to be the group's last new album. Entitled *Innuendo*, it entered the UK charts at No 1 earlier this year and was followed more recently by a compilation, *Greatest Hits II*, which also topped the UK chart. The current single *The Show Must Go On*, which has been in the chart for the last six weeks, has a decidedly valedictory flavour and is accompanied by a video stitched together from old footage of Queen. In a nostalgic sequence of vignettes, Mercury's enduring generosity of spirit and his arch sense of humour continue to shine through.

"I don't expect to make old bones," Mercury once said. "What's more, I really don't care. I certainly don't have any aspirations to live to 70. It would be boring."

Freddie Mercury, rock star, was born on September 5, 1946. He died of complications from AIDS on November 24, 1991, aged 45

RONNIE SPECTOR

———— • ————

Style-setting lead singer of the Ronettes, who had a string of hits in the Sixties and the Rolling Stones as their support band

Ronnie Spector (left) with bandmates Estelle Bennett and Nedra Talley

The Times, January 13, 2022

The best thing Ronnie Spector ever did was to record with Phil Spector. The worst thing she ever did was to marry him.

In the studio they made sweet music together, as Phil produced Ronnie and her group the Ronettes singing some of the most enduring hits in 1960s pop, cloaking her voice in his celebrated "wall of sound" on hits such as *Be My Baby, Baby I Love You* and *Walking in the Rain*.

Once they married there was only disharmony, physical abuse and mental torment as he became her nemesis. Jealously imprisoning her in his 23-room mansion in Beverly Hills, he surrounded the property with barbed-wire fences and guard dogs and confiscated her shoes to prevent her from leaving.

He also halted her singing career and when she protested he pulled a gun on her. In the basement of the mansion he kept a gold coffin with a glass top and told her it was intended as her tomb if she ever left him.

"I wasn't allowed to go anywhere," she recalled. "I never saw a movie. I never did anything because everything was brought to me."

She started drinking heavily and volunteered for rehab just to get out of the house. When she drove off to AA meetings, her husband placed a life-size dummy of himself alongside her in the car. After four years of this nightmarish marriage, by 1972 Ronnie was at the end of her tether and escaped through a broken window, barefoot and leaving behind all her personal belongings. "I knew that if I didn't leave I was going to die there," she said.

After her escape Phil Spector threatened to hire a hitman to kill her unless she gave up the royalties from their recordings together. He also forced her to surrender custody of their three adopted children, Donté and twins Louis and Gary, whom he had surprised her with one Christmas as a "present".

In the divorce settlement that followed she was awarded just $25,000, a second-hand car and five years of alimony. It was not until 2001 after a 15-year court battle that the injustice was corrected when Phil Spector was ordered to pay his ex-wife $1 million in royalties. It was almost certainly a fraction of what she was due.

For Ronnie it was a journey from wide-eyed innocence into nightmarish experience, for nothing summed up the joyful spirit of 1960s teenage girl-pop better than the records Ronnie made with her sister Estelle and cousin Nedra Talley as the Ronettes. "I'll make you happy, baby, just wait and see/ For every kiss you give me I'll give you three," she sang in *Be My Baby*. Despite everything she had been through, the song's magic never faded for her. "I was so much in love," she recalled in 2013, on the 50th anniversary of the day in 1963 when she had recorded the song with Spector in a Hollywood studio. "That energy comes back to me every time when I'm singing *Be My Baby*."

The song was later used in the opening sequence of the movies *Dirty Dancing* and Martin Scorsese's *Mean Streets*, while Brian Wilson nominated *Be My Baby* as his favourite song of all time and wrote *Don't Worry Baby* for the Ronettes to sing as a follow-up. Phil Spector jealously turned it down and Wilson recorded the song instead with the Beach Boys.

When Spector died in prison, where he was serving a sentence for murder, Ronnie valiantly preferred to recall the good times rather than the abuse. "When I was with Phil Spector in the recording studio, I knew I was working with the very best," she said. "Meeting him was like a fairytale. I loved him madly, and gave my heart and soul to him."

Until he decided to shut down her career, Ronnie was riding the crest of a wave with the Ronettes. When the group made their first tour of Britain in 1963, they were the headliners and the Rolling Stones were the support group.

It was the start of a long friendship with Keith Richards, who positively drooled over her long black hair, teased up into a gravity-defying beehive, while her kohl-blackened eyes stared out seductively from under her fringe – a look that Amy Winehouse would later imitate.

"The first time I ever went to heaven was when I awoke with Ronnie asleep with a smile on her face. We were kids. It doesn't get any better than that," Richards wrote of their affair in his 2010 memoir *Life*.

He later sang a duet with her on her 2006 album *The Last of the Rock Stars* and inducted her into the Rock & Roll Hall of Fame, declaring that her voice could penetrate "right through a wall of sound".

The Beatles were equally smitten and she fended off the attentions of John Lennon, who invited her to his room at New York's Plaza Hotel on the group's first American tour in 1964. She took the other two Ronettes with her and they sat around playing records.

Two years later the Beatles picked the Ronettes as their support act on their final US tour. Although Ronnie did not marry Spector until 1968, by then she was living with him, and he refused to allow her to join the tour. Her place was taken by her cousin Elaine Mayes.

He had become so possessive that he could not bear to think of other men looking at her on stage. "We weren't afraid to be hot. That was our gimmick," Ronnie wrote in her 2004 memoir *Be My Baby: How I Survived Mascara, Miniskirts, and Madness.* "We squeezed our bodies into the tightest skirts we could find. Then we'd get out on stage and hike them up to show our legs even more."

Her story had parallels with that of Tina Turner, who was similarly forced to flee from an abusive husband who controlled her professional and private lives.

Both women showed a resilience in rebuilding their careers to become symbols of survival and, like Turner, Ronnie found enduring happiness in her second marriage, in 1982, to Jonathan Greenfield. Some 15 years her junior, he acted as her manager and survives her, along with their sons, Austin and Jason.

Veronica Yvette Bennett was born in New York's Spanish Harlem in 1943, the younger of two daughters. Her mother, Beatrice, was of Cherokee and African-American heritage and her father, Louis, came from White Irish-American stock.

Inspired by 1950s doo-wop groups such as Frankie Lymon and the Teenagers, the two Bennett sisters and their cousin Nedra sang at school hops and dances before landing a residency at the Peppermint Lounge, a hip Manhattan nightspot where both the twist and go-go dancing were said to have been invented.

Known initially as Ronnie and the Relatives and with a look fashioned by Estelle, who had a job on the cosmetics counter at Macy's, the trio's early singles flopped. Their fortunes looked up after Estelle contacted Spector, who had just produced a No 1 hit with another girl group, the Crystals, and asked for an audition.

When the trio began singing *Why Do Fools Fall in Love,* Spector leapt from his chair, pointed at Ronnie and shouted: "That's it! That's the voice I've been looking for!" He tried to sign her as a solo act until her mother, who acted as chaperone on the group's tours, made it clear that her teenage daughter wasn't signing for anyone unless her older sister and cousin were part of the package.

After escaping from Spector, she toured for a while as Ronnie and the Ronettes with two new members but was injuncted from singing her old hits by her ex-husband, who owned the copyrights.

Her 1980 debut solo album *Siren* failed to chart and it was not until 1986 that she returned to the limelight with Eddie Money's hit *Take Me Home Tonight*, on which she not only sang the refrain but was the subject of the lyric: "Take me home tonight/ Listen honey, just like Ronnie sang, 'Be my little baby.'"

In later years she presented an annual Christmas show, based on the Spector-produced versions of songs such as *I Saw Mommy Kissing Santa Claus*, *Frosty the Snowman* and *Sleigh Ride* which she recorded with the Ronettes.

She also covered *Back to Black*, the signature song of Amy Winehouse, who cited Ronnie as one of her main inspirations and turned up to see her in concert.

"She was in the audience looking just like me while I sang her song. It scared me," Ronnie recalled. "I saw a tear out of her eye and it made me cry. Six months later she was dead. I was devastated."

Away from music she enjoyed painting at home in rural Connecticut, where she claimed to lead "a very bland life, shopping twice a week, running errands and cooking. I don't even sing in the shower."

Yet on stage she was transformed. "Everything else disappears except the faces in the crowd," she said. "It's like I have no kids and I'm not even married. I'm married to the audience."

Ronnie Spector, singer, was born on August 10, 1943. She died of cancer on January 12, 2022, aged 78

BB KING

Virtuoso blues guitarist and singer whose career was languishing until,
in the late 1960s, his work was championed by British rock musicians

The Times, May 16, 2015

BB King was the last and arguably the greatest of the original
bluesmen to emerge from the cotton plantations of the Mississippi
Delta. His name was synonymous with the blues for more than 60
years; quite literally so, for his initials represented not his birth
names but the sobriquet "Blues Boy", which he earned as a street
musician in Memphis in the 1940s and which remained with him as
he became the grand old man of the blues, known to fellow
musicians as "the Chairman of the Board".

In later years King become an eminent symbol of popular music's
racial integration and helped to turn the blues into a universal
language, after he had been lionised by Eric Clapton and other
prominent White rock musicians.

He performed at jazz and rock festivals, on college campuses, in Las Vegas nightclubs and on primetime television. He toured the world as a blues ambassador, performing in Africa and Asia and even visiting the Soviet Union; the Moscow news service Tass reported that more than 100,000 attended his concerts in Russia in 1979.

But it was not always so and even as he became an international blues superstar, a part of him never really left the so-called "chitlin circuit", the network of small-town clubs, ghetto theatres, dance halls, roadhouses and juke joints where in his early years he played almost exclusively for Black audiences.

It was a gruelling lifestyle for although he enjoyed considerable success on the "race" chart – later renamed the R&B chart – he made little money from his early recordings and for many years his income came primarily from touring. Throughout the 1950s he played more than 300 one-night stands per year and, in an interview towards the end of the decade, he claimed that he had never experienced racial discrimination as he had only ever played for Black audiences. "While the civil rights movement was fighting for the respect of Black people, I felt I was fighting for the respect of the blues," he said.

All that changed with the blues-rock explosion of the late 1960s, spearheaded by groups such as Cream, who raided old blues recordings for their material and updated the songs with a dash of rock'n'roll energy and attitude. This sent rock fans back to the original bluesmen to discover where the music had come from. King was perfectly placed to capitalise, but the new-found interest came as a shock to him. He recalled playing the Fillmore West, San Francisco's premier rock venue, for the first time in 1967: "It seemed to be 98 per cent White so I thought maybe we had gone to the wrong place. I was kind of frightened because I was considering how I would go over, whether the people would like me."

He need not have worried. He received a rapturous ovation and it was the turning point in his career. Two years later he toured with the Rolling Stones and he went on to perform with numerous rock artists, from U2 and Clapton to Van Morrison and Elton John. King was blues royalty. Invited to attend a reception hosted by the Queen and Prince Philip at the British embassy in Washington DC, a coterie of admirers gathered around him, leading one of his fellow guests, the Rev Jesse Jackson, to quip that "more people are lining up to see the King than the Queen".

Franchised clubs bearing his name opened in New York, Los Angeles, Nashville, Las Vegas and elsewhere, and a BB King Museum was established in his hometown of Indianola, deep in the heart of the Mississippi Delta. Fittingly, the museum was housed in a former cotton industry warehouse where King had worked as a teenager, and sited on a street where he had once played on weekends for tips, until a new career opened up when he realised that "sometimes I made more money on Saturday than I made all week driving a tractor".

Pride of place in the museum went to his electric guitar, "Lucille", an instrument that became almost as famous an icon of the blues as King himself. He first gave his guitar the name as a result of an incident when he was playing a dance hall in Twist, Arkansas in 1949. After a fight broke out between two men in the audience over a woman named Lucille, a pail of kerosene was knocked over and the wooden building caught fire.

King fled the stage to safety but when he realised he had left his guitar behind, he rushed back inside the burning building, risking his life to rescue the instrument. He gave the guitar its name to remind him never to be so foolhardy again. After the original "Lucille" was stolen from the boot of his car, he worked his way through 17 more of her descendants. The guitar manufacturers Gibson even marketed a BB King-approved customised model under the name Lucille.

He was married twice, to Martha Lee Denton from 1946 to 1952 and to Sue Carol Hall from 1958 to 1966. Both marriages were childless and ended in divorce, unable to survive his devotion to touring and to "Lucille". The dissolution of his second marriage inspired one of his biggest hits, *The Thrill Is Gone*. "Real-life songs, where you feel the hurt and heat between man and woman, have cash value," he noted.

He fathered 15 children by 15 different women, noting that: "I haven't always had a halo around my head." In his autobiography,

Blues All Around Me, he wrote: "I make my move to women who seem kind and gentle, sympathetic and beautiful in ways beyond what most people can see. I want a soft shoulder, a soft caress. I didn't think of the consequences of having children." He was unapologetic about his failed marriages and relationships. "About 15 times, a lady has said, 'It's either me or Lucille.' That's why I've had 15 children by 15 women."

Yet he supported all of his children, 11 of whom survive him. Shirley King, his eldest surviving daughter, is a singer who tours as "Daughter of the Blues" and his youngest daughter, Claudette King, performs as "the Bluz Queen". Two other daughters – Karen Williams and Rita Washington – have been involved in legal battles for guardianship of their father's estate, while a fifth, Patty King, has served time in jail for a drugs offence.

He continued to maintain a punishing schedule of around 250 live appearances per year until the 1990s, when he finally announced he was cutting down. He gained his private pilot's licence in 1963 and often flew himself to concerts until his insurance company asked him to stop when he turned 70. He continued to tour and perform and his "retirement" was relative. "I don't want to go fishing every day, so what else is there for me to do?" he said on his 80th birthday.

He was born Riley King into a family of sharecroppers on a plantation near the small town of Itta Bena, Mississippi in 1925. His parents separated when he was a child, and he was partly raised by his maternal grandmother. As a boy he sang in the gospel choir at Elkhorn Baptist Church in Kilmichael. From the age of six or seven he was working six days a week picking cotton, milking the cows and working at the plantation owner's house.

He bought his first guitar around the age of 12 and accompanied the Famous St John's Gospel Singers, but soon discovered there was more cash in playing the blues. As he later recalled: "When I played gospel, people would pat me on the shoulder and tell me I was going to be good one day. But when somebody asked me to play a blues song, they would also give me a tip."

In 1946 he moved to Memphis, where he roomed with his

cousin, the blues singer Bukka White, who gave him crucial advice on how to make his way in the world: "He said, 'If you're going to be a blues musician, always dress like you're going to the bank to try to borrow money.'" But as a callow youth from the backwoods, King struggled in the big city and within a few months he had retreated back to Mississippi to drive a tractor.

He returned to Memphis at the end of 1948, this time better prepared. He won a regular slot as a performer and DJ on a local radio station, where his duties included singing a jingle in praise of a health tonic called Peptikon. As a result, he acquired the sobriquet "The Peptikon Boy", although it was not long before he became known as "The Beale Street Blues Boy", which in turn evolved into "Blues Boy King", and finally "BB King".

He made his recording debut in 1949 and his commercial breakthrough came in 1951 when he topped the "race" chart with a version of Lowell Fulson's *Three O'Clock Blues*. Further hits followed with *Every Day I Have the Blues* and *Sweet Little Angel*.

By the mid-1960s, as Black music lovers increasingly defected to the youthful, urban sounds of Motown, the blues, with its unwelcome reminders of segregation and rural poverty, was in decline. King was also in financial difficulties thanks to a chronic gambling addiction, the theft of his copyrights by less than scrupulous record companies and producers and a failure to pay his taxes, which resulted in years of wrangling with the Internal Revenue Service.

Salvation came in unlikely form as a collection of mostly British rock musicians reinvigorated the blues and created a new market for its original practitioners. By the 1970s, King was acknowledged as one of the all-time great guitar virtuosi, his playing characterised by fluid single-string runs with subtle use of vibrato and sustain to create a "singing" style in which his own voice seemed to duet with "Lucille".

When Love Comes Around, a duet with U2, introduced King to yet another generation in 1989; Bono had written the song specifically for him after watching one of King's concerts in Dublin. A duets album with Eric Clapton released in the 2000s also won glowing reviews and a Grammy award.

As old age approached, King's Falstaffian girth steadily increased, but his playing and singing remained as majestic as ever. By the time he made his farewell British tour in 2006, he was too frail to stand and played from a seated position. His ample frame had also shrunk, as he was ordered to diet in order to control his long-term diabetic condition. By the time his career finally wound down, it was estimated that he had clocked up more than 15,000 performances.

In a business not always noted for such qualities, he was a famously kindly and courteous man. According to David Ritz, the co-author of his biography: "Civility is the cornerstone of BB King's character."

BB King, guitarist, singer and songwriter, was born on September 16, 1925. He died on May 14, 2015, aged 89

DAVID CROSBY

— • —

*Iconoclastic singer, songwriter and guitarist with the Byrds and
the supergroup Crosby, Stills, Nash & Young, whose life alternated
between highs and lows*

The Times, January 19, 2023

David Crosby butted heads with his colleagues in every band he
ever passed through, but when he made music with them the
abrasiveness was replaced by a rich and mellifluous harmony.

First as a founder member of the Byrds and then with Crosby,
Stills, Nash & Young, he helped to define the sound of American
soft rock, creating the template for the Eagles and hundreds of
other West Coast bands and troubadours who followed.

His facility for melody and harmony when he sang was as great
as his tendency towards turbulence and trouble in his private life.
Although he remained an unreformed hippy who preached a genial
philosophy of love and peace all his life, he was stubborn and

opinionated, did not know how to bite his tongue and was not a man to back down in an argument.

It led to repeated fights that resulted in him being thrown out of the Byrds at the height of the group's success and falling out with Stephen Stills, Graham Nash and Neil Young as rock music's first "supergroup" disintegrated in a clash of competing egos wrapped up in a blizzard of cocaine.

A libertine with an insatiable appetite for the forbidden, he became one of rock'n'roll's most notorious junkies, narrowly defying death on several occasions and serving time in prison in the 1980s.

When his addictions caught up with him, he underwent a liver transplant in 1994, paid for by Phil Collins because Crosby's habits had left him broke (by the time he conquered his cocaine addiction he had squandered more than $2 million on the drug).

Yet the songs he wrote, including *What's Happening* and *Everybody's Been Burned* for the Byrds and *Guinnevere* for Crosby, Stills & Nash, were magical and inventive, and his bandmates knew that the sweet harmonies he brought to their compositions always made them better songs.

David Van Cortlandt Crosby was born into a prosperous, liberal family, the son of Aliph (née Van Cortlandt Whitehead), the granddaughter of a bishop, and Floyd Crosby, a Hollywood cinematographer. His father was blacklisted during the McCarthyite era and the youngster grew up a natural rebel.

He toyed with becoming an actor but, inspired by the burgeoning folk scene of the time, spent the early Sixties freewheeling his way around the clubs in Greenwich Village, New York. He then moved to Coconut Grove, Florida, where there was also a thriving scene, before returning to the West Coast.

By 1964 the Beatles' invasion of America was in full swing and Crosby was entranced. So too was Roger McGuinn, who was working as a studio musician. They joined forces in Los Angeles with Gene Clark and Chris Hillman to form the Byrds.

Their first single, *Mr Tambourine Man*, was sufficient to establish them as one of the most influential groups of the decade, marrying a sound derived from their shared love of the Beatles with Bob

Dylan's more sophisticated lyrics and topped with their own sublime West Coast harmonies.

Folk rock had been born, and further hits followed with *Turn! Turn! Turn!*, *So You Want to Be a Rock'n'Roll Star* and *Eight Miles High*, which ran into radio bans as one of the first drug songs of its time.

By 1967, however, Crosby's bandmates were describing him as "insufferable" and clashing egos between him and McGuinn resulted in the former being sacked, the conflict reaching a head over Crosby's song *Triad*, about a ménage à trois, which the rest of the group refused to release.

He drifted north to San Francisco and spent his time hanging out with members of the Grateful Dead and Jefferson Airplane, who released the controversial *Triad*.

In Florida that year he discovered an unknown folk singer called Joni Mitchell, and they became lovers. He helped her to get a record deal and produced her first album, though his womanising made their relationship short-lived.

On another trip to Florida in 1968 he bought an ocean-going yacht called the Mayan, borrowing £15,000 from Peter Tork of the Monkees to pay for it. Sailing became his main passion other than music, and he kept the boat until 2014.

About the same time Crosby also teamed up with Graham Nash from the English group the Hollies, and Stephen Stills, whose band Buffalo Springfield was in the process of breaking up. All three were fine songwriters, their voices meshed perfectly and they became rock's first "supergroup", made up of refugees from already successful bands.

Their first album, *Crosby, Stills & Nash*, was released in the summer of 1969 and included Crosby songs such as *Long Time Gone* and *Guinnevere*. The sound was mostly acoustic (they themselves called it "wooden music") and, flying in the face of the heavier, "progressive" rock of the time, it was a breath of fresh air that generated an entire new acoustic movement.

Within months, Neil Young, a former colleague of Stills in Buffalo Springfield, had joined and they played their second-ever live concert as a quartet at Woodstock. By the time they took the stage it was 3.30am and, with the likes of Jimi Hendrix, Janis Joplin and Sly Stone watching from the wings, Stills told the crowd: "We're scared shitless, man."

They triumphed over adversity and the day after the festival Crosby, appearing on the *Dick Cavett Show* with Mitchell and members of Jefferson Airplane, described the festival as "incredible ... probably the strangest thing that has ever happened in the world".

Yet at the height of their success Crosby was struck by an appalling personal tragedy. On the day the album went gold in America, his girlfriend Christine Hinton was killed in a car crash.

He retreated to his boat and undertook a long voyage but the band carried on and their first album as a quartet, *Déjà Vu*, released in 1970, was another instant classic.

A live album, *4 Way Street*, followed but the band fell apart, mostly due to tension between Young and the other members. Crosby recorded a solo album, *If I Could Only Remember My Name*, with a glittering cast of West Coast musical luminaries including Jerry Garcia, Grace Slick and Mitchell. Derided in some quarters at the time as self-indulgent, it subsequently came to be regarded as perhaps the definitive recording of the loose, jamming style that characterised the San Francisco scene at its best.

Crosby made more records as a duo with Nash but a further CSNY album, to be called *Human Highway*, was aborted in 1973 amid renewed acrimony, although the quartet managed to remain on speaking terms long enough for a reunion tour in 1974.

By the late 1970s Crosby had fallen out with most of his old friends, including Mitchell, his career was in a tailspin and he was chronically addicted to free-base cocaine and heroin. His role was almost marginal in such reunion albums as *CSN* (1977) and *Daylight Again* five years later.

Selling almost everything except his yacht to fuel his drug habit, there were repeated arrests until in 1983 he was sentenced to five years in jail. On appeal he was allowed to enter a rehabilitation centre, but he was returned to prison after absconding.

Abandoned as a hopeless case by even his closest friends, jail was his salvation: he emerged in 1986 free of drugs and the following year married Jan Dance, his long-time partner and former fellow addict. He also began making meaningful music again with *Oh Yes I Can,* his second solo album (18 years after the first) and a CSNY reunion album, *American Dream.*

Yet his troubles were not over. In 1990 he had a near-fatal accident on his Harley-Davidson motorcycle, and in the mid-1990s, after years of substance abuse and previously undiagnosed hepatitis C, he almost died from liver failure. A transplant was arranged in the nick of time. He also had type 2 diabetes.

He detailed his troubled life in the frank and revealing autobiography *Long Time Gone* and, restored to full artistic health, made further solo albums. *Thousand Roads* in 1993 was co-produced by Phil Collins and was followed two years later by a live album, *It's All Coming Back to Me Now.* There were also further CSN albums in the Nineties with *Live It Up* and *After the Storm.*

In 1995 his life took a remarkable turn when his wife gave birth to a son, Django Crosby. About the same time he also discovered the existence of another son, James Raymond, who had been born in the 1960s to a casual girlfriend and adopted.

To Crosby's delight, he discovered that Raymond was a session musician in Los Angeles and together they formed a group, CPR. Their first album appeared in 1998.

Jan, Django and James survive him, along with a daughter, Erika, from a relationship with Jackie Guthrie, and a second daughter, Donovan Crosby, by his former girlfriend Debbie Donovan.

Crosby, Stills, Nash and Young also finally reunited for *Looking Forward* (1999), their first album as a quartet in a decade and only their third studio recording. Their first tour since the Seventies followed in 2000.

In 2019 Crosby was the subject of a documentary, *Remember My Name,* which did not gloss over his flaws. Several of the contributors had disobliging things to say, but no one was more brutally honest about him than he was about himself as he described how his former bandmates Stills, Nash and Young had found him impossible to work with. Stills was the only band member who continued to talk to him.

On a happier note, he and Mitchell patched things up in recent years to the extent that they would even have dinner together occasionally. His final album, *For Free*, was released last autumn: the title track was a cover of one of her songs. It was the third album that he had co-written and produced with his son James. By then he had twice been inducted into the Rock & Roll Hall of Fame, but he had also been obliged to sell the rights to his back catalogue.

Crosby was white-haired by that stage but still had his trademark walrus moustache and he still smoked home-grown cannabis every day.

He also still had a high-pitched giggle that he deployed when discussing his 80th birthday with *The Guardian*. "I expected to be dead when I was about 30," he said. "Hehehehe!"

David Crosby, rock musician, was born on August 14, 1941. He died after a long illness on January 18, 2023, aged 81

KEITH MOON

*Outrageous and eccentric but highly talented drummer with the
rock band, "The Who"*

The Times, September 9, 1978

Keith Moon, without question among the most talented
rock'n'roll drummers in contemporary popular music, was found
dead in bed at his flat in Mayfair on Thursday. He was 31. An
unrelenting iconoclast with a reputation for wild behaviour, Moon
was also one of the more enigmatic figures of popular music in the
past two decades. His outrageous behaviour was seen by many as
disguising a perceptive and sensitive personality.

Keith Moon's aggressive drumming style, which sometimes
depended on the use of two bass drums as well as dramatic play
with the cymbals, played a vital part in the international success of
his rock'n'roll group "The Who".

The group was formed in 1962 under the name The Detours in
Shepherd's Bush, London, and its original four-man membership

did not change throughout its history. Moon was a decisive factor in their success. Originally identified as rebellious "mods" in the middle 1960s, with songs like *My Generation* and *The Kids Are Alright*, they progressed in the 1970s to the much-admired rock opera *Tommy* and *Quadrophenia*. Their work was at least partly inspired by Moon's ability to retain a sense of what ordinary teenagers of his generation thought and felt.

As "The Who" became more and more successful internationally, often rivalling the slightly longer-established Rolling Stones for the much vaunted title of the "Greatest Rock'n' Roll Band in the World", so Moon's connection with his London roots and his family began to fray. In their endless and persistent travels Moon often took refuge in bizarre acts, including driving a Rolls-Royce into a hotel swimming pool, and wiring explosives to a hotel door, as well as drinking heavily.

Close friends regarded this behaviour as a persistent attempt to disguise his basic uncertainty, and he remained in the rock fraternity as a figure most admired and liked as a person.

Moon's body was discovered by his Swedish fiancée, Annette Walter-Lax; their engagement was announced last week. His first marriage ended in divorce, after nine years in 1975.

Keith Moon, drummer, was born on August 23, 1946. He died of a drug overdose on September 7, 1978, aged 32

SINÉAD O'CONNOR

Controversial and troubled but prodigiously talented Irish singer
best known for her moving rendition of Nothing Compares 2 U

The Times, July 26, 2023

When Sinéad O'Connor appeared at a star-studded tribute concert
at Madison Square Garden in 1992, she was meant to sing Bob Dylan's
I Believe in You, a tender ballad of love and devotion.

Instead, she delivered an angry version of Bob Marley's *War*, for
which she was booed and jeered. As she ran off the stage, she had to
be consoled by the avuncular figure of Kris Kristofferson, who held
her in a bear hug while she sobbed.

It was just one of many troubled moments in a troubled career,
yet her choice of song was fitting. Throughout her life, O'Connor
seemed to be permanently at war, whether it was with her family,
the Catholic Church, the music industry or the world in general.

Above all, she frequently appeared to be at war with herself. On
hits such as *Nothing Compares 2 U* she sang like an angel but she was

haunted by demons and her life became a harrowing personal psychodrama, played out in the public glare of the media.

She carried the pain of a troubled and abused wild child into adulthood. Sometimes this produced great music, but peace and redemption eluded her.

There were four marriages, all of which ended in divorce, abortions, custody battles over her children, numerous breakdowns, spells in psychiatric hospitals and suicide attempts. Diagnosed with bipolar disorder, she spent years on various prescription drugs, including lithium.

It was a tragic waste of a potentially stellar talent that reached its defining moment when at 23 she topped charts around the world with a brilliant, poignant arrangement of Prince's *Nothing Compares 2 U*, accompanied by a compelling video that starkly framed her shaven head in dramatic close-up with a single tear rolling down her cheek. She later revealed that the tear was real and she had been thinking about her dead mother, with whom she had had a fiery and at times violent relationship.

The performance won her four Grammy nominations, although typically she boycotted the ceremony and became the first artist ever to refuse an award. She said her no-show was a protest against "extreme commercialisation". In truth it was another manifestation of the war she seemed to have declared on everything and everyone, including herself.

If anybody told or even asked her to do something, she made it a point of contrarian principle to do the exact opposite. When she was a young woman starting out in music, Nigel Grainge, who had just given O'Connor her first recording contract, gently advised her that if she stopped wearing her hair short and dressed in a more feminine style, it would be easier to sell her to the record-buying public. In response she went straight out and had her head shaved and bought a pair of bovver boots.

Once she had scored her first hit, she struggled to cope with the pressures of her new-found celebrity. "I don't like being famous. I don't like the effect it is having on my life," she said. Stardom undoubtedly amplified her emotional fragility. She put it more bluntly in her 2021 autobiography *Rememberings*. She was, she admitted, "as nutty as a fuckin' fruitcake and as crazy as a loon" long before she became a star. *The Guardian* called her book "a tremendous catalogue of female misbehaviour".

A series of outrageous public outbursts led the tabloid press to rename her "Sinéad O'Controversy". She declared her support for the IRA and opined that "people like Thatcher and Ian Paisley should be shot". Saddam Hussein was no worse than George Bush, she said during the 1991 Gulf War.

When on tour in America she refused to appear if *The Star-Spangled Banner* was played before her concerts, radio stations banned her records and Frank Sinatra expressed a desire to attend one of her concerts in order to "kick her ass".

To her credit, she never lost a sense of humour in her distress. When protesters hired a steamroller to crush piles of her albums outside her record company HQ in New York, she donned a wig and sunglasses and joined them, even giving an interview to a news crew in which she claimed to have come from Saratoga to add her patriotic voice to the protest.

Similarly, when the rap star MC Hammer said she should be kicked out of America and he would personally pay her fare home, she sent him a £2,600 bill for her first-class air ticket back to Dublin.

When she tore up a photograph of Pope John Paul II and denounced the Vatican as "a nest of devils" live on television in 1992, she received death threats. As she fled America she donated the five-bedroom house with a swimming pool that she had purchased in the Hollywood Hills to the Red Cross and asked that the money should go to children in war-torn Somalia.

It was the fruition of a promise she had made in childhood when she had confessed to a priest that she had stolen money from a charity collecting box. He told her that if she promised to give the money back when she got a job she would be "square with God".

Some attributed her controversial outbursts to attention-seeking but it seemed that she could not help herself and a psychologist suggested she suffered from coprolalia, a compulsion to shock that was beyond her control. "I don't do anything in order to cause trouble. It just so happens that what I do naturally causes trouble," she said.

Her love-hate relationship with the Catholic Church was rooted in her childhood experience, when at 13 after repeated truancy from school and an arrest for shoplifting she had spent 18 months in a Magdalene laundry run by the Sisters of Our Lady of Charity, during which she endured "unbelievable panic and terror and agony".

Yet she suggested that if she had not been a singer she would like to have been a priest and in 1999 she was ordained in a rebel Tridentine Catholic sect and for a while was known as "Mother Bernadette Marie".

Her calling did not last long and was just one manifestation of a promiscuous spiritual longing. She flirted with paganism, Rastafarianism and Buddhism and in 2018 converted to Islam. Taking the name Shuhada Sadaqat, she was photographed wearing a hijab and called her conversion "the natural conclusion of any intelligent theologian's journey".

Her relationships were similarly complicated. She claimed to be bisexual and there were numerous affairs, including one with Peter Gabriel, and four husbands. In 1987 she married John Reynolds, her drummer, when she was pregnant with his son Jake. The marriage was short-lived but they remained on good terms and continued to be musical collaborators.

Her daughter Roisin was born in 1995, the result of a relationship with the Irish journalist John Waters. She insisted that he had merely been a "sperm donor" and a bitter custody battle ensued.

In 2001 she married the journalist Nick Sommerlad. They divorced and in 2004 she had her third child, Shane, with the Irish musician Dónal Lunny. She had another son, Yeshua, with Frank Bonadio, the estranged husband of the Irish singer Mary Coughlan.

In 2010 she married for a third time, to Steve Cooney, a musician, but they separated within a year. She met her fourth husband, Barry Herridge, an Irish therapist, through the internet and they married in Las Vegas in 2011. Within days she was back online reporting that they were no longer together.

For a while her children lived with her in a rented house in Dublin, but after another breakdown, her eldest son, Jake, by now an adult, organised a family intervention. Shane was placed with foster parents and Yeshua went to live with his father. O'Connor berated her family on social media, telling them, "You killed your mother. You stole my sons."

She is survived by Jake, Roisin and Yeshua. Shane took his own life last year at the age of 17. A week after his suicide, O'Connor was admitted to hospital after tweeting that she also intended to take her own life.

Sinéad Marie Bernadette O'Connor was born in Glenageary, Ireland, in 1966 and named after the wife of the Irish president, Éamon de Valera, and Saint Bernadette of Lourdes. Her father, Sean O'Connor, was an engineer who later trained to become a barrister. She had a tempestuous relationship with her mother Marie (née O'Grady), particularly after her parents separated when she was eight. After her father was denied custody of the five children he became chairman of the Divorce Action Group, which campaigned for the rights of fathers.

Her older brother, the novelist Joseph O'Connor, recalled their mother's "extreme and violent abuse, both emotional and physical" towards her daughter and it left profound scars. She wrote about the experience in several songs and in adulthood spoke out in support of abused children.

Four of the five children went on to have creative careers. Her sister Eimear O'Connor is a noted art historian and her brother Eoin O'Connor a successful painter.

At 13 Sinéad went to live with her father but he was unable to control her waywardness and she was placed in a Magdalene laundry. She later moved to a Quaker boarding school, where she was encouraged by her Irish language teacher Joseph Falvey to record a demo of the songs she had begun writing.

On leaving school she joined the Irish band Ton Ton Macoute but after her mother died in a car crash in 1987 – a loss that despite their difficult relationship left her devastated – she moved to London, where she recorded her debut album, *The Lion and the Cobra*. It made her an instant sensation as the album went gold, spawned the hit single *Mandinka* and earned her a first Grammy nomination. The follow-up album, *I Do Not Want What I Haven't Got* (1990), was even better and included *Nothing Compares 2 U*.

It was the highlight of her career, artistically and commercially, and amid the chaos of her dysfunctional life, her music suffered. During one bout of manic depression, she sold all her guitars and announced that she would never play again. She did, but although her voice remained potent, there were long gaps between her records and she lost artistic focus. Later releases included a misfiring reggae album and a collection of "sexed-up" versions of traditional Irish folk songs. After *I'm Not Bossy, I'm the Boss* (2014), produced by her first husband John Reynolds, there were no more albums but she made occasional fleeting reappearances, most recently singing *The Skye Boat Song* over the opening credits of the 2023 season of the TV series *Outlander*.

She once said that on her tombstone she wanted only her name and mobile phone number, so that everyone would "know I am still contactable, though I'm elsewhere".

Sinéad O'Connor, musician, was born on December 8, 1966. She died of undisclosed causes on July 26, 2023, aged 56

ELVIS PRESLEY

———————●———————

*Singer known as "The King" and remembered as one of the earliest
and greatest exponents of rock'n' roll music*

The Times, August 17, 1977

Mr Elvis Presley, who died yesterday at the age of 42, will be remembered as one of the earliest and greatest exponents of rock'n'roll music, whose recordings of *Blue Suede Shoes*, *Hound Dog* and *Heartbreak Hotel* establish the music's otherwise fitful claim to be a 20th-century art form.

Presley was not the first to play rock'n'roll, nor can he be numbered among its faithful adherents, but such details have long become irrelevant in the immensity of his legend. To his own generation and to others born after his career began, to the uninformed as well as the aficionado, Elvis Presley remained "The King". A new art form, a youth revolution, was not among the objectives of Presley or his promoters.

He was launched in the middle Fifties as a money-making confection with a life, possibly, of six months. It was inconceivable that the catchpenny excesses of the moment, the slicked hair and shaking torso, the guitar, flashed and flourished and spun, would create a style to fascinate millions of young people for 20 years. As a symbol, Presley dominated rock music, pop art and unnumbered private ways of life; as a person, he was largely untroubled by mortality. That he himself never did or said anything remotely outrageous, significant or even interesting has only added to the purity of his myth.

Elvis Aron Presley was born in 1935 in the small town of Tupelo, East Mississippi. His parents were poor, eking out a precarious sharecropper living as factory workers or farm hands. Elvis was one of identical twin boys; his brother Aron died at birth. Throughout his childhood, a doting affection was lavished on him, especially by his mother Gladys. Elvis, in return, became devoted to his mother, and was deeply affected by her death in 1958. It was propitious that he should have grown up in that region of the American South. The lands around the Mississippi River, for all their outward dreariness, have fostered two distinct and vital musical cultures. From the Negro people came slave and work songs, later formalised into the blues. White people too evolved music to express their superior caste, with fine clothes and sentimentality and rapid banjo and guitar picking. The two styles met, but did not coalesce, at the city of Memphis, with its rich merchants and its depressed hinterland, nurturing the blues tradition of the famous, and infamous, Beale Street.

The Presley family moved to Memphis when Elvis was ten, living first in one room, then in an apartment house for poor Whites. Elvis had received a musical education no greater than any Southern boy, picking up the rudiments of guitar playing and singing in church or at county fairs. When he left school, it was to work as a truck driver. At the age of 19, he was signed to the local Sun record label by its proprietor, Sam Phillips, who had heard him singing in a record-your-voice machine. Phillips was the first to see the possibilities in a White boy who could sing Black music: it was Phillips who encouraged Presley to develop a style unlike anything ever heard in Country and Western music. The result was *That's All Right*, released on the Sun label in 1954.

Presley might nonetheless have enjoyed a regional popularity merely but for the intervention of "Colonel" Tom Parker. A man in his forties, of doubtful fairground antecedents, Parker had already gauged what convulsions were threatening American popular music. In a market hitherto dominated by crooners and ballad singers, new and violent noises could be heard, compounded partly by boogie and bebop, partly by rhythm and blues and other Negro styles traditionally stigmatised as "race" music. Already, the appearances of a former dance band called Bill Haley and the Comets were providing scenes of hysteria among young people.

With masterly timing, Parker wrested Presley away from Sun and signed him to the wealthy RCA label: under Parker's personal and exclusive management, the young man from Tupelo was launched upon the world.

From 1956 to 1958 Presley's music and his appearance became the scandal of America. He was universally denounced as an immoral influence on the mobs of girls who shrieked for him at his concerts, who tore at his clothes and covered his cars with lipstick. A new species, the "teen-ager", became the preoccupation of the American establishment, and Elvis was condemned as the embodiment of its rebellion and cleanliness. Every record that Presley made generated fortunes: *Heartbreak Hotel* alone stayed for eight weeks at No 1 in the American hit parade. Merchandising empires were built up around his name. Films followed: *Love Me Tender*, *Jailhouse Rock*, *King Creole*. The sale of guitars rose to unprecedented figures. And all proceeded under the skilful tutelage of Colonel Parker, orchestrating "Elvis the Pelvis", his gold suits, his pink suits and gold Cadillac cars, together with intriguing glimpses of a quiet, religious and respectful Southern boy.

His fame grew subsequently in England but Parker, cautious of the fate of other teen idols, saw to it that he played no concerts here. Rumours of his coming were to recur, however, throughout his career. It was Parker's most adroit piece of management which brought about the end of the Presley golden age. In 1958 Elvis entered the army for two years' service. That potential disaster was converted, with the aid of the military authorities, into a commercial transfiguration.

The film *GI Blues* signified the birth of a new Elvis: rebel and outcast no longer, but an all-American hero, clean-cut and close-cropped and dutiful. The years that followed his discharge were devoted to the playing of this anodyne part. Throughout the early and middle sixties, Presley was cast in a series of second-rate musical films. His recording output, with such notable exceptions as *Return to Sender* or *His Latest Flame*, entered the same decline.

His public grew accustomed to his remoteness. Inordinately rich, he lived as a recluse in the mansions he had built for himself, maintaining a squad of his former army friends to be his aides and to allay the boredom of his wealth.

In 1967 he married Priscilla Beaulieu, an army officer's daughter whom he had met in Germany. They had one child, Lisa Marie. The marriage was dissolved in 1972. Although the influence of rock'n'roll appeared to wane during the sixties, it was to provide the stimulus for most of the next generation of young musicians, including the Beatles.

Inevitably the commercial "rock revival" brought Presley out of retirement, first on a television show, then by personal appearances in the Las Vegas clubs. Overweight, self-conscious and self-mocking, he seemed astonished by the ovation which he received.

The standard of his records improved, though inclining to middle-of-the-road pop. As he passed the age of 40, surrounded by countless youthful imitators, his command of the hit parade had been restored.

His private life remained largely a matter of speculation. There were rumours concerning his erratic temper, his indifference to beautiful women, his diffidence, his preoccupation with his mother and with religion. That he never visited England was felt by many to be a betrayal of his most faithful audience; to others it was part of his incalculable fascination. His total record sales are estimated at 150 million copies. He leaves behind clubs and associations dedicated to impersonating his voice and appearance. What lay behind the music was never clear, if indeed there was anything at all. But merely by innuendo, he is assured of his place in history.

Elvis Presley, singer and actor, was born on January 8, 1935. He died of a heart attack on August 16, 1977, aged 42

ARETHA FRANKLIN

———————•———————

Peerless if sometimes "difficult" diva known as the Queen of Soul,
whose voice tingled spines and made presidents cry

The Times, August 16, 2018

"American history wells up when Aretha sings," Barack Obama observed after witnessing Aretha Franklin's performance at the Kennedy Center in Washington in 2015.

Her voice certainly had the power to make the presidential tear ducts well up; during the concert Obama wept openly as she sang her soulful 1967 hit *(You Make Me Feel Like) A Natural Woman.*

A long-time fan, Obama also booked Franklin to sing at his first inauguration, but he was far from the only incumbent of the White House to be moved by the emotional heft of Franklin's spine-tingling voice.

Jimmy Carter boogied on the balcony while she sang; Bill Clinton made a personal request for her to perform at his inauguration concert; and although Franklin was a lifelong Democrat, in 2005 George W Bush awarded her the Presidential Medal of Freedom, America's highest civilian honour.

"Aretha is still the best singer in the world, bar none. She finds meanings in lyrics that even the composers didn't know they had," Bush declared.

Yet it was America's first Black president who most eloquently encapsulated Franklin's significance, not merely as the world's sassiest female singer, but as an indomitable icon of Black womanhood. "Nobody embodies more fully the connection between the African-American spiritual, the blues, R&B, rock'n' roll – the way that hardship and sorrow were transformed into something full of beauty and vitality and hope," Obama wrote.

"When she sits down at a piano and sings *A Natural Woman,* she can move me to tears because it captures the fullness of the American experience and the possibility of synthesis, reconciliation, transcendence."

Franklin's peerless voice combined the fervour of gospel, a jazz-like sophistication and an unparalleled emotion that seemed to emanate from deep within her being. It was often said that if extraterrestrials landed a spaceship on Earth and wanted to know the meaning of soul, the best definition would be to play them one of Franklin's recordings.

Her finest work came in the 1960s and early 1970s when she embarked on a red-hot streak with unforgettable hits such as *Respect, I Never Loved a Man (the Way I Love You), Chain of Fools, I Say a Little Prayer, Rock Steady, Think* and *A Natural Woman,* a body of work that represents one of the towering pinnacles of 20th-century popular music and which came to define the art of soul singing.

She remained the benchmark by which subsequent female singers were judged, from Whitney Houston to Beyoncé. For all their undoubted qualities, none was ever found to be quite as regal as the original "Queen of Soul".

The quality of Franklin's later work was patchy and she developed a reputation for being difficult and demanding. David Ritz – initially hired to ghost a sanitised autobiography – later described a life racked by insecurities and characterised by tantrums, rages and jealousies.

"She was afraid she wasn't good enough as a singer, pretty enough as a woman or devoted enough as a mother," her younger sister and backing singer Carolyn Franklin told Ritz. "I don't know what to call it but deep, deep insecurity. Her style was to either drink away the anxiety or, when that stopped working, disappear for a while, find her bearings and go right back onstage and wear the crown of the impervious diva."

In interviews, which she gave rarely and reluctantly, she developed the disconcerting superstar tic of referring to herself in the third person. "Aretha is a woman like any other woman," she told *The Sunday Times* in 2014.

The magnitude of her talent was rivalled only by the size of her ego. When she worked with the singer Luther Vandross she treated him like an employee rather than a collaborator. She called him "Vandross" and insisted that he addressed her as "Miss Franklin".

Yet such petty foibles could not detract from the fact that her landmark recordings made her status unassailable as one of the great divas of the age. Like her fellow African-American singers Ray Charles and Stevie Wonder, she left behind the limitations of musical genre to become a legend in her own lifetime.

As a popular entertainer she could sing anything – literally. At the 1998 Grammy awards, Pavarotti called in sick with a sore throat. Given 20 minutes' notice, Franklin stepped in and delivered a deathless version of *Nessun Dorma* in his stead.

Several of her songs became feminist and civil rights anthems, although, more than that, they transcended gender and race to become celebrations of a shared humanity. Perhaps the most potent of all was her rearrangement of Otis Redding's *Respect*, which she recorded at the age of 25 and which – after several years of unfulfilled promise – became her signature tune and gave Franklin her first No 1 hit.

Redding had recorded the song as a plea. Franklin transformed it into a demand and added her own brilliant, semi-improvised tropes to the lyric, such as the chorus in which she spelt out letter-by-letter "R-E-S-P-E-C-T, find out what it means to me" and the thrilling "Sock it to me, sock it to me, sock it to me" refrain.

Her delivery – "as precise an artefact as a Ming vase", as one critic put it – was so monumental that when she had finished recording the vocal her gobsmacked backing musicians stood as one and applauded. It was an unprecedented show of appreciation on the part of seen-it-all-done-it-all session players whose habit was to work to the clock on union rates.

When Redding sang his version during the most famous performance of his career at the Monterey Pop Festival that summer he acknowledged that Franklin's genius meant that the song was no longer his property. He introduced *Respect* as a composition "that a girl took away from me, a friend of mine, this girl she just took this song".

Respect made Franklin an overnight star. She went on to have 112 singles in the American charts, including 17 in the Top Ten, making her the most charted female artist in history. She won 18 Grammys, sold more than 80 million records and was the first female performer to be inducted into the Rock & Roll Hall of Fame.

She had famously larger-than-life appetites for sex, shopping and food, bordering on addictions. Never as svelte as, say, Diana Ross, she fought a losing battle with her weight, which increased considerably after she stopped smoking in the early 1990s.

At home in Detroit – which she left with decreasing regularity in later years – she enjoyed cooking. "I do a great chicken and dressing and I like banana puddings and peach cobbler," she said. "But if you mess up, you can gain a lot of weight. The most difficult thing for me to give up was ham hocks and greens."

When she recorded a version of *Nothing Compares 2 U*, the Prince song turned into a hit by Sinéad O'Connor, she even added a line about how not even "a strawberry sundae or ham hocks and greens" could compare.

Her weight issues took a toll and her health was not helped by a bizarre view of what constituted exercise. "I have my fitness regime where I walk the big superstores – Kmart and Walmart," she said. "I walk the whole store. Sometimes twice if it's not a superstore. I don't do it with the cart. Security people mind the cart and I do the walking."

She is survived by four sons, several of whom followed her into the music industry. After becoming pregnant at the age of 12 by Donald Burk, a boy she knew at school, she gave birth to her first child – named Clarence after her father – in 1955. By the time she was 14 she had a second child, named Edward after his father, Edward Jordan. Both children took her family name and were brought up by Franklin's grandmother, Rachel, and by her elder sister, Erma.

There were also stories that at about the same time Franklin had a liaison in an Atlanta motel room with the soul singer Sam Cooke, almost twice her age, after he had crooned his way into her heart singing *You Send Me*. Her third child, Ted White Jr, was born in 1964 and is a guitarist who sometimes played in his mother's backing band. He is known professionally as Teddy Richards. Her fourth son, Kecalf Cunningham, the child of her road manager Ken

Cunningham, was born in 1970 and is a Christian rap artist.

Her first husband, Ted White, whom she married in 1961, was described by Franklin's fellow singer Bettye LaVette as "a gentleman pimp". Using the earnings of his prostitutes to invest in Franklin's career, White became not only Franklin's husband, but also her manager – and her abuser. She went to great lengths to hide the bruises. "She wanted the world to think she had a storybook marriage," said her brother Cecil, who succeeded White as Franklin's manager. "She was having all those hits and making all that money. She was scared of rocking the boat, until one day the boat capsized and she nearly drowned."

They separated in 1968, by which time Franklin was drinking heavily, "using booze to numb the pain of her lousy marriage", according to Ruth Bowen, her long-time booking agent. During a concert in Columbus, Georgia in 1967, she fell off the stage and broke her arm. It was officially reported that she had been blinded by the stage lights, but Bowen knew it was caused by alcohol.

She married her second husband, the actor Glynn Turman, in 1978 and briefly became stepmother to his three children from a previous marriage. They separated in 1982 and divorced two years later.

She also had a long-running and typically volatile affair with the Temptations singer Dennis Edwards. "She was the Queen of Soul and I think at times she saw her boyfriends like her servants," he noted tartly.

In 2012 she announced that she was marrying Willie Wilkerson, a long-term friend and confidant with whom she had begun a relationship in 1988. She even revealed the designers of her bridal outfit (Donna Karan, Valentino and Vera Wang), but later called off the wedding without explanation.

Aretha Louise Franklin was born in 1942 in a shotgun shack in Memphis, Tennessee. Her mother, Barbara (née Siggers), sang and played the piano in church where her father Clarence LaVaughn – known as CL – Franklin was a preacher. The couple had four children together in addition to children born to both outside their marriage.

When Aretha was four, the family moved to Detroit, Michigan, where her father became pastor of the New Bethel Baptist Church, but within two years her mother had left owing to her husband's infidelities. She died shortly before her daughter's tenth birthday.

Her father's emotional sermons denouncing segregation and White supremacy earned him a name on the gospel circuit and in the civil rights movement. When Martin Luther King was in Detroit he stayed at the Franklin family home. Aretha later sang at King's funeral.

As an accomplished pianist, by the age of 12 she was singing and playing in the New Bethel Church and accompanying her father on the road with his travelling "gospel caravan".

Despite being a man of the cloth, it was a sexually liberated environment. "I got a kick outta seeing how God's people were going for it hard and heavy every which way," Ray Charles said of Franklin's church. "I was just surprised to see how loose they were." It was even rumoured – incorrectly – that the Rev Franklin was the father of Aretha's first child.

Having dropped out of school, she made her first gospel recordings at the age of 14. In 1960 she informed her father that she wanted to sing secular pop material and signed to Columbia Records. Feeling obliged to explain herself to her churchgoing fans, she wrote: "I don't think that in any manner I did the Lord a disservice when I made up my mind to switch over. After all, the blues is a music born out of the slavery day sufferings of my people."

At Columbia she came under the influence of the veteran producer John Hammond, who three decades earlier had discovered Billie Holiday and Count Basie. Although her voice was already a gloriously soulful instrument, her career never really took off during the six years she spent on the label, as Hammond attempted to turn her into a Holiday-styled jazz singer.

Her breakthrough finally came in early 1967 after signing with Atlantic Records. Jerry Wexler, the label's in-house producer, immediately took her to the Fame Studios in Muscle Shoals, Alabama, where they recorded the funk-filled *I Never Loved a Man (the Way I Love You)*.

With a sensual vocal performance that to this day retains its capacity to send shivers down the spine, it was the pivotal moment in Franklin's career and heralded the start of a golden run, the soulful intensity of her voice seemingly enhanced by her increasingly troubled personal life. Drinking heavily and with her abusive marriage collapsing, she was arrested in a Detroit parking lot for creating a disturbance, missed concerts and walked offstage in distress in the middle of a gig in St Louis. The promoter announced that she had suffered a nervous breakdown.

"I think of Aretha as Our Lady of Mysterious Sorrows," wrote Wexler, who produced most of her hits during the 1960s and 1970s. "Her eyes are incredible, luminous eyes covering inexplicable pain. Her depressions could be as deep as the dark sea. I don't pretend to know the sources of her anguish but anguish surrounds Aretha as surely as the glory of her musical aura."

In the 1970s she made a stunning return to her gospel roots with an album recorded in a Baptist church in the Watts district of Los Angeles, featuring the voices of her father and the noted gospel preacher the Rev James Cleveland.

Later she updated her sound via glossy duets with George Benson, Annie Lennox, George Michael, Elton John and Whitney Houston. There was even a hip-hop makeover via collaborations with Lauryn Hill and Puff Daddy, while she became first choice to sing the American national anthem at key sporting events.

A fear of flying meant that in later decades she did not perform outside North America and the next tantrum was never far away. That she exploded with jealous fury when Beyoncé described Tina Turner as "the Queen" at the 2008 Grammy awards suggested that, far from mellowing with age, the advancing years had made her more prickly than ever.

Yet throughout it all, the voice continued to sing out with unrivalled soulfulness. "I don't care what they say about Aretha," said Billy Preston, who often performed with her. "She can go into her diva act and turn off the world. But on any given night, when that lady gets her body and soul all over some righteous song ... you'll know that she's still the best."

Aretha Franklin, singer, was born on March 25, 1942. She died of pancreatic cancer on August 16, 2018, aged 76

GENESIS P-ORRIDGE

*Reliably outrageous musician, performance artist and provocateur
who founded the cult experimental band Throbbing Gristle*

The Times, April 24, 2020

"Gen, don't even try and get them to understand you," the film-maker Derek Jarman once told Genesis P-Orridge.

It was advice from a fellow provocateur that he followed all his transgressive life. Confrontation rather than understanding seemed to be P-Orridge's objective, from the abrasive swirl of noise he made with his band Throbbing Gristle to an insistence on being known as "s/he" and "he/r".

The cultural commentator Christopher Partridge once characterised P-Orridge's work as a "confluence of pornography, violence, death, degradation, the confrontation of taboo subjects, noise and paganism". P-Orridge would not have had much argument with that; he saw himself as an amalgam of Aleister Crowley, William S Burroughs and Johnny Rotten.

His work was highly influential in avant-garde circles. As the leader of the conceptual performance art troupe COUM Transmissions in the mid-1970s he received grants from the Arts Council and the British Council and performed at the Institute of Contemporary Arts (ICA) in London. His show featured pornography and presented nappies as works of art. "Public money is being wasted here to destroy the morality of our society," the Conservative MP Sir Nicholas Fairbairn complained in the Commons. COUM lost their grants.

By then, however, P-Orridge had created a rock band designed to take his performance art to "a more street level". He named the group Throbbing Gristle after a slang term for an erect penis. The line-up included his girlfriend Christine Newby on guitar. He gave her the name Cosey Fanni Tutti.

"TG", as they were known, set out to make the transgressions of the Sex Pistols and other punk groups appear tame. Throbbing Gristle's material – they were not songs exactly – explored mass murder, mutilation and deviant sex. One piece referenced Charles Manson and featured the recorded confession of a murderer. The music was a rebarbative collage of dissonant guitars and tape loops with P-Orridge's dystopian vocals. The group came to define a sub-genre of alternative rock style known as industrial music and influenced a range of acts from Nine Inch Nails to Marilyn Manson.

The band folded in 1981 following a messy end to P-Orridge's relationship with Cosey Fanni Tutti. On the rebound, he married Paula Brooking, a supermarket cashier whom he met when she was 16. As Paula P-Orridge, she played drums in his next band, Psychic TV. They came close to having a hit with *Godstar*, about Brian Jones of the Rolling Stones, but were thrown off course in 1992 by a Channel 4 documentary that falsely claimed P-Orridge had been involved in satanic rituals. Police raided his home and headlines such as "Cage This Evil Monster" followed. It was true he had founded a network of occultists called Thee Temple ov Psychick Youth, but the more lurid accusations were groundless and Channel 4 was forced to retract them.

P-Orridge escaped to California with his wife and their two daughters, Caresse and Genesse. When the marriage collapsed he found himself the single father of two girls. He attended meetings at their school in a silver miniskirt and thigh-high boots. He subsequently got remarried to Lady Jaye (née Jacqueline Breyer), a New York dominatrix. After abandoning "the binary divisions of gender", both underwent surgical alteration with breast implants and hormone therapy in an attempt to resemble each other. They called it the "Pandrogeny Project", sharing clothes and make-up. She died of cancer in 2007.

Born in Manchester in 1950, he began life as Neil Andrew Megson, the son of Muriel, a housewife, and Ronald Megson, a travelling salesman who played drums in an amateur jazz band. He grew up in Essex, Cheshire and Warwickshire, where he attended the fee-paying Solihull School, an experience he likened to being "mentally and physically tortured".

In 1968 he began a degree in social administration and philosophy at Hull University, where he won a poetry competition judged by Philip Larkin. Influenced by the radical student politics of the time, within a year he had dropped out and moved to London, where for three months he lived in a hippy commune. It was a chaotic and unsatisfying experience that, for the only time in his adult life, persuaded him to give normality a try. He returned to the family home and took a job in his father's office. "Neil Megson, clerk" was never going to work, though, and he soon returned to Hull and launched COUM.

He and Newby lived in a derelict warehouse. Photographs at the time show him looking like a Wolfie Smith-styled suburban Che Guevara.

Asked to define his life, he answered, "When in doubt, be extreme."

Genesis P-Orridge, musician, was born on February 22, 1950. He died of leukaemia on March 14, 2020, aged 70

LES MCKEOWN

●

*Bay City Rollers frontman, whose life veered dramatically
between highs and lows*

The Times, April 23, 2021

As a consummate hedonist, Les McKeown ought to have been
in his element as the lead singer of the Bay City Rollers. In the mid-
1970s "Rollermania" seemed unstoppable and as the band's teenage
heart-throb, he had the pop world at his feet. Hit records such as
Shang-a-Lang, *Bye Bye Baby* and *Give a Little Love* set the Bay City
Rollers on the way to record sales of 120 million, generating income
estimated to be worth more than £5 billion in today's money.

Everywhere McKeown and his bandmates went they were mobbed
by frenzied screaming girls, all dressed like their heroes in tartan
trousers worn at half-mast, accessorised with a tartan scarf tied around
the wrist. Nobody stopped to question how ridiculous this crime against
fashion looked. For Rollers fans, and there were millions of them, the
uniform was as compulsory as the one they had to wear to school.

The Rollers did their bit to help to boost Britain's ailing balance
of payments by repeating their domestic success in the global
marketplace and going to No 1 everywhere from the US to Japan.
That they were, in terms at least of screaming fans, the world's
biggest band since the Beatles was no exaggeration, as even the Fab
Four's former producer Sir George Martin acknowledged. "Nowadays
it is difficult to appreciate the excitement of the Beatles' breakthrough,"
he wrote in 1977. "My youngest daughter, Lucy, once asked me about
them. 'You used to record them, didn't you, Daddy? Were they as
great as the Bay City Rollers?'"

For a while McKeown relished the fame, the sex, the drugs and the
money. Even the fraction of the cash that filtered down after rapacious
managers, agents, record executives and other hangers-on had taken
their cut, there was enough to buy a big house in Edinburgh, in which
he installed his parents, and a turbo-charged Ford Mustang 351.

Then it all went horribly wrong, beginning with a day in 1975 when at the wheel of his Mustang McKeown knocked down and killed a 76-year-old Edinburgh neighbour, Euphemia Clunie. He was initially charged with causing death by dangerous driving but subsequently convicted on the lesser charge of driving recklessly, fined £150 and banned for a year.

Those who knew him said he was never quite the same again but he was told by the Rollers' management to get over it. "They didn't see it from a helpful, human way," McKeown recalled many years later. "It wasn't 'We're going to get through this together', it was more 'We need you on stage tomorrow, so you better stop fucking crying.'"

On the back of their American success, by 1978 the group had relocated to Los Angeles, where an increasingly unhappy McKeown spent much of his time taking cocaine with Led Zeppelin's John Bonham and The Who's Keith Moon, both of whom would be dead from their excesses within two years.

By then the Rollers' popularity was tailing off, eclipsed by punk and disco. The offer of an American children's TV series was eagerly accepted as a way of reviving their appeal, but McKeown objected. For his pains he was bounced out of the group. In some ways it came as a relief but, as he swiftly discovered, the fallout was cruel. The way the group's finances had been set up meant that he lost almost everything, including his house, which was repossessed, forcing his parents to move into a hotel.

The only asset he didn't lose was his sense of humour. He formed a new backing band, which he named Leslie McKeown's Ego Trip and his first post-Rollers solo album was titled *All Washed Up*. He came to hate everything to do with the Rollers and realised that being in the UK's first manufactured boy band was never what he had wanted in the first place. "It wasn't really me standing there having to smile on *Top of the Pops*," he complained. It was "someone created by a manager and *Jackie* comic".

His musical heroes were not David Cassidy and the Osmonds, but David Bowie and Freddie Mercury. He longed to be a cool rock'n'roll star, not a bubblegum pop marionette having to escape out of the back window of his house into a waiting van to avoid the pubescent girls outside the front door ready to rip the clothes off his back.

Being in the Rollers "brought a darkness that I can't get rid of", he told *The Guardian* in a candid interview in 2005. "It's relentless. It's sitting there right on your shoulder, just waiting. And it's talking to me, saying the world's shite."

By then he was drinking a bottle of whisky a day, sometimes two. He was convicted of driving while drunk and leaving the scene of an accident, banned for 18 months and fined £1,000. Arrested for drug possession, he told the police he had no idea what the cocaine they found in his wallet was doing there because it should have been up his nose.

Living modestly in a two-bedroom flat in Hackney, his dark mood was not helped by a protracted legal dispute of Dickensian complexity over unpaid royalties. It was the Bay City Rollers' misfortune that their success came in an era in which only managers, producers and record companies knew where the money went and youthful pop stars were fobbed off with pocket money and discouraged from asking awkward questions.

"We were barely out of our teens and simply trusted that the adults around us had our best interests at heart," McKeown told *The Times*. "They told us we were making lots of money, and we were, but we didn't know that it was for everyone else but us."

It was suggested that the band's members were collectively owed £50 million but when the legal battle was eventually settled out of court, it was reported that each band member received just £70,000.

McKeown finally turned a corner in 2008 when he went into rehab at the urging of his Japanese-born wife Peko Keiko, whom he met in a London sushi restaurant in 1978. "The wife got to me just in the nick of time," he said after his treatment. "I didn't really want to go. I was supposed to be there for two weeks and stayed for four months. When I came back from it I said sorry to everyone I had pissed off."

Leslie Richard McKeown was born in Edinburgh in 1955 to Florence (née Close) and Stephen McKeown, a deaf soldier from

Ballymena, who later became a tailor and helped to create the Rollers' tartan uniform. He attended Forrester High School, joined the Boys' Brigade and tried to join the merchant navy at 15. Instead he found work as an assistant in a recording studio.

When he was recruited to join the Bay City Rollers at the end of 1973, he signed a contract in the back of a car without reading it and never saw it again. The band's instant success swiftly turned into a nightmare tale of fear, loathing and exploitation at the hands of manager Tam Paton who marketed them as a wholesome, milk-drinking boy band but was himself a notorious sex predator who was later jailed for indecency with teenage boys.

Paton drove the band relentlessly while he raked in the profits and plied his young charges with drugs to keep them going when they flagged.

In what came to be known as "the curse of the Rollers", few emerged without scars of one sort or another. The collective history of band members in later years was littered with suicide attempts, heart attacks, bankruptcy, legal battles, mutual loathing and, in the case of one member, a child porn conviction. *The Sunday Times* called the Rollers' experience a cautionary tale based on "the classic Greek model of destiny, hubris and nemesis".

Ultimately, how five unremarkable teenage boys from Edinburgh with modest talent were groomed to become, for a brief time, as big as the Beatles remains one of pop's most baffling mysteries. Yet Rollermania created the template for all of the manufactured boy bands which followed, from Take That to One Direction.

Given that McKeown was stuck with his past, while in rehab he underwent hypnosis in an attempt to convince himself that being in the band had, after all, been a blessing rather than a curse.

"I used to think the worst thing that ever happened to me was being in the Bay City Rollers. Now I think it is the best," he insisted when he re-emerged. Whether he truly meant it is another matter.

Les McKeown, pop star, was born on November 12, 1955. He died suddenly at home of undisclosed causes on April 20, 2021, aged 65

*Les McKeown (front left) with bandmates Alan Longmuir,
Derek Longmuir, Stuart Wood and Eric Faulkner*

MARVIN GAYE

———————•———————

Soulful singer who helped shape the sounds of Motown in the 1960s

The Times, April 3, 1984

Marvin Gaye, the American soul singer and songwriter, died in a shooting accident in Los Angeles on April 1. He was 44. Gaye had been involved with the Motown recording company from its earliest days and was in the vanguard of the expansion of soul music's popularity. His biggest hit was the single *I Heard It Through the Grapevine*, which was released in 1968.

Born the son of a preacher in Washington on April 2, 1939, Gaye sang and played the organ in church as a child. Singing with street-corner vocal groups led him to form his own group, the Marquees, in 1957; two years later he joined the Moonglows. Shortly thereafter the group was heard in a Detroit club by Berry Gordy, who signed him to a contract with his newly formed company, Motown Records.

The story of Motown's success is virtually the story of soul music's rise and, after starting out as a drummer on some of the label's earliest hits, Gaye assumed a leading role, thanks to his flexible voice – modelled on that of Sam Cooke – and to his natural elegance as a stage performer. By the time he left the company in 1982, he had averaged two hit records a year over two decades, among the best known being *How Sweet It Is (To Be Loved by You)*, *Ain't No Mountain High Enough* and *You're All I Need to Get By*. Gaye frequently brought original thought to bear on his music. The album *What's Going On*, released in 1971, broke away from the enclosed forms and careful arrangements associated with Motown, as well as from the prevailing degree of artistic supervision, so successfully that others (notably Stevie Wonder) were encouraged to follow suit. It set a fashion, too, in its acute but non-dogmatic observation of the social condition of Black Americans.

Gaye's later recordings explored extended forms and complicated orchestrations to considerable effect, while the last record of all, the enormously successful *Sexual Healing*, proved that soul could retain its impact within a style of arrangement borrowed from electronic pop music.

Marvin Gaye, singer, was born on April 2, 1938. He was shot and killed by his father on April 1, 1984, aged 44

MEAT LOAF

◆

Larger-than-life singer and actor known for his multimillion-selling
album Bat Out of Hell *as well as for his theatrical stage performances*
and his fibs

The Times, January 21, 2022

When Marvin Aday was 13 years old, he clumsily trod on the foot
of his American football coach, who, in the anger of the moment,
turned on the overweight boy and called him a "meat loaf". The jibe
was taken up by his classmates and when he turned up at school the
next day, the name had been daubed on his locker.

Recognising that there was no point in protesting against the
innate cruelty of adolescent boys, Aday stoically accepted the nickname
and set about turning it to his advantage, creating the brash, larger-
than-life personality that would in adulthood make Meat Loaf one
of the biggest-selling names in American rock music.

A combination of a theatrical stage presence modelled on
Marlon Brando and a bombastic musical style that borrowed the

Rolling Stones' swagger made Meat Loaf's 1977 kitsch tour de force, *Bat Out of Hell*, one of the most successful debut albums of all time, with sales estimated at in excess of 43 million.

The album stayed in the charts for nine years and was still selling strongly decades after its release, a rock'n'roll behemoth that found new fans in every new generation. Operatic in its ambition, Aday alleged that the title track was one of only two pieces of music that required the singer to conclude by hitting three successive high Cs; the other, he said, was by Wagner.

Like many of his claims, it was unverifiable, and the exaggerated melodrama of his music was frequently echoed in the self-mythologising of his public pronouncements. The awkward, unathletic, overweight boy who had trodden on his football coach's foot created an indestructible, derring-do persona: he claimed to have had concussion 18 times in various mishaps, been in eight car wrecks and to have repeatedly diced with death in planes that came to earth with a bump, including a private jet that made an emergency landing at Stansted in 2006 after losing its front wheel.

For decades his official biography knocked four years off his age and he claimed in his autobiography to have been present when President Kennedy was shot, seeing him arrive at Dallas Airport and later turning up at the hospital to see Jackie Kennedy get out of the fateful car in which her husband died.

Sometimes he made up stories for the sheer hell of it or to test the media's gullibility: he once told Sky Sports that he was a lifelong supporter of the English football club Hartlepool United. The story was swallowed so unquestioningly that it was even falsely reported that he was house-hunting in the vicinity. He subsequently admitted – with what degree of veracity we cannot be sure – that he had picked Hartlepool because he had been amused by the folkloric tale that during the Napoleonic Wars the people of the town had hanged a monkey, believing it to be a Frenchman.

More credible was his insistence that he had never wanted to be a rock star and had hoped for a career as an actor. "I never figured on music. I was originally cast in *One Flew Over the Cuckoo's Nest* as Billy Bibbit, but there was a writer's strike," he said.

After appearing in a stage production of *The Rocky Horror Picture Show* in Washington, he was cast in the film version, which in 1974 brought him to London. His account of his time spent filming in Britain was embroidered with characteristically colourful detail. "I had the time of my life," he said. "I made friends with a Pakistani taxi driver. He was a member of the Playboy Club and he took me. You could gamble there in those days. I went in with £40 and came out with £23,000 – I was rich, dude! I went and bought an apartment."

Three years later came *Bat Out of Hell*, which elevated him to a place among rock music's highest earners, although he continued to hanker after an acting career and was content to take a drop in his usual headliner's fee in order to do so. Perhaps his most notable film role came in David Fincher's *Fight Club* (1999). "Actors are the people I'm most comfortable around and the people I find more real," he said. "We're doing *Fight Club*, Brad Pitt's making $20 million, I'm making $300,000, but it doesn't make any difference because when we're working together it's not about the money, it's about the scene. We're equal."

The blurring of the lines between rock stardom and acting made his music unique and among his fellow rock singers perhaps only Queen's Freddie Mercury rivalled his melodramatic theatricality. The songs on *Bat Out of Hell* and its two sequels, *Bat Out of Hell II: Back into Hell*, and *Bat Out of Hell III: The Monster Is Loose* were written by Jim Steinman, and their working relationship, he suggested, was more like that between an actor and a playwright than a singer and a songwriter.

Meat Loaf was a role he invented and based on a method-acting technique he learned from the drama coach Lee Strasberg, in which he adopted a different persona for different songs. "I'm not listening to myself sing. I'm into the character, I'm into pictures," he said. "It's called image method acting. I have a movie rolling in my head when I'm singing."

He happily admitted that Steinman's compositions on *Bat Out of Hell* were "bombastic, over the top and self-indulgent"; but he insisted "all these things are positives". Yet their relationship was not an easy one and at one point Steinman's manager sued Meat Loaf for several million dollars, forcing him into bankruptcy.

If it was a "marriage made in hell", they were repeatedly forced back together by mutual dependence. "Some people say, 'If it wasn't for Steinman, Meat Loaf wouldn't be where he is,'" the singer admitted. "Other people go, 'If it wasn't for Meat, Jim wouldn't be where he is.' I think they're both right."

It was while working with Steinman on the follow-up to *Bat Out of Hell* in 1978 that Meat Loaf met his first wife, Leslie Edmonds. They were married within a month and he adopted her daughter, Pearl, from a previous marriage, who later went on to sing in her stepfather's backing band. The couple had a second daughter, Amanda Aday, who became a television actress. The family regularly accompanied Meat Loaf on tour and while the two girls were young they slept in guitar cases which conveniently doubled as carry-cots. His marriage to Leslie was annulled after 23 years in 2001 and he married Deborah Gillespie in 2007.

While his children were growing up, he coached baseball as a volunteer at their schools. He also enjoyed a moment of sweet revenge on the football coach who had called him "meat loaf", when, during a charity softball game at Yankee Stadium, he hit a ball out of the park for a home run. The way he told it, the home run meant more to him than any of his chart-topping hits.

Born in the motor city of Detroit, for much of his career he claimed to have been born in 1951, although it later transpired that his birth year was 1947. His father, Orvis Aday, was an alcoholic police officer who spent his hours off-duty on drinking binges that lasted for days at a time. When he failed to come home, Meat Loaf's mother, Wilma, a schoolteacher who also sang in a gospel quartet, would drive around the Dallas bars looking for him.

He was educated at a Christian college and used his considerable bulk to advantage as a shot putter, until one day he got in the firing line of a fellow competitor and was hit in the head by a 12lb shot.

When his mother died of cancer in the mid-1960s he inherited a substantial sum which he used to rent an apartment in Dallas. Locked in one of the deep depressions that would afflict him all his life, he spent several months there as a recluse before he moved to Los Angeles in 1966.

Despite his claim that he had set out to be an actor rather than a musician, he immediately formed a band called Meat Loaf Soul, which changed its name a year later to Popcorn Blizzard. The band toured extensively, opening for such names as Pink Floyd and The Who. But it wasn't enough to pay the rent and in 1969 he took a job as a parking lot attendant at the Aquarius Theatre in Los Angeles, where the musical *Hair* was about to open. Asked to audition, he was cast as Ulysses S Grant, a role that led to a recording contract with Motown, for whom he recorded an album of duets with the singer Shaun "Stoney" Murphy, a fellow refugee from *Hair*.

Yet it was hardly the big time: he claimed to have been paid an advance of $6.25, and when the album sold poorly he rejoined the cast of *Hair*. Further theatrical work followed when he played Buddha in the musical *Rainbow* and then landed a part in the off-Broadway show *More Than You Deserve*, written by Jim Steinman and Michael Walker.

It was the start of a long association with Steinman and the pair spent three years plotting *Bat Out of Hell*, while he continued with his theatrical work, serving as John Belushi's understudy in the satirical *National Lampoon* show on Broadway.

The songs' pseudo-operatic excesses were hard to sell and were rejected by half a dozen record labels before Sony offered him a deal. Accompanied by a suitably overwrought video and described by one critic as "a bizarre and grandiose version of heartland America, in which ordinary lives are made mythic by gothic melodrama", *Bat Out of Hell* became a huge seller and spawned four hit singles including the title song, *You Took the Words Right Out of My Mouth*, *Two Out of Three Ain't Bad* and *Paradise by the Dashboard Light*.

Success brought with it problems. He fell off stage, broke a leg and spent the rest of the tour performing from a wheelchair. He started drinking heavily, developed a cocaine addiction, had a nervous breakdown which left him unable to sing, threatened to kill himself by jumping off a building and fell out with Steinman. "I spent seven months trying to make a follow-up with him and it was an infernal nightmare," his partner complained. "He had lost his voice, he had lost his house and he was pretty much losing his mind."

When he re-emerged in 1981 his comeback album, *Dead Ringer*, topped the charts in Britain but barely scraped the Top 50 in America. As a result he concentrated his career in Europe, becoming a British media personality whose attempts at dieting were extensively chronicled and who was recruited to appear in the Duchess of York's team in a celebrity fundraising edition of the TV show *It's a Royal Knockout*. It was not entirely well received. He also claimed that during filming he had had a shoving match with the Duke of York, who warned him about flirting with his then wife, and that he promptly told the duke, "I don't give a shit who you are."

Meat Loaf's declining record sales took a major upswing in the 1990s when he reunited with Steinman on *Bat Out of Hell II*. The critics derided the record as overblown and out of date, and *Rolling Stone* voted it the "most unwelcome comeback of the year". But the album went on to sell more than 15 million copies, led by the hit single *I'd Do Anything for Love (But I Won't Do That)*, which reached No 1 in 28 countries.

An appearance in the Spice Girls movie *Spice World* endeared him to an adolescent audience not even born when he had first topped the charts; his other film appearances, including in *Wayne's World* and *Fight Club*, kept him in the public eye while he sorted another legal battle with Steinman, who had registered *Bat Out of Hell* as his own sole trademark. Meat Loaf sued for $50 million. They settled out of court and then made *Bat Out of Hell III* together.

In later years Meat Loaf suffered considerable health issues, but illness failed to stop him touring and he continued to perform with lung-busting ferocity. He collapsed during a concert at Wembley Arena in 2003 and was diagnosed with a heart disorder, and there were further collapses on stage in 2012 and 2016. Those predicting his imminent demise were out by six years. In death as in life, it seemed, he had defied the odds.

Meat Loaf, rock singer, was born on September 27, 1947. He died of Covid-19 on January 20, 2022, aged 74

SYD BARRETT

———————•———————

Founder of Pink Floyd and inspiration for the band's early albums who became a recluse after suffering a mental breakdown

Syd Barrett (second from right) with bandmates Nick Mason, Rick Wright and Roger Waters

The Times, July 11, 2006

In the early days of Pink Floyd, Syd Barrett was the group's undisputed leader. His psychedelic and often whimsical style of songwriting perfectly encapsulated the heady spirit of the late 1960s and the hippy dream. Barrett's compositional method has been called naive, but it is perhaps better described as childlike, often effortlessly inhabiting the worlds of dream, mystery and the subconscious.

He was a wonderfully instinctive guitarist, and his highly original use of slide and echo was able to translate the hypnotic atmosphere that Pink Floyd generated on stage to the albums they created in the studio. These are memorable as few others of their era are.

But Barrett then fell victim to the darker side of those heady times, as his copious indulgence in hallucinogenic drugs pushed an already fragile psyche over the edge.

After dominating Pink Floyd's early material and writing their first two hit singles, by 1968 he found himself forced out of the group on account of his erratic behaviour. Without him, they went on to become one of the biggest-selling acts of the 1970s and 1980s, while his output was restricted to two strange but compelling solo albums, which reflected his precarious mental state and are today regarded as cult classics.

After that, the rest was silence, as he became a recluse and abandoned all involvement in music. Yet although he did not release another record after 1970, he continued to exert an eerie fascination for generations of future musicians – perhaps because his fate reminded them of the slender thread by which creative talent can hang.

The son of a Cambridge pathologist, Roger Keith Barrett fell in love with rock'n'roll in the late 1950s while at Cambridge High School. He earned the nickname "Syd" at a local jazz club, after a drummer of the same name, and by the early 1960s was in his first group, Geoff Mott and the Mottoes.

The line-up also included future Pink Floyd colleague Roger Waters. After a brief spell in another local R&B band, Those Without, Barrett moved to London in 1964 to attend Camberwell Art College.

There he was reunited with Waters in a new band, which already included the drummer Nick Mason and Rick Wright on keyboards. After trying various names, including the Spectrum Five and the Tea Set, they settled upon the Pink Floyd Blues Band.

Barrett had coined the name as a fusion of two grizzled bluesmen called Pink Anderson and Floyd Council, although hippy romantics will always prefer the story he later told of the name being transmitted to him by a flying saucer while he was sitting on Glastonbury Tor.

At first, the group played mostly R&B covers. But Barrett had begun experimenting with LSD in 1965 and the experience began to inspire his own songwriting. As the nascent post-beat, drug-based hippy subculture gathered pace throughout 1966, Pink Floyd – as they were now called – effectively became its house band. The R&B covers gave way to Barrett's quirky songs and long, improvisational "space" epics, with titles such as *Interstellar Overdrive* and *Astronomy Domine*.

By early 1967 all of the main record labels were looking to sign one of the new psychedelic groups. Pink Floyd, who had built a sizeable following at all-night underground London clubs with names such as Middle Earth and UFO, were top of most A&R men's lists and, after turning down a deal with Polydor, they were snapped up by EMI.

Not that the company was totally aware of whom or what it had signed. When the group were introduced to the label's executives, one of them reportedly demanded to know which one was Pink. EMI was also concerned by the band's druggy image and felt obliged to issue a press statement insisting that the term "psychedelic" referred to the effect created by the light show which accompanied the Floyd's live performances, and that it had no connection with drugs.

The band had already recorded *Arnold Layne* with the producer Joe Boyd before signing, and the song became Pink Floyd's first single. Despite Barrett's lyrics about transvestism, it somehow escaped a BBC ban and reached No 20 in the charts. The follow-up, *See Emily Play*, did even better. It reached No 6, found the band miming on *Top of the Pops* and was later covered by David Bowie. The two songs were undoubted masterpieces of early psychedelic pop and are the bedrock of claims that Barrett was a "genius".

Pink Floyd's debut album, *The Piper at the Gates of Dawn*, followed in August 1967. With its title borrowed from a chapter heading in *The Wind in the Willows*, the record marked the high tide of the "summer of love". But by now Barrett's behaviour was growing increasingly erratic. He was ingesting LSD on an almost daily basis and began missing gigs. When he did turn up, he often resembled a zombie on stage who would play one note all night.

As the main songwriter, there was also pressure on him to come up with another hit. The third Pink Floyd single, *Apples and Oranges*, contained flashes of his earlier inspiration but failed to chart. Stories began to circulate that all was not well in the Floyd camp, and by the autumn of 1967 the rest of the band were determined that Barrett had to go.

There was a half-hearted attempt at a compromise when the guitarist David Gilmour, an old Cambridge friend with whom

Barrett had spent the summer of 1965 busking in the South of France, was recruited to bolster their live performances, with the intention that Barrett should concentrate on writing songs. But he seemed incapable even of that, and halfway through the recording of their second album, he was ousted for good.

When *Saucerful of Secrets* was released some months later in June 1968, Barrett's contribution was still there. But his spectral presence only served to make it clear that he had ceased to be the driving force long before he was kicked out. The album concluded with his *Jugband Blues*, a song with a harrowing lyric in which he appeared to be describing his own mental illness.

After receiving psychiatric treatment in a Cambridge hospital, he was coaxed back into the studio and spent 15 months intermittently recording his first solo album, *The Madcap Laughs*. In contrast to Pink Floyd's elaborate arrangements, the songs sounded threadbare and even slapdash, and recording them was a maddening process.

Peter Mew, the EMI engineer who worked on the sessions, described Barrett as "not on the same planet as the rest of us". Gilmour and Waters, perhaps feeling guilty for pushing him out of Pink Floyd, eventually offered Barrett assistance to salvage something from the tortured sessions. Eventually released at the beginning of 1970, somehow it worked and *The Madcap Laughs* includes some hypnotic and ethereal moments, such as *Golden Hair*, a James Joyce poem set to music by Barrett.

Almost immediately, Barrett began work on a second album, *Barrett*, with Gilmour as producer. On its release that summer, he even attempted a return to the stage. But four songs into the set, he decided he wasn't enjoying himself and put down his guitar and walked off. It later emerged that he had returned to Cambridge and was living in the basement of his mother's house.

There was one more attempt in 1972 at putting a new band together, called Stars, but they fell apart when he stopped turning up for gigs. A last effort at recording some new songs in 1974 was aborted when it became obvious to all concerned that his muse had finally deserted him. It was the end of his musical career.

Yet he was far from forgotten. In 1975 Pink Floyd paid tribute to him in a song called *Shine On You Crazy Diamond* on their multiplatinum *Wish You Were Here* album. The lyric poignantly remembered how in earlier days his eyes had "shone like the sun" but now looked "like black holes in the sky". He had turned up during the recording sessions for the album at Abbey Road and his old bandmates had not even recognised him.

He spent the rest of his years living quietly in Cambridge, although for a time he also kept an apartment in Chelsea. His royalties from early Pink Floyd recordings ensured that he did not need to work and he passed much of his time painting. Fans who hunted him down found a remote, balding and heavy-set man who was unwilling – or unable – to talk.

In 1987 the *News of the World* knocked on his door and ran a two-page account of what it said were the effects on him of taking LSD. It claimed that long-term drug use had left him virtually unable to string a sentence together. Some of Barrett's family and friends were upset by the story, but there could be little doubt that drugs had indeed been a significant factor in his terrible decline.

The following year, his former Pink Floyd colleague Rick Wright expressed the view that "if he hadn't had this complete nervous breakdown, he could easily have been one of the greatest songwriters today".

Such comments only helped the legend to grow. In 1988 previously unreleased solo material was issued on the album *Opel*. Five years later his collected solo works were repackaged in a lavish three-CD box set. In 2001 came another compilation, *Wouldn't You Miss Me? – The Best of Syd Barrett*. A biography, *Crazy Diamond*, written by Mike Watkinson and Pete Anderson, was first published in 1991, and an updated edition – including reports of new "sightings" by fans – appeared ten years later.

Yet Barrett remained uninterested until the end. An offer from Atlantic Records in the mid-1990s of £200,000 for "three or four songs" to be recorded at his convenience in his living room was ignored. And although he was said to have found some contentment in later years, his death brings to an end one of the most enigmatic and saddest stories in rock'n'roll.

Syd Barrett, Pink Floyd founder and songwriter, was born on January 6, 1946. He died on July 7, 2006, aged 60

BRIAN JONES

———————●———————

*Charismatic, long-haired and hard-living guitarist, who was
a founding member of the Rolling Stones*

The Times, July 4, 1969

Mr Brian Jones, guitarist until only a month ago with the Rolling
Stones pop group, died yesterday. He was 27.

Lewis Brian Jones was born in Cheltenham on February 28,
1942, and educated at Cheltenham Grammar School, where he
stayed until he was 18, completing both O-levels and A-levels. He
came to London in 1962 and met Mick Jagger, then a student at the
London School of Economics, and Keith Richards, and together
they formed the nucleus of the pop group that came to be known as
the Rolling Stones.

In his own words, their musical influence was formed by the
imported American records of Muddy Waters, Jimmy Reed and Chuck
Berry, which they used to play by day and try to imitate by night. Jones
was a talented musician who, apart from playing rhythm guitar with
the group, had mastered the organ, saxophone and piano. The three
original members of the group were joined by Charlie Watts, at that
time drummer with Alexis Korner, and Bill Wyman, and the Rolling
Stones, as most of their fans knew them, came into existence.

From the beginning their attitude was uncompromising. While
other groups were projecting a clean-cut, energetic and youthful
image, the Rolling Stones were openly rebellious. Their hair was
longer and their clothes apparently dirtier than their contemporaries
– it was a style which was to have a crucial influence on the
development of pop music in Britain and America. Brian Jones's
wide grey-green eyes fringed by his long blond hair became an
important part of the group's public image. In Europe he was almost
as quickly identified as Mick Jagger.

While the group's recording career went from success to success
– beginning with *Come On*, their first hit record, and a reputation

assured with the Lennon and McCartney composition *I Wanna Be Your Man* – their brushes with the law increased. In October 1967 Jones himself was sentenced to nine months' imprisonment for admitting the offence of possessing cannabis and allowing his flat to be used for the purpose of smoking it. In December, after an appeal, his sentence was changed to a fine of £1000, together with three years' probation.

Last year, Jones was again fined after being found guilty of unlawful possession of cannabis. Indeed Brian Jones's personal life was less settled over the past year and tensions within the Rolling Stones were growing. The group's last No 1 record, *Jumpin' Jack Flash*, was released in June last year, and Brian Jones does not feature on their new record released last week, for early last month he finally left to be replaced by another guitarist.

In the group's six years of success, Brian Jones was a constant source of musical invention and ability within the group. He was also the most talkative of the group, but over the past two years he had suffered from feelings of persecution and unhappiness. He felt that his relationship with his personal brand of music was threatened and he was about to form a new group.

Brian Jones, guitarist, was born on February 28, 1942. He drowned in a swimming pool on July 3, 1969, aged 27

CHARLIE WATTS

•

Mild-mannered Rolling Stones drummer who grumbled about fame and was baffled by the excesses of his bandmates' rock'n'roll lifestyle

The Times, August 25, 2021

Watts may have been the most mild-mannered member of the Rolling Stones, but he saw red when Mick Jagger made the mistake of possessively referring to him as "my drummer".

It happened one night in Amsterdam in 1984 and according to Keith Richards's autobiography, the drummer hauled Jagger up by his lapels and gave him a punishing right hook that sent him sprawling across a table laden with platters of smoked salmon.

Self-effacing and low-maintenance as he was, Watts had his pride and Jagger's slight had pushed him too far. The next day Watts was still so angry that he told Richards, "Fuck it, I'm gonna do it again," and had to be physically restrained by his bandmate.

It was a rare explosion by the normally placid Watts, and Jagger was careful never to disrespect his drummer again. The Stones rode the losses of Brian Jones, their founder member, and bassist Bill Wyman, but Jagger thereafter always insisted that there could "never be a Rolling Stones without Charlie".

As a counterweight to the flamboyance of Jagger and Richards, Watts's phlegmatic presence was a vital ingredient in the Stones' often volatile chemistry. Yet in many ways he was an unlikely member of a group that in its pomp boasted of being the rowdiest, noisiest, nastiest rock'n'roll band in the world. Despite six decades in the job, Watts never seemed entirely comfortable with being a rock star. "He's modest and shy and the idea of stardom horrifies him. He's a very secretive man," Richards said.

Throughout his life he preferred jazz to rock music and he was the closest thing to a conservative Rolling Stone. The phrase sounds like an oxymoron, but Watts was a creature of habit who valued stability above rock'n'roll mayhem.

While his bandmates dressed like outlaws, Watts was a style icon who preferred smart Savile Row tailoring, well-polished brogues and expensive eau de cologne. *The Daily Telegraph* and *Vanity Fair* both voted him in their lists of the world's best-dressed men.

His watchword was constancy. He spent almost 60 years in the same band and was faithfully married to his wife, Shirley, for more than half a century. When the Stones weren't touring the world he ran his own jazz combo. With characteristic loyalty the line-up included his childhood next-door neighbour, whom he had known since he was three years old.

The low-key informality of club gigs with his jazz mates was in stark contrast to the circus extravagance that surrounded a Stones tour and he relished the absence of hoopla. "It's great because you just walk on, start the set and at the end you can go home," he observed.

On the road with the Stones, Watts displayed a distaste if not a disdain for the rock'n'roll lifestyle. While others partied wildly, he avoided the temptations of the road and spent his time sketching his hotel room and its furnishings. He claimed to have drawings of every room in which he had ever stayed and deadpanned that on non-concert days he could often be found going to bed about the same time that Keith Richards and Ronnie Wood were getting up.

"We won't do this again. At least I won't. It's too much," he told *The Times* at the end of one of the group's gargantuan world tours in the late 1990s. But then he admitted he had been saying that at the end of every tour since 1972.

Nobody believed him, least of all himself, but his grumbling became part of his routine. Asked to describe his own character, he replied: "Miserable most of the time, sitting in the back, moaning about things", a reply that drew on the spirit of the 1950s radio comedy *It's That Man Again* and its famous catchphrase: "It's being so cheerful as keeps me going."

His protests reached a peak when the Stones headlined Glastonbury for the only time in their career in 2013. "I don't want to do it but everyone else does," he grumbled. "I don't like playing outdoors and I certainly don't like festivals."

He played the gig, of course, and was still on the road with the Stones in 2021, when he was forced to bow out of an autumn tour after an operation for an unspecified medical condition. "I say I'll retire and then I have two weeks off and my wife says, 'Aren't you going to work?'" he said.

If his temperament was conservative, he was also a genuine English eccentric with a passion for collecting things he could never use. He never learnt to drive but had a garage full of vintage cars. According to Richards he bought a 1936 Alfa Romeo "just to look at the dashboard".

When Jagger introduced the band in concert and the spotlight was turned on Watts, the drummer acknowledged the applause with nothing more than an apologetic shake of his leg and the briefest of paradiddles on his snare drum. Stones fans loved him for his stoicism and the eruption of the crowd was in inverse proportion to the minimalism of his response. "For the band, I want everyone to love us and go crazy, but when I walk off, I don't want it. I never could deal with it and still can't," he said.

Yet his swinging, rhythmic drumming style suited the Stones to perfection. He eschewed the flashy and self-indulgent drum solos favoured by the likes of Led Zeppelin, but his indestructible beat powered the Stones' 1960s pop hits such as *(I Can't Get No) Satisfaction, Get Off of My Cloud* and *19th Nervous Breakdown* and grounded the monstrous riffs on such rock classics as *Jumpin' Jack Flash, Honky Tonk Women* and *Brown Sugar.*

"Charlie's always there, but he doesn't want to let everybody know," Richards said. "People think Mick and Keith are the Rolling Stones. But if Charlie wasn't doing what he's doing on drums, that wouldn't be true at all. You'd find out that Charlie Watts is the Rolling Stones."

Born Charles Robert Watts in 1941 in north London during the Blitz, he grew up in a "prefab" in Wembley after being bombed out of the family home. His father, Charles Watts, was a lorry driver and his mother, Lillian, a housewife.

He grew up listening to his father's Frank Sinatra records and fell in love with jazz at an early age. After an early abandoned affair with the banjo, he cited *Walkin' Shoes* by the American saxophonist Gerry Mulligan as the piece of music that convinced him to become a drummer.

By then he had failed his 11-plus and was at Tyler's Croft Secondary Modern School, where he showed some talent as an artist and on the sports field as a footballer and cricketer.

His parents bought him his first drum kit when he was 14 and while other teenagers were dancing to Elvis Presley and Chuck Berry, Watts was listening to records by Duke Ellington and Charlie Parker in his bedroom with his next-door neighbour Dave Green.

By the age of 16, both were playing together in a local jazz combo while Watts attended Harrow art school. Green was still playing bass in the jazz band Watts ran as a side project from the Rolling Stones more than 60 years later.

By 1961 Watts was playing the London jazz clubs with the likes of Chris Barber, and met the British blues pioneer Alexis Korner, who asked him to join his band Blues Incorporated, where he met Jagger, who occasionally guested as a singer.

Jagger also had his own group which already included Richards and Jones, but lacked a regular drummer. When Watts was asked to join in the summer of 1962, he refused, preferring his secure job as a designer in an advertising agency. He subsequently admitted that at the time he was convinced rock'n'roll "wasn't going to last five minutes". Six months later he relented and Watts made his first public appearance with the Rolling Stones in January 1963 at the Flamingo Club in Soho. Yet he still stubbornly refused to give up his day job until the Stones signed their first recording contract with Decca later that year.

For a while he lived with Jagger, Richards and Jones in an infamously sordid flat in Chelsea. But after the Stones had scored their first chart hits with *Come On* and *I Wanna Be Your Man*, he moved to an apartment overlooking Regent's Park and married his art student girlfriend, Shirley Shepherd. Fearing his marriage would upset the Stones' army of screaming teenage female fans, he figured that the fewer people who knew the better and didn't even tell his bandmates or Andrew Loog Oldham, the Stones' manager.

Domesticity reinforced his image as the quiet and unostentatious Stone. While Jagger and Richards got themselves into endless high-profile scrapes, Watts did his best to stay aloof from the group's "lock up your daughters" notoriety, determined to maintain his privacy, even as he was required to live his professional life in full public view.

On the group's first trip to Australia in 1965, eschewing the attraction of groupies and hangers-on, he spent more money on long-distance phone calls home every day to Shirley than he earned on the tour.

By that year, he had used his share of the proceeds from the group's growing list of chart-topping hits to become one of the first of rock music's country squires, buying a 16th-century timbered mansion in Sussex once owned by Lord Shawcross. The couple's daughter, Seraphina, was born there in 1968. She was later expelled from Millfield School for smoking cannabis and has spent much of her adult life abroad, living in Bermuda for many years and now in Rhode Island.

The hippy era found Watts cast as a square peg in a psychedelically decorated round hole. "I hated all that. To me the 1960s was Miles Davis and three-button suits," he said. While the other band members experimented with mind-expanding drugs, Watts declined to join them and felt alienated when Jagger, Richards and Jones were all busted for drugs.

He was also deeply unhappy when the Stones were forced to become tax exiles in 1971. Quintessentially English in his tastes, he spent a miserable year living in Vaucluse in France while the Stones recorded the druggy *Exile on Main St* album at Richards's rented house on the Riviera.

Returning to Britain at the earliest opportunity, he subsequently bought an estate in Devon, where he stabled horses and took up breeding sheepdogs.

Having survived the drug scene of the 1960s unscathed, for reasons he was never fully able to explain he started taking heroin in the 1980s. "I had never done serious drugs when I was younger but at this point in my life I went, 'sod it, I'll do it now'," he recalled. "Looking back, I think it was a midlife crisis. I became totally another person and I nearly lost my wife and everything over my behaviour."

His haggard, smack-haunted look led to him acquiring the nickname "Dracula" but he cured himself of his addictions after taking a potentially fatal fall down a flight of stone steps while under the influence. "I was in the cellar getting a bottle of wine and it brought it home to me how far down I'd gone," he said. "I thought, enough is enough. So I stopped drinking, smoking, taking drugs – everything, all at once."

His sobriety was sorely needed, for by the time he had straightened himself out there were other destructive forces tearing the Stones apart. When a ruinous rift between Jagger and Richards resulted in them not speaking to each other for several years in the mid-1980s, Watts was cast in the role of arbitrator. The punch with which he laid out Jagger notwithstanding, it is unlikely that without his diplomatic skills the Stones would have survived.

As the Stones embarked upon a series of box office-breaking world tours in later years, Watts found a new role, putting to use his early training as a graphic designer to help create the band's elaborate stage sets.

Despite his moaning about life on the road, he admitted that he could not envisage doing anything else. "This band doesn't mean everything to me and I don't really care if it stops," he observed in the 1980s, when the Stones weren't even halfway through their long and colourful existence. "But I don't know what else I'd do. I think I'd go mad."

Charlie Watts, Rolling Stones drummer, was born on June 2, 1941. He died on August 24, 2021, aged 80

KEITH FLINT

—•—

*Anarchic frontman of the Prodigy, whose terrifying antics on stage
made him Britain's most notorious pop star since Johnny Rotten*

The Times, March 4, 2019

Every generation needs its iconoclastic provocateurs whose
music is guaranteed to generate parental shouts of "Turn that noise
down!" For those coming of age in the 1990s the role was played
with enthusiastic diabolism by Keith Flint and the Prodigy.

When the band topped the charts in 1996 with *Firestarter*, the
song was accompanied by a video in which Flint, covered in satanic
tattoos, eyes bulging wildly and his hair teased into Beelzebub-like
horns snarled into the camera about being a "trouble starter".

Tapping into pop music's carefully cultivated lineage of outrage
from the Rolling Stones to the Sex Pistols, the lyrics were malevolent,
the music raucous and the image fearsome, with Flint cast as the
Johnny Rotten of his generation. When the video was shown on
Top of the Pops, the BBC was inundated with more complaints than

it had known since the heyday of punk.

The next year *Smack My Bitch Up*, which rose to No 8 in the UK charts, was accompanied by a video that seemed to glorify drink-driving, cocaine snorting, vandalism and casual sex.

When questions were raised in parliament about the song's misogyny, the band responded that "most people have had nights out like that". Despite being banned by the BBC, the film won best dance video at the MTV Music awards. The song was later voted the most controversial of all time in a survey conducted by the Performing Rights Society. Among those who objected to the song were the Beastie Boys, who a decade earlier had themselves been dubbed "the world's nastiest pop group" by the tabloid press.

When another hit single, *Baby's Got a Temper*, extolled the virtues of the "date rape" drug Rohypnol, many began to suspect a certain cynicism in the band's relentless desire to shock. "How very risqué and rebellious," Sarah Cohen of BBC Radio 6 Music remarked. "Or, more likely, how very shrewd and calculating."

Emerging from the wastelands of Essex at the height of the chemically enhanced underground rave scene in the early 1990s, the Prodigy swiftly became crowd-pleasing favourites at the all-night free rave parties and festivals that the Conservative government attempted to outlaw in the Criminal Justice and Public Order Act.

The legislation even contained a clause that defined the kind of music played by the band and others at illegal raves as "wholly or predominantly characterised by the emission of a succession of repetitive beats". Whitehall's description of rave music was the subject of much hilarity at the time and the Prodigy responded with a song titled *Their Law*, on which they defiantly sang: "Crack down at sundown/ Fuck 'em and their law."

Known as the godfathers of rave and "the premier dance act for the alternative masses", the Prodigy crossed into the mainstream to become one of the most commercially successful of all electronic dance acts, with worldwide record sales estimated to be in excess of 30 million.

Flint revelled in his notoriety and suggested his goals in life were to live out his ultimate sex fantasies with "lots of babes", have every part of his body pierced and dye his hair every colour of the rainbow. His favourite pastimes ranged from "going out all night on wild benders" to "photocopying my bum".

A tattoo on his stomach bore the legend "Inflicted", a reference to the line "I'm the self-inflicted mind detonator" in *Firestarter*. Having the tattoo done, he bragged, had felt "like he was on an altar being ritualistically scarred by a satanic beast". On the band's flights to the US, where the Prodigy topped the American album charts with 1997's *The Fat of the Land*, Flint was infamously a nightmare. One of his favourite tricks was to make erotic sculptures out of in-flight food to embarrass the cabin crew and, on one occasion, he had to be restrained from kicking down the door to the cockpit.

He was unrepentant. "I'm sorry if I offend little kids, but this is just me," he said in a rasping Essex accent. "I just love it when I see the faces of these stuffy executives who look me up and down wherever I go."

Yet like so many of pop music's bêtes noires, there was another side to Flint. A great lover of animals and the natural world, he rescued a sick hedgehog at school and took it home to nurse. He was devastated when the creature died. He was also an enthusiastic twitcher and built a large pond to attract birds to the garden of his Tudor house in the village of Dunmow, Essex. His other joy was a rare species of apple tree. He was described as "kind and caring" by his neighbours; one said that Flint had given him a bottle of whisky on his 80th birthday.

Over time, the outrage engendered by the Prodigy diminished, for it was hard to remain shocked once *Firestarter* had become a fixture in provincial karaoke bars. Instead, Flint found himself the inspiration for a Lucozade advert, in which one swig of the energy drink turned a geriatric lookalike from a docile grandad into a rampaging "twisted firestarter".

Long after the rave scene declined, the Prodigy remained hugely popular and the band's 2018 album *No Tourists* became their sixth to enter the UK charts at No 1.

Away from music Flint was a keen motorcyclist. He raced in club competitions, riding his Honda FireBlade at speeds of up to 180mph, and owned Team Traction Control. It competed in the

British Superbike Championships and within a year of formation was winning Isle of Man TT races.

At the height of the Prodigy's notoriety, Flint dated the TV presenter Gail Porter, who attained an infamy of her own when her naked image was projected onto the Houses of Parliament by *FHM* magazine. She described him as "lovely and gentle", although she admitted that when her mother met him she was rendered "speechless" by his green mohican haircut. They broke up in 2001. In 2006 he married Mayumi Ka, a Japanese DJ who performed as DJ Gedo Super Mega Bitch. They were reported to be separated at the time of his death.

In 2014 Flint became the proprietor of the Leather Bottle pub in Pleshey, near Chelmsford, Essex, taking over when the inn was threatened with closure. He was a popular landlord and kept a jar in which customers were required to put a pound every time they made a "firestarter" joke when he lit the pub's fire. He left in 2017 without explanation, pinning a sign on the door that simply said: "Due to unforeseen circumstances the pub is closed today. Sorry for any inconvenience."

Keith Charles Flint was born in 1969 in Redbridge, east London, the son of Clive Flint, an engineering consultant whose father was a German Jewish immigrant, and his wife, Yvonne. By the mid-1970s the family had moved to middle-class, lace-curtained suburbia in Springfield, Essex, where Keith grew up in a quiet cul-de-sac.

He attended The Boswells School in Chelmsford. Clearly intelligent, he was also disruptive and hyperactive. He fashioned his hair into a mohican and tore around the neighbourhood on a motorbike, but friends also recalled that he was polite and well brought up. "When he visited my house he always called my mum Mrs Williams," one school contemporary said. The teacher whom he hit with a rolling pin during a cookery class remembered him less fondly. Eventually, he was excluded and sent to a "special school".

Flint left at 15 with no qualifications and moved to nearby Braintree. He was working as a roofer in 1989 when he met Liam Howlett, a DJ, at a local rave club called the Barn. Howlett suggested they form a group with the MC and vocalist Maxim. The Prodigy's debut single, *Charly*, sampled a public information advert from the 1970s and reached No 3 in the UK singles chart in 1991.

Initially Flint merely danced on stage. "I never planned for Keith to become a singer," Howlett said. "I didn't even know he was capable of singing until he asked to have a go at *Firestarter*. The Prodigy was always about me doing the beats and the others doing their thing on stage." Flint's first vocal became their defining moment. He later formed his own band, which he called Flint.

In an interview in 2009 he conceded that "I can be quite self-destructive when left on my own, which is something I have to keep a check on."

Keith Flint, singer, was born on September 17, 1969. He died suddenly on either March 3 or 4, 2019, aged 49

PETE SHELLEY

———•———

Songwriter, lead singer and guitarist for one of the best-loved bands of the punk era, Buzzcocks

The Times, December 8, 2018

One cold and dismal day in early 1976, Pete Shelley was sitting around in the student union common room, idly thumbing through a copy of the *New Musical Express* when he came upon the words: "Don't look over your shoulder, but the Sex Pistols are coming."

The sentence, contained in a review of one of the unknown band's first gigs at London's Marquee Club, leapt off the page at him. As he read on and learnt more about the noisy, anarchic new phenomenon called punk, he knew he had to find out more.

Two days later, Shelley and a college friend, Howard Devoto, borrowed a car and drove 200 miles south from Manchester to London in search of the Sex Pistols. They located them playing a gig in support of Screaming Lord Sutch, not in the capital but 30 miles west along the M40 in High Wycombe.

"We saw them and we chatted with them and thought, well, it would be easier if they came up and played in Manchester rather than groups of us coming down to London," Shelley said.

Struggling to get bookings, Malcolm McLaren, the group's Svengali-like manager, agreed to Shelley and Devoto's offer: they would organise a Sex Pistols gig in Manchester if the band they were putting together called Buzzcocks could be the support act.

Shelley and Devoto raised £32 to rent a room at the Lesser Free Trade Hall, but by the time of the gig in June 1976 they still hadn't found a permanent bassist and drummer, and had to drop off the bill. The gig went ahead without them and was successful enough for the Pistols to return for a second engagement six weeks later. By then, Shelley and Devoto had recruited bassist Steve Diggle and drummer John Maher, and Buzzcocks were ready.

It was a seminal moment in the expansion of punk from a

London-based cult into a national movement. The Sex Pistols brought with them a posse of journalists and when the reviews appeared, Buzzcocks were catapulted to national attention.

Two months later, McLaren returned the compliment by inviting Buzzcocks to make their London debut supporting the Sex Pistols at a two-day punk festival in the 100 Club, which became an even more significant stepping stone in the emergence of punk as a musical force.

Yet there seemed little prospect of Buzzcocks landing a recording contract. "Record company scouts just didn't venture up to Manchester. The place felt like the tide had gone out," Richard Boon, the group's manager, noted.

Slowly the idea of putting out their own record began to take shape. Over the 1976 Christmas holiday, Buzzcocks recorded three songs written by Shelley and Devoto, which they put out on their own label called New Hormones, for their *Spiral Scratch* EP.

The sound was ramshackle to the point of amateurishness – as were the efforts of Shelley and his bandmates to market and distribute the record. Borrowing £500 from friends and parents, they pressed 1,000 vinyl copies and assembled at Devoto's flat to slot the discs by hand into the sleeves, which featured a grainy photo of the band taken on a Polaroid instant camera. They then took a box of them to the Manchester branch of Virgin, which accepted 25 copies. Virgin sold the records for 99p each, with 60p going to the band. When the first 1,000 copies had sold out, Jon Webster, the shop's manager, lent them £600 to press some more.

Spiral Scratch reached John Peel, who played it on the radio, and the music papers made it "single of the week". The record eventually sold 16,000 copies and made the Top 40. In a way, it epitomised the spirit of punk even more viscerally than *Anarchy in the UK*.

The Sex Pistols were signed to a big label and recorded with a budget to match; Shelley and his Buzzcocks represented the DIY ethos of punk. They pioneered an indie movement operating outside the orbit of the mainstream record companies. Within months there were dozens of punk bands making their own records and releasing them independently.

The production and musicianship on *Spiral Scratch* may have sounded amateur, but therein lay its appeal. *Boredom* became an early punk anthem with a lyric that went: "You know me, I'm acting dumb/ You know the scene, very humdrum/ Boredom, boredom, boredom" and a three-note guitar solo played by Shelley on a Woolworth's guitar, which debunked the pomposity of prog-rock and the mythology of the guitar hero playing one thousand notes a minute. "After we'd finished it, we fell about laughing," he recalled. Punk, in Shelley's view, was not a style of music but an attitude. "It was something that people could do themselves. Rather than being a passive consumer, you became an active part in it."

The initial Buzzcocks line-up lasted barely a dozen gigs before Devoto returned to college, leaving Shelley as lead vocalist, songwriter and undisputed band leader. After signing to United Artists, the group created some of the best-loved music of the punk era with hits such as *Orgasm Addict, What Do I Get?* and *Ever Fallen in Love (With Someone You Shouldn't've)*, written by Shelley about his unrequited love for a friend called Francis.

When the group broke up in 1981, Shelley launched a solo career with the single *Homosapien*, which was banned by the BBC for its references to gay sex. In interviews he described a sexuality that "tends to change as much as the weather". Certainly, the ambiguity of gender in his lyrics was an influence on others including Morrissey, whom Shelley accused of "stealing" his ideas.

His fellow Buzzcock, Steve Diggle, subsequently suggested he had only "dabbled" in homosexuality during a phase because "anything that was controversial in 1976 was welcome to the table". Shelley claimed early in his career that his relationships with women were problematic because of his "erratic emotions and insane jealousy". After the break-up of one youthful love affair, he claimed to have attempted suicide by taking an overdose.

He later married twice. First he wed Miniko, a Japanese fan he met backstage after a gig. They lived for several years in Camden, north London, before she returned to Japan, where she lives with their son Alex, who works in computer software. He is survived by his second wife, Greta Varep, an Estonian illustrator who grew up in

Canada, whom he married in 2011. After visiting her relatives in Estonia, Shelley fell in love with the country's tranquillity and the couple moved to Tallinn in 2012. He proudly reported that he was learning the local language by watching *The Simpsons* with Finno-Ugric subtitles.

He was born Peter Campbell McNeish in 1955 in Leigh, Lancashire, the son of Margaret, a mill worker, and John, a fitter at a colliery. He passed his 11-plus and, after grammar school, enrolled at Bolton Institute of Technology on an electronics course. After deciding that he didn't want to spend his life "repairing TVs" he switched to philosophy and European literature.

It was on the college noticeboard that Shelley saw an advert placed by Devoto, then known as Howard Trafford, wanting to form a band. The result was Buzzcocks. Name changes were de rigueur in punk circles at the time, but rather than the brutality of "Rotten" or "Vicious", Shelley named himself after a romantic poet.

After the Fine Young Cannibals covered *Ever Fallen in Love* in the late 1980s and took the song into the Top Ten, the royalties paid for Shelley to re-form the band. It transpired that Kurt Cobain was a huge fan and Buzzcocks were invited to support Nirvana on their final tour, before Cobain shot himself. Shelley later rerecorded *Ever Fallen in Love* himself with an all-star line-up including: Roger Daltrey, David Gilmour, Elton John and Robert Plant, as a tribute to John Peel, with proceeds going to Amnesty International.

His band also gave its name to the long-running BBC TV comedy panel quiz *Never Mind the Buzzcocks*. When Shelley appeared on it, host Mark Lamarr introduced him by saying that without him "there'd be no Smiths or Radiohead and this show would be called *Never Mind Joan Armatrading*".

Pete Shelley, musician, was born on April 17, 1955. He died of a suspected heart attack on December 6, 2018, aged 63

JIM MORRISON

———————•———————

Poetic and erratic singer and songwriter for the rock band the Doors

The Times, July 4, 1971

Mr Jim Morrison, whose death in Paris last Saturday was reported yesterday, lived much of his life like any dime novelist's idea of a rock'n'roll star. In his prime every performance was a ritual, a mock crucifixion enacted in skin-tight black leather and reaching its climax with the scream of "We want the world and we want it now!"

Born 27 years ago in California, Morrison formed his band, the Doors, when he met organist Ray Manzarek in Italy in 1965. The following year they began playing in Los Angeles, and became one of the first of the American "New Wave" bands to catch on with the public. Their biggest hit single was *Light My Fire*, and their albums were consistent bestsellers. Morrison's writing for the band often flirted with quasi-literary imagery, and his stage appearances contained a strong element of theatre.

The music itself was never as strong as the band's collective imagination suggested: Morrison was in fact not a good singer, and possessed a very limited technical and emotional range. It was his face, with its look of a fallen angel and his agonised bearing which drew him so many admirers. Recently the band's power waned drastically. Their appearance at last year's Isle of Wight festival was a disappointment, and Morrison talked of returning to his first love, films.

Jim Morrison, singer and songwriter, was born on December 8, 1943. He was found dead in a bathtub on July 3, 1971, aged 27

NINA SIMONE

Tempestuous soul singer, who enjoyed a 50-year career,
but left America because of racism

The Times, April 22, 2003

In the pantheon of great soul singers, Aretha Franklin was always known as "the queen" and Nina Simone "the high priestess". But Simone was also a jazz and blues singer, and came from a proud tradition of Black female American singers who traced their lineage back to Bessie Smith and Billie Holiday.

One of the most distinctive voices of the latter half of the 20th century, she was capable as a live performer of spine-chilling intensity. She also displayed a wayward unpredictability, but this only served to heighten her artistic mystique.

One of eight children, she was born Eunice Kathleen Waymon in 1933 at Tryon in North Carolina. By the age of seven she was playing piano and organ and singing with her sisters in the church choir. But the racial prejudice that was endemic in the Deep South of the 1940s had an early and lasting effect upon her. Years later she described as the formative event of her life a piano recital she gave in the local library at the age of 12, at which her parents were asked to stand at the back because they were Black.

With the financial support of the local Black community, which shared a collective pride in her precocious talent, she was sent to a girls' boarding school and then to the Juilliard School of Music in New York. Her classical training came to an abrupt halt at 21, however, when she was refused a scholarship by the Curtis School of Music in Philadelphia. For the rest of her life she believed this was due to her race.

Out of necessity she took an engagement at the Midtown Bar and Grill, Atlantic City in July 1954. On the first night she played classical and gospel selections on the piano without once opening her mouth. The following night, Harry Seward, the club owner, told her that either she sang or she was out of a job. She began a reluctant singing career and three years later she was performing jazz and blues at Carnegie Hall. "I'm where you always wanted me to be but I'm not playing Bach," she wrote to her parents.

Her first album, in 1958, was a phenomenal debut, including *I Loves You, Porgy,* her first million seller, and *My Baby Just Cares for Me.* Ranging across gospel, jazz, blues and cabaret standards, she worked for several labels until she switched in 1963 to Philips, which was run by her long-time friend and mentor, Willy Langenberg. Seven albums followed in a prolific four years and it was during this period that she recorded some of her angriest and best songs, including *Old Jim Crow* and *Mississippi Goddam,* which became virtually a civil rights anthem.

There was also a spine-tingling version of Billie Holiday's *Strange Fruit,* a song she later stopped singing because it upset her too much.

At the same time she also developed into a powerful writer, as witnessed by the remarkable *Four Women,* a mini-novel in song, painting powerful portraits of four Black women of different backgrounds and generations.

She was a close friend and ally of both Malcolm X and Dr Martin Luther King, and sang *We Shall Overcome* at King's side on many of the great civil rights marches of the 1960s. Souvenirs of both men continued to hold pride of place in the living room of her home in the south of France until her death.

She left America at the end of the 1960s, claiming that both the FBI and the CIA had files on her and she could no longer stand the racism. At the time of this self-imposed exile, she was enjoying the most commercially successful period of her career, with big pop crossover hits such as *Ain't Got No, I Got Life,* from the musical *Hair,* and a cover of the Bee Gees' *To Love Somebody.*

For the next 25 years she moved restlessly around the globe, living in Barbados, Liberia, Egypt, Turkey, Holland and Switzerland before she finally settled in Aix-en-Provence in 1994. It was the first house she had ever owned.

After she left America, albums continued to appear sporadically, the best of them being *Baltimore* in 1978. But she missed playing live (even though she was capable of insulting and abusing her audience when she did) and during the 1980s she began touring again. When Chanel appropriated *My Baby Just Cares for Me* for a television advert, a new generation discovered her music and she became a symbol of late-Eighties jazz cool.

She married twice and had one daughter but she led a troubled personal life. She suffered four miscarriages and had difficult relationships with a string of powerful and often violent men. In her autobiography, *I Put a Spell on You*, she recounted how she was beaten by her manager and husband Andrew Stroud. There was also an affair with Earl Barrow, the prime minister of Barbados. Then in Liberia, where she lived for four years in the late Seventies, she was assaulted and hurt so badly by the man she was living with that she had to go to hospital.

She next became engaged to CC Dennis, a prominent local politician, with equally unhappy consequences. When she was out of the country, Dennis married someone else – and he was killed by an assassin's bullet during the 1980 coup.

She was volatile and highly-strung, and her artistic career was littered with no-shows, walk-outs, fights and tantrums. "If you're a Black woman and you stand up for yourself people say you're difficult," she said when asked about her reputation. But the stories about her were manifold. She once cancelled a London concert without notice because she was "distressed" over an injury to her dog. It was reported in 1988 that she had closed a business meeting by pulling a knife, and in 1996 she was given a suspended sentence by French magistrates for firing an air-rifle at two boys playing in the swimming pool of a neighbouring villa. She claimed they were making too much noise.

She had suffered from ill health for several years and employed a live-in nurse. But she continued to perform, last appearing in Britain in August 2001 at the Bishopstock Festival. By then, she freely admitted she was only doing it for the money, but she was still guaranteed a rapturous reception wherever she played.

Nina Simone, singer, was born on February 21, 1933. She died on April 20, 2003, aged 70

ALVIN STARDUST

———•———

Pop singer who had a run of hits in the 1970s and cultivated a menacing image that was far removed from his real personality

The Times, October 24, 2014

With his quiff and sideburns, black leather and permanent scowl, Alvin Stardust revived and repackaged the original mean-and-moody spirit of rock'n'roll for a youthful audience that had not been born when the likes of Elvis Presley and Gene Vincent patented the style.

Stardust was as kitsch as his glam-rock name but he enjoyed considerable chart success in the mid-1970s with hits such as *My Coo Ca Choo, Jealous Mind, Red Dress* and *You, You, You*, as teen audiences thrilled to "the man who never smiles".

He even sported a pair of decidedly threatening-looking black leather gloves, although this part of his image was explained by an accident with a bottle of black hair dye just before his debut on *Top of the Pops*. Somehow he had to hide his blackened hands.

Stardust became famous enough to be chosen to appear in a TV commercial for road safety, extolling the virtues of the Green Cross Code. "Hey. You must be out of your tiny minds," he told two careless young pedestrians.

However, the menacing image was entirely manufactured. Stardust – whose real name was Bernard William Jewry – was an old-school Tin Pan Alley entertainer of enduring versatility who once remarked that "showbiz is no different to any other kind of job whether it's working as a banker or shop assistant". His career continued for more than 50 years in various incarnations and guises as he proved himself to be the master of reinvention.

By the time he emerged as Alvin Stardust in the 1970s, he already had two careers behind him, first as the lead singer of the early 1960s group Shane Fenton and the Fentones and then, when their fortunes waned, as the manager of artists such as Lulu and the

Hollies. Later, he continued to make the chart in the 1980s with hits such as *Pretend* and *I Feel Like Buddy Holly*.

When the hits tailed off, he took to the nostalgia circuit and moved into TV and theatre, appearing in the soap *Hollyoaks*, and starring on stage in *Godspell*, *David Copperfield* and *Chitty Chitty Bang Bang*.

Stardust spent the last 30 years of his life contentedly as a born-again Christian in the Sussex village of Loxwood, where he performed to raise funds for the village hall and primary school. His third wife, the actress Julie Paton, whom he met while they were touring in *Godspell*, appeared with him on stage as a backing singer, dressed in black leather, platform boots and a Stetson. Sir Cliff Richard is a godparent to their teenage daughter, Millie.

He was previously married to Iris Caldwell, the sister of the singer Rory Storm and an ex-girlfriend of George Harrison and Paul McCartney. His eldest son from his first marriage, Shaun Fenton, is the head teacher at Reigate Grammar School. His second son from his first marriage is the producer and DJ, Adam F.

In the 1980s he was married for eight years to the actress Liza Goddard, with whom he had a daughter, Sophie, who runs a graphic design business. "I wasn't especially a fan of his music but I was bowled over by his charm," Goddard said. "At home he didn't wear the quiff, he brushed his hair normally: he was going through a mellow phase." Their marriage broke down when she found it difficult to come to terms with his conversion to Christianity. "He was converted by a group of people in a train carriage," she said. "At Waterloo, the cleaner found them on their knees praying. Alvin came home and said, 'I've found God.'"

Born in the East End of London in 1942, he grew up in Mansfield, Nottinghamshire, where his mother let out rooms to performers at the local Palace Theatre. Jewry boarded at Southwell Minster Grammar, and was given his first guitar on his 12th birthday. At 15 he took the instrument with him to see Buddy Holly and the Crickets play in Doncaster and talked his way backstage, where he and Holly played an impromptu version of *Peggy Sue* together. Holly then signed the guitar and over the next few years he added the signatures of Gene Vincent, Chuck Berry, Bill Haley, the

Beatles and the Rolling Stones. The guitar was subsequently lost but he found it again, decades later, at his mother's home after her death. He promptly insured it for £2 million.

Tragedy struck his first group, Johnny Theakstone and the Tremeloes, when in 1960 the lead singer died suddenly. Shortly before his death, Theakstone had sent a demo tape to the BBC under the name Shane Fenton. When his parents received a reply, offering him a slot on Brian Matthew's *Saturday Club*, they asked Jewry if he would take the place of "Shane Fenton" and play in his friend's memory.

The radio appearance led to a recording contract with Parlophone and several minor hit singles. When the Beatles made them sound dated, he broke up the group and spent the rest of the 1960s in management.

His career did not revive until 1973 when he met Michael (later Lord) Levy, then the owner of Magnet Records. Levy's business partner, the songwriter Peter Shelley (not to be confused with Pete Shelley of Buzzcocks), had already written and recorded *My Coo Ca Choo* under the name Alvin Stardust, but he had no desire to be a star and when the record charted, Shelley and Levy had to find someone else to play the part. For the second time in his career, Bernard Jewry was asked to step into someone else's shoes. The single rose to No 2. But the follow-up, *Jealous Mind*, again written by Shelley, went to No 1, moving John Lennon to declare: "I'm so glad for Shane, he really deserves this success; he's a great bloke and performer."

Even at the height of his success the singer was less than comfortable with the Alvin Stardust image and complained that being "the man who never smiled" left him lonely and isolated. He recalled hearing that he had gone to No 1 in a hotel in Tokyo: "I remember looking round and realising I had absolutely no one to share it with. The rest of the band were downstairs in the bar, and I was doing my moody, untouchable routine, locked in my room. I got two bottles of champagne from the mini-bar, shook them up and showered them all over my balcony."

Alvin Stardust, pop singer, was born on September 27, 1942. He died of cancer on October 23, 2014, aged 72

RAY CHARLES

───────●───────

*Singer, songwriter and pianist regarded as one of the most
influential musicians of the modern age*

The Times, June 11, 2004

There is hardly a strand of modern popular music whose course
has not been affected by the colossal and unique talent of Ray
Charles. A musician who defied categorisation, he was fluent in all
three of the basic musical forms of Black America – jazz, blues and
gospel – and by welding them into a new, coherent whole he created
the genre that became known as soul.

That taken care of, he turned his attention to the notoriously
closed world of country, which he cracked apart with the truly
remarkable *Modern Sounds in Country Music*, a million-seller in 1962.

The singular authority of his rough-hewn, R&B vocal style had
an immense impact on the English and Irish pop singers of the
Sixties – Joe Cocker, Steve Winwood, Van Morrison and Eric Burdon
of the Animals were among those who cited him as a formative

influence – while his songs were recorded by artists like the Rolling Stones (*I'm Movin' On*) and John Mayall's Bluesbreakers with Eric Clapton (*What'd I Say*).

As recently as January 1990, Charles was to be found riding high in both the UK and US charts with the single *I'll Be Good to You*, a collaboration with Quincy Jones and Chaka Khan.

The obstacles to such a long and distinguished career were formidable. He was born Ray Charles Robinson in 1930 in Albany, Virginia, the result of an extramarital affair conducted by his father Bailey Robinson. When Robinson Sr flew the coop soon afterwards to marry yet another woman, responsibility for the care of his infant son was divided between his former wife and his former lover.

Glaucoma rendered Charles blind at the age of six, though not soon enough to spare him the trauma of seeing his younger brother drown in a washtub accident the year before. At seven, and now living in Greenville, Florida, he was sent to Florida's State School for the Deaf and Blind in St Augustine. While there he developed a keen interest in music, consolidating an early skill on the piano and learning to play the clarinet, saxophone and trumpet as well as how to read and write music in braille.

When he was 15 his mother died suddenly and Charles struck out from school and home with the intention of making a living as a musician. "Times and me got leaner and leaner," he later recalled, "but anything beats getting a cane and a cup and picking out a street corner."

After various cross-country swings he moved to Los Angeles in 1949, where, with mixed results, he made his first recordings, adopting the professional name of Ray Charles in order to avoid confusion with the boxer Sugar Ray Robinson. Despite some early successes in the R&B chart with *Baby, Let Me Hold Your Hand* (1950) and *It Should Have Been Me* (1953), it was with the release in 1954 of *I've Got a Woman* that Charles began an epoch-making series of recordings, including *Hallelujah I Love Her So, This Little Girl of Mine, Night Time Is the Right Time* and *Drown in My Own Tears*.

By applying a searing dose of gospel spirituality (what was known as his "sanctified" singing style) to a decidedly secular line of lyrics, while honing some of the hottest jazz-blues keyboard riffs ever committed to vinyl into concise three-minute statements, Charles reshuffled the deck of popular music idioms with results that were no less revolutionary than those achieved when Elvis Presley first mixed up elements of rockabilly, country and R&B to create rock'n'roll.

Once he had cracked the American pop Top 10 with his call and response classic *What'd I Say* in 1959, Charles enjoyed many spectacular successes including the No 1 hits *Georgia on My Mind* (1960) and *Hit the Road Jack* (1961). His spell of greatest popular acclaim in Britain came during the country period which followed, and included a No 1 in 1962 with *I Can't Stop Loving You* (also No 1 in America), along with appreciable chart success for *Your Cheating Heart* (1962) and *Take These Chains from My Heart* (1963).

Such richly rewarding adventures did not keep Charles away from the jazz arena. He made two celebrated recordings with vibraharpist Milt Jackson of the Modern Jazz Quartet – *Soul Brothers* (1958) and *Soul Meeting* (1962). An album recorded with the Count Basie Orchestra minus Basie in 1961, *Genius + Soul = Jazz*, provided further confirmation of a supreme talent that knew no boundaries.

Sadly, like so many gifted musicians before and since, Charles saddled himself with a heroin addiction, and on December 3, 1966 he was convicted on charges of possessing both heroin and marijuana and given a five-year suspended prison sentence and a $10,000 fine and put on probation for four years.

It was around this time that the magic began to fade. The Beatles and the Rolling Stones had spearheaded a British rock invasion of the American charts, while a new wave of soul stars, all of them influenced by Charles's example, had risen in his wake, among them Sam Cooke, Otis Redding and the inimitable James Brown.

Charles stepped back from the cutting edge, becoming more of a mainstream cabaret entertainer. He enjoyed hits with lush arrangements of the Beatles' tunes *Yesterday* and *Eleanor Rigby*, and invariably turned his concert performances into bland extravaganzas featuring a huge orchestra and all the Las Vegas trimmings.

A cameo appearance in the 1980 movie *The Blues Brothers* opened his account as an actor, and throughout the Eighties he guested on several American television series, including *Moonlighting, St Elsewhere* and *Who's the Boss*. At the start of the decade, his renewed enthusiasm for country music led to a recording contract with the Nashville division of Columbia. But his versatility remained such that in 1983, the year he scored a big country hit with his album *Wish You Were Here Tonight*, he also headlined the 30th Kool Jazz Festival in New York alongside Miles Davis and BB King. In 1985 he played a leading role, together with Michael Jackson, Bruce Springsteen and most of the American popular music elite, in the recording of USA for Africa's *We Are the World*.

By the time President Clinton awarded him with a National Medal of Arts in 1993 for his contribution to American cultural life, Charles was a distinguished and decorated music business veteran, as well as a millionaire with a mansion and even a private jet.

On a less exalted but more pervasive level, his singing was featured in an advertising campaign for Diet Pepsi, and in 1994 he was signed up as the star of a series of car adverts, which gave rise to the bizarre sight of a smiling, blind man in a bright red convertible, confidently making his driving debut at the age of 63 (albeit amid the deserted terrain of the Great Salt Lake in Utah).

Although his record output dwindled, he continued to tour throughout the 1990s, cutting a fragile but spry figure on stages around the world. He made regular visits to Britain, sharing a bill with Van Morrison at Wembley Arena in 1996 and playing a one-off show at the Hammersmith Apollo in 2001.

At the time of his death, Charles was working to complete an album of duets with such talents as Elton John, Willie Nelson and Norah Jones. It is due to be released later this year. Despite some loss of strength in the upper register, the rich and expressive timbre of his voice and the perfection of his timing remained to the end, testament to the enduring talent of a performer who was so clearly in a class of his own.

Ray Charles, singer, songwriter and pianist, was born on September 23, 1930. He died of liver failure on June 10, 2004, aged 73

GLEN CAMPBELL

———————•———————

*God-fearing country star who mixed the Bible with sex and cocaine
and whose many musical hits included* Rhinestone Cowboy

The Times, August 9, 2017

In an image that captured the dichotomy of his life, Glen Campbell revealed in his autobiography that at the height of his fame he spent his nights hoovering up lines of cocaine while reading the Bible.

He titled the book *Rhinestone Cowboy* after one of his biggest hits, in which he sang: "There's been a load of compromisin' on the road to my horizon." Although he had not written the lyric, it was, as a metaphor, as autobiographical as anything in his memoir. A God-fearing, scripture-quoting evangelical who said grace before meals, Campbell made his name singing middle-of-the-road country-pop ballads, but his penchant for drugs, drink and wild women rivalled the feral appetites of the most hedonistic rock'n'roller.

A man of many parts, he carved out a career as a brilliant session guitarist in which he backed Frank Sinatra and Elvis Presley, the Beach Boys and the Monkees before he ever became a star. Looking like a true all-American cowboy – "as blonde as the sun and solid as a bale of hay", as one critic said of his beefcake physique – he also appeared in several films, most notably *True Grit* with John Wayne.

Yet he was best known for his faultlessly smooth tenor voice on a memorable string of hit records that included *Wichita Lineman, By the Time I Get to Phoenix, Galveston* and *Gentle on My Mind*, in a career in which he sold more than 45 million records. His appeal lay in the way he effortlessly bridged the worlds of country music and pop – although he insisted that he was "not a country singer, but a country boy who sings".

Many of his biggest hits were written by Jimmy Webb, to whose poetic lyrics Campbell brought an aching sense of melancholy. In *Wichita Lineman* he poignantly sang of hearing the ghost of an absent lover "singin' in the wire", while *By the Time I Get to Phoenix* was the story of a broken affair in which he imagined the daily routine of the woman he had left behind.

Such songs played subtly on themes of loss, longing and memory, and it was a sad irony that after a farewell tour in 2011 Campbell was no longer able to sing them because Alzheimer's disease robbed him of his ability to remember the words.

By then his wild days were long behind him, a reformation that he attributed to God, but more practically to his fourth wife, Kim Woollen, a Radio City Music Hall dancer, who issued him with an ultimatum after they married in 1982. "He would fall down drunk five nights a week, just pass out," she recalled. "I thought, 'I can't take it any more.' We had tiny children, and I thought, 'I'm not going to expose my children to some drunkard coming home and being mean.'"

She forced him to kick first the cocaine and then the booze, but there were relapses and in 2003 he spent ten days in jail for driving under the influence. He told the officer who arrested him that he wasn't drunk, but had been "over-served" and then kicked him in the thigh. He served his time in Phoenix, Arizona, in a jail where the inmates were shamed by being made to wear pink underwear. On his release his wife asked the sheriff to autograph a pair of pink prison-issue boxer shorts and kept them as a warning. "Glen straightened up after that," she said.

When they met on a blind date at the Waldorf in New York, Campbell was in a high-profile and mutually destructive relationship with Tanya Tucker, another country singer and fellow cocaine addict. Tucker was 21; he was in his early forties. They recorded hits together and brawled, broke up and got back together as the gossip columns had a field day chronicling their drug-fuelled antics, including a suicide attempt by Tucker and a near-fatal overdose by Campbell while the couple were freebasing cocaine.

She told reporters that he was "the horniest man I ever met" and claimed that in a violent outburst he had knocked her teeth out. He denied this allegation, but admitted: "In our sick slavery to things of the flesh, we were either having sex or fighting. We even fought during sex once or twice."

His first marriage at the age of 17 to his pregnant 15-year-old girlfriend, Diane Kirk, lasted five years. She gave birth to his daughter Debby. When they divorced in 1959 he married Billie Jean Nunley, a beautician with whom he had three children: Kelli, Travis and Kane. By the time they divorced in 1976 he was having an affair with Sarah Barg, the wife of his friend Mac Davis, who wrote *In the Ghetto* for Elvis Presley and several songs for Campbell. They married in 1976, but divorced three weeks after the birth of their only child, Dillon Campbell. With his fourth wife he had three further children, Cal, Shannon and Ashley, who all played or sang in his band.

Life was sometimes complex. When he was moved to a care facility in 2014 his daughter Debby and son Travis went to court seeking to wrest control of his care from his wife, who they alleged was refusing to allow them to see him.

He was born Glen Travis Campbell in a small farming community near Delight, Arkansas, the seventh son among 12 children. His father, Wesley, a sharecropper of Scottish ancestry, and his mother, Carrie, were devout members of the Church of Christ. Campbell was an active member of the congregation until his fourth wife introduced him to a Messianic synagogue that follows the Old Testament, but believes that Jesus is the Messiah.

He got his first guitar at the age of four, which was a $5 instrument from a mail-order catalogue. When he needed a capo to clamp to the frets to change key, his father fashioned one out of a corn on the cob and a rubber band: "All I ever wanted to do was play the guitar; singing was a sideline," Campbell said. "And once I had that capo in place, I didn't look back."

The family home had no electricity; he learnt to copy songs by listening to a country station on an old battery radio. By his mid-teens he had moved to Albuquerque, New Mexico, to play in his uncle's western swing combo, the Dick Bills Band. In 1960 he moved again to Los Angeles, where his burgeoning reputation as one of the hottest guitar pickers in town soon earned him a place in the Wrecking Crew, an informal grouping of A-list session players. The work was plentiful and lucrative. In 1963 he calculated that he played on 586 sessions. His ringing guitar tone became a cornerstone of Phil Spector's epic "wall of sound", heard on hits such as the Righteous Brothers' *You've Lost That Lovin' Feelin'*. He also played on Sinatra's *Strangers in the Night*.

"We were all in the studio together, Frank and the band, and we did the whole song in two takes. They spliced together the best bits of both versions for the final record," Campbell recalled. Yet he was so star-struck that he couldn't stop staring at the singer throughout the session. A disconcerted Sinatra eventually turned to the producer and asked: "Who's the fag guitarist over there?"

Despite the awkwardness of their introduction, they went on to become friends. On one occasion when Campbell was playing golf in the Bob Hope Classic in Palm Springs, where Sinatra had a home, he invited him to stay in his house. "I asked him, 'Which one?' He had three of 'em," Campbell said. He also played on sessions for the Beach Boys. When Brian Wilson retired from performing live to concentrate on songwriting, Campbell replaced him. He stayed with the group for 18 months and played on their 1966 masterpiece, *Pet Sounds*. His performances with the Beach Boys persuaded Capitol Records, who had signed him as a solo act in 1962, to start putting promotional muscle behind him. His breakthrough came in 1967 with *Gentle on My Mind*, which won four Grammy awards, shared between Campbell and the song's writer, John Hartford. From that moment top composers wanted to write for him. He had hits with *Dreams of the Everyday Housewife* and the title song of *True Grit*, in which John Wayne picked him to play his sidekick, La Boeuf.

He shared Wayne's conservative politics and at the height of the Vietnam War protests Campbell intemperately suggested that draft-card burners "should be hanged". He later performed at the White House for President Nixon and for Ronald Reagan at the Republican National Convention in 1980. Shortly after, he was involved in an altercation with an Indonesian government official over the seating arrangements on a flight and told him that he was going to "call my friend Ronald and ask him to bomb Jakarta".

By then he was in what he called the doldrums of his career and was consuming quantities of cocaine and whiskey that would have killed anyone with a less robust constitution. He admitted that even when he sang *The Stars and Stripes* for the president he was "higher than the notes we were singing".

He blamed his addictions on the pressures of his solo career; when he was a session player he claimed he had been so busy that there was no time for drugs. "I was hanging out with the wrong crowd, and they were handing me things they said would 'knock my head off'. It was silly but I didn't have any stability," he explained. "After a couple of failed marriages, it became a habit. So I got down on my knees and prayed. And, eventually, I got rid of those demons." His other recreation was somewhat healthier: he was a fanatical golfer and celebrity host of the Los Angeles Open from 1971 to 1983.

When he announced in *People* magazine in 2011 that he was suffering from Alzheimer's disease he was praised for his courage in going public. Yet the signs were becoming apparent and critics were asking awkward questions about the state of his health: one had written of a recent concert performance that he appeared "unprepared at best and disorientated at worst". In the interview in which he made the announcement he struggled to recall details of his life and could not remember his age.

This year his wife said he could no longer play the guitar, but continued to sing, although the words were gibberish. "It's not a melody that we recognise," she said. "But you can tell that it's a happy song and he has a song in his heart."

Glen Campbell, guitarist and singer, was born on April 22, 1936. He died of Alzheimer's disease on August 8, 2017, aged 81

GEORGE HARRISON

―――――――――●―――――――――

Quiet and self-effacing Beatle who became the most complete musician in the group, and later built a career as both solo artist and film producer

The Times, December 1, 2001

At the apogee of the Beatles' domination of the pop music scene it was a commonplace that the group's youngest member, the shy and self-effacing George Harrison, was completely eclipsed by the other three. True, from the earliest days he was contributing such identifiably individual compositions as *Don't Bother Me* and *I Need You* to the band's phenomenal success. And his later *Here Comes the Sun* became virtually a Beatle anthem and remains a buskers' favourite.

Yet the impression remained that Harrison's modicum of talent was utterly overshadowed by the prodigious creative output and performing brio of John Lennon and Paul McCartney, and that as a character he could not hope to match the ebullient, limelight-loving Ringo Starr. Whereas the other members of the group were so clearly organic to its evolution and manifestly the true authors of the seismic revolution the Beatles encompassed in pop music in the early Sixties, Harrison could give the impression of having hopped on the bandwagon by accident – of being the one member of the Beatles who could have been exchanged for almost any other guitarist without noticeably detracting either from the band's impact or its style.

As the years went by, this impression was seen to be mistaken. Though never a flamboyant performer, Harrison emerged as a much more complete musician than might have been suspected from his early years. This was not merely a matter of the inevitable evolution which would have been expected to accompany the Beatles' own progressive growth. Harrison was a highly disciplined individual. He worked at the guitar in a way many rock'n'roll players do not, once they have achieved success, and as a result he became a most accomplished player.

When he progressed to transcendental meditation it was not a mere flirtation with those "exotic" spiritual exercises of the East which became so fashionable among the young as the Sixties progressed. Harrison made a serious attempt to understand this new experience and his introduction of the sitar into occidental pop was no stunt but a direct result of a thoughtful study of Indian raga.

Thus, when the Beatles broke up in 1970, it was no surprise to those who had followed the input into the band of this quiet and likeable man that he had no difficulty whatsoever in forging for himself a solo career. It was of course inevitable that the distraught fans of the disintegrated group would have been ready to give a sympathetic welcome to any of them as individual performers.

But Harrison forged a solo path very much along lines he wanted to go, and was seen to be accomplished enough not to need to be simply an "ex-Beatle". Creative energies which had already been trying to assert themselves against Lennon, McCartney and Starr before the band's break-up, found a ready outlet after that event.

Yet the limelight was very far from being a necessity to Harrison. Indeed, he tended to recoil from it. There were long periods in the 1980s when he withdrew from pop's "front line" and involved himself in such activities as film producing, a preoccupation first given impetus by his financial rescue of the Monty Python comedy, *Life of Brian*. Formula One racing was one of his great recreational enthusiasms and he was a familiar sight at Grand Prix circuits around the world. He was a close friend of many of the drivers and had played the guitar with Damon Hill and Jacques Villeneuve, drummed with Eddie Jordan and taught Gerhard Berger the ukulele. Latterly, in failing health, he had lived quietly at his home at Henley-on-Thames.

George Harrison was born in 1943 in Liverpool, the youngest of three sons. He was the only member of the Beatles to come from a large family, and the only one whose home life had been relatively uneventful. His father, Harold, was a bus driver and part-time trade union official.

He attended Dovedale Primary School in Liverpool – the same school as Lennon, though they never met there – and then the Liverpool Institute, where he met McCartney. By his own account, Harrison had little academic bent. He passed no O-levels, indeed his school decided not even to enter him for the English Language paper after he had scored a spectacular 2 per cent in the mock exam. School, in general, was not a particularly positive influence on his development.

At a period when the first wave of 1950s rock'n'roll – with its heroes Bill Haley, Elvis Presley and Buddy Holly – was running into the sands, to be replaced momentarily by a species of languorous and formulaic balladeering, many teenagers were turning to skiffle to recapture the excitement and raw energy of pop's early days. Harrison became a devotee of the skiffle king Lonnie Donegan, particularly of his recording of *Rock Island Line*. He taught himself to play the guitar, rehearsing every chord until his fingers bled.

In this he had active encouragement from his mother, Louise, not a woman to be frightened of the new subculture. When her manifestly unacademic offspring muttered about being in a group she had the sense to see that it would be the best thing for him.

McCartney had joined Lennon's school group, the Quarrymen, in 1956. Later he took the 15-year-old Harrison along to play with them. Friends were surprised that Lennon and McCartney, who were obviously so bright and original (though no one could yet discern what they were bright and original at), should be interested in Harrison.

Younger and less mature, and without their artistic interests, he seemed an unpromising product of working-class Liverpool. His work as an apprentice electrician in a Liverpool department store contrasted markedly with their student existence. They, however, recognised his hard-won accomplishment on the guitar.

Lennon, McCartney and Harrison were soon established as a trio of local beat-group players and personalities. Until 1960, when they went to play in Hamburg, and Harrison was able to give up his job forever, they played at parties, coffee bars, teenage dances or just in each other's homes, for a few shillings a night and more often than not for nothing.

In Hamburg nightclubs, where they played over the next two years, they developed a sound of their own which was unlike anything then popular in Britain. It was a song recorded by them in Hamburg that brought them to the attention of Brian Epstein, who was then running the record department of a shop in Liverpool. His perseverance helped to get them a record contract with Parlophone in 1962, when every other major British record company had turned them down.

At this point the Beatles fired their then resident drummer, Pete Best, and took on Ringo Starr, just in time for their first recording, *Love Me Do*, which was released in October 1962. By the end of the year it had reached the Top 20, the first of an astonishing string of hits which, with their artless lyrics and singable melodies, seemed to revitalise pop music overnight.

The phenomenon soon dubbed Beatlemania exploded in the summer of 1963. For three years the Beatles attracted hysterical crowds in every country they played in. The record sales were enormous, the Beatles were used to sell every kind of merchandise and they were mobbed wherever they went. The Beatles were not only an astonishing success in America but they wrested the palm from the country where rock'n'roll had been born. After the Beatles it was never again possible for British bands to think of themselves as the poor relations of pop. Even the prescription transatlantic accent ceased to be a sine qua non for pop singers.

Harrison had started composing in 1963. His first song, *Don't Bother Me*, appeared on *With the Beatles*, their second LP, and from 1965 onwards he had at least one song on every album. Nevertheless he tended to leave Lennon and McCartney to do the bulk of the composing, while he concentrated on his role as lead guitarist. To this he brought a certain intensity which was extremely valuable when the others were larking about.

This latent strength of character was soon to assert itself in other ways. He was the first to articulate the perception that touring was a drag, that he was fed up with being a Beatle and that he resented the inroads on his private life of constant press attention. In 1966, the group stopped touring.

In 1965 he and the other Beatles had been appointed MBE, in a gesture which was designed to underline the progressive nature of the Labour government of Harold Wilson. The following year, Harrison's satirical *Taxman*, which mocked both Wilson and Edward Heath, was an indication of his underlying feelings about the proceedings.

The 1966 album *Revolver* also included his jangling sitar number *Love You To*, which perhaps foreshadowed the inner tensions that were to break up the group. In a sense it was not a Beatles song at all, but a George Harrison song which the others had allowed on to the record.

Harrison had led the way to Indian culture, first going to the subcontinent with his wife, the former model Pattie Boyd, whom he married in 1966. Throughout the group's two-year association with Maharishi Mahesh Yogi and transcendental meditation he applied himself most assiduously, passing on to the others what he had learnt.

As well as taking up the sitar, Harrison taught himself to read and write Indian music, a considerable achievement for someone with neither a Western musical training nor any academic background. As he saw it, it was the only way to get Indian musicians to play the Indian-style songs which he had started to compose. The style not only affected the Beatles' music throughout 1967 and 1968, but was an influence on the sound of popular music everywhere.

Harrison's contribution to the album *Sgt Pepper's Lonely Hearts Club Band* (1967) was his Indian-style *Within You Without You*, a number both musically challenging and lyrically innovative. His 1968 lament, *While My Guitar Gently Weeps*, was one of the finest songs on the two-LP "White Album", while his final contributions to the group's music were the songs *Here Comes the Sun* and *Something*, on what was to be their last recorded album, *Abbey Road* (1969; *Let It Be* had been recorded earlier, though it was not released until 1970). With Lennon spending time on other projects, *Abbey Road* was mostly the work of McCartney and Harrison. *Something* was rated one of the greatest love songs of all time by Frank Sinatra, and was covered by many other performers.

With the break-up of the Beatles, Harrison was at last free to record some of the backlog of songs that he had accumulated during the Beatle years, when they had been overlooked in favour of McCartney's and Lennon's. His triple album *All Things Must Pass* (1970) outsold the first solo efforts of any of the other Beatles, thanks in part to the success of the single *My Sweet Lord*. However, after some years of litigation, a court ruled that Harrison had "unconsciously plagiarised" an old record by the Chiffons, *He's So Fine*, and he was forced to surrender all royalties from the single.

In 1971, Harrison organised two benefit concerts for the relief of famine in the newly created state of Bangladesh, enlisting the help of such singers and performers as Bob Dylan, Ravi Shankar, Eric Clapton and Ringo Starr. This spawned another triple album and served as the model for the later star benefit concerts such as Live Aid in 1985. In the meantime Harrison's until then idyllic marriage to Pattie Boyd, for whom he had written two songs, had foundered when she left him for his friend Eric Clapton. This created a hostility between the two musicians which lasted many years.

Thereafter Harrison continued to play the guitar and sing, appearing on more than 20 albums by musical friends, sometimes content to be almost a session player. But he had a hit with the 1981 single, *All Those Years Ago*, which was recorded with McCartney and

Starr as a tribute to Lennon, who had been shot dead in New York by an obsessive fan the previous year.

Over the next few years Harrison became interested in film-making and production. The Monty Python comedy team had always been personal heroes and when their film *Life of Brian* struck financial trouble, he came to their aid, baling out the film, which went on to become a huge commercial success after its release in 1979. Thereafter, Harrison's production company, HandMade Films, made a number of movies, including *Time Bandits* (1981), a fantasy starring John Cleese, Sean Connery, Ian Holm and Ralph Richardson; *Water* (1985), a frenetic comedy featuring Michael Caine, Leonard Rossiter and Billy Connolly; and *Shanghai Surprise* (1986), a somewhat uncertain adventure romance starring Madonna and Sean Penn. *Withnail and I* (1987), a studiedly seedy comedy featuring the life of two out-of-work actors in a dilapidated country cottage, was not initially a commercial success, but later emerged as a cult classic. Harrison sold the company in 1994.

In 1987 Harrison unexpectedly topped the charts again with his album *Cloud Nine*, following the success of the single *Got My Mind Set on You*. And in 1988 he formed an ad hoc supergroup, the Traveling Wilburys, with Bob Dylan, Roy Orbison, Tom Petty and Jeff Lynne. Their jokey and good-natured debut album was a novelty success, with each member composing for the group and taking a turn as lead singer – Harrison went under the name of "Nelson Wilbury". After Orbison's death, a second album appeared without him.

When the pressure of public nostalgia and the demands of the collectors' market prompted the surviving Beatles to compile the Anthology videos and records of unreleased material in the late 1990s, Harrison was reported to be the least keen, but was eventually won over. Last year a compilation of Beatles No 1 singles, *1*, sold millions of copies.

During the 1990s Harrison fought a draining battle against throat cancer. He blamed the affliction "purely on smoking". Latterly he spent much of his time behind the high walls of his home at Friar Park, Henley-on-Thames, tending the garden, which had been a long-time passion. It was there in the early hours of

December 30, 1999, that he and his second wife, Olivia Trinidad Arias, whom he had married in 1978, were attacked by an intruder and Harrison suffered serious stab wounds. Last July he underwent further treatment for cancer in Switzerland. He died in Los Angeles.

Harrison is survived by his second wife, Olivia, and by their son Dhani.

George Harrison, MBE, guitarist and composer, was born on February 25, 1943. He died of cancer on November 29, 2001, aged 58

LOU REED

— • —

Rock'n'roll pioneer who fronted the Velvet Underground and launched
a solo career that yielded some of his most enduring songs

The Times, October 28, 2013

Lou Reed was one of rock'n'roll's most original, if wayward, artists. He lived much of his life close to the edge and his songs frequently inhabited a demi-monde in which drugs, mental breakdown, attempted suicide and nihilism were common currency. His work was infuriatingly uneven, often difficult and at times he was given almost to self-parody. Yet his most inspired moments, both with the seminal Sixties band the Velvet Underground and in his long and varied solo career, qualify him as one of the most influential musicians of the past fifty years.

With the Velvet Underground in New York he shaped the punk scene for a generation before embarking on years of wild, make-up-clad excesses with David Bowie. His hymn from that time to misfits and transgender people, *Walk on the Wild Side*, gave him his biggest commercial success. Although latterly he had swapped drugs for coffee and t'ai chi he continued, almost relentlessly, to perform and compose music.

Born Lewis Allan Reed, he grew up in Long Island, New York and began to play rock'n'roll in high-school bands in his teens. A disturbed personality was diagnosed early and at the age of 17 he was sent by his parents for electro-shock treatment in an attempt to cure him of severe mood swings.

He took a creative writing and journalism course at Syracuse University and then worked for Pickwick Records as a contracted songwriter. It was low-grade stuff – cheap cash-ins on current hits sold in the budget supermarket bins – but his talent became apparent when one of his compositions, *The Ostrich*, released under the name the Primitives, became a minor hit. A group was swiftly assembled to promote the record which included John Cale and the two men went on to form the Velvet Underground.

While the West Coast groups of the time were embracing peace and love, between 1966 and 1970 the New York-based Velvets made four powerful albums which explored the darker side of human nature. They became darlings of the New York avant-garde scene, taken up by Andy Warhol, who made them an integral part of his Factory arts collective and part of the Exploding Plastic Inevitable, an early multi-media experiment in theatre, music and dance. Warhol produced the group's first album *The Velvet Underground & Nico*, and also designed its distinctive cover, a peel-off banana based on one of his screen prints.

Although it was recorded in 1966, the album did not appear until the following year after several major labels had rejected it due to its lyrical content. *Heroin* and *I'm Waiting for the Man* were blatant drug songs while *Venus in Furs* dealt with sado-masochism. Released at the height of the "summer of love", its urban intensity was out of step with the spirit of the times and it was doomed to commercial failure. Yet subsequently it was to become one of the most influential debut albums in rock – prompting the claim that although hardly anybody bought it, "everyone who did formed a band".

With the departure of the German singer Nico and the ending

of Warhol's role, Reed tightened his control as both main songwriter and lead vocalist. *White Light/White Heat*, the second album, was released in 1968 and featured radical experiments in atonality and such uncompromising compositions of gothic horror and black humour as *Sister Ray* and *The Gift*.

Internal conflicts led to the departure of Cale, the group's most accomplished musician, and Reed was very much in charge on the third album, 1969's quieter and more introspective *Velvet Underground*. The following year saw the release of *Loaded*, which included *Sweet Jane*, one of Reed's best songs, but new member Doug Yule was pulling in a more commercial direction and by the time the album was released Reed was ready to quit.

In August 1970 after a gig at Max's Kansas City (a performance later released as a live album), Reed returned to his parents on Long Island. In one of the oddest career diversions in the history of rock he stayed two years, allegedly working in his father's accountancy firm for 40 dollars a week.

He resurfaced in London in 1972 to record his debut solo album, *Lou Reed*, which surprisingly featured members of the overblown progressive rock band Yes. David Bowie, then at the height of his Ziggy Stardust glam-rock phase, was a more congenial soul mate and they began working together. 1972's *Transformer*, which featured a heavily made-up Reed on the cover in the style of the period, was produced by Bowie and his guitarist Mick Ronson. It included two of Reed's most enduring songs in *Perfect Day* and *Walk on the Wild Side*, which became a hit after the censors at the BBC surprisingly missed the song's obvious reference to oral sex.

Reed and Bowie became inseparable companions and lurid stories filtered out of their hedonistic excess and debauchery. Yet, in what was to become a career trademark, Reed retreated from the commercial success of *Transformer* to make the darker, less accessible concept album *Berlin*. It was unappreciated at the time but is now seen as a lost masterpiece. The same cannot be said of the lacklustre and disco-ish *Sally Can't Dance* and although the live album *Rock'n'Roll Animal* earned him a gold disc, 1975's *Metal Machine Music* was an impenetrably avant-garde double set which was described memorably by one critic as "four sides of whines, whistles, feedback and screams". It sold so badly that for a time his record label, RCA, withdrew it from the catalogue.

The general opinion was that Reed had lost it but his career, now largely based in Britain, took an upturn when the London Palladium banned him in 1977 for his "punk image" and he was an early hero to the likes of the Sex Pistols and the Clash. He perversely continued to follow good albums with the downright dire – the excellent *Coney Island Baby* with the listless *Rock'n'Roll Heart* and the powerful *Street Hassle* with the underwhelming *Growing Up in Public*. Yet despite this erratic output, his reputation continued to grow. Having been embraced by the punks, he then became a mentor to such post-New Wave groups as Joy Division.

In the Eighties he branched out on some unexpected collaborations. He appeared in a cameo role in Paul Simon's film *One-Trick Pony*, sang on a Kurt Weill tribute album, had a hit with the old Sam & Dave hit *Soul Man* and co-wrote songs with the salsa performer Rubén Blades. By the end of the decade he was working with Cale again on *Songs for Drella: A Fiction*, which they performed as a tribute to Warhol.

But his own work remained uneven as ever and fans had to wait until the end of the decade for a fully satisfying album with 1989's *New York*, which displayed strong flashes of his old sharp and caustic wit.

He followed it encouragingly with 1992's *Magic and Loss*, which made number six in the British album charts, his highest ever placing. In the same year he published a book of poems entitled *Between Thought and Expression* and was made a Knight of the French Order of Arts and Letters by the French culture minister Jack Lang.

Already once divorced (from Sylvia Morales), he and the respected avant-gardist Laurie Anderson became partners in the mid-Nineties and the union inspired a creative renewal. Reed appeared on Anderson's 1994 album *Bright Red*, while her influence was apparent on his own 1996 offering *Set the Twilight Reeling*.

Despite the fervent wishes of fans, the prospect of a full-scale Velvets reunion was never a realistic one. In 1993 the original line-up had re-formed for some acclaimed shows but tensions again surfaced between Reed and Cale. Except for a one-off in 1996 when the Velvets were inducted into the Rock & Roll Hall of Fame, they did not play together again.

Reed then wrote an album devoted to the poet Edgar Allan Poe and a few years later *Hudson River Wind Meditations*, inspired by t'ai chi, returning to rock on his 2011 album with Metallica, *Lulu*. In recent years he had performed with Metal Machine Trio, a group which he set up in 2008, as well as a new generation of artists such as Gorillaz.

In 1997 Reed's song *Perfect Day* was famously adopted by the BBC for promotional purposes. BBC executives seemed deaf to the strong suggestions that the song was about heroin use.

Lou Reed, singer and songwriter, was born on March 2, 1942. He died on October 27, 2013, aged 71

GINGER BAKER

Virtuoso drummer in Cream who would seethe at the mention of Led Zeppelin, and who drove through the Sahara to kick his drug habit

The Times, October 7, 2019

By his own admission Ginger Baker was "an obnoxious git". He was truculent, rude, abrasive, arrogant, prone to outbursts of physical violence and the lash of his tongue could be even more vicious than his fists.

Eric Clapton, who played with Baker in his salad days in Cream and Blind Faith, admitted that he was "scared" of him and there was no mellowing in the autumn of his years. When a documentary film was made about his turbulent life in 2012, it was appropriately titled *Beware of Mr Baker*. The opening scene showed him attacking Jay Bulger, the film's director, with a walking stick and breaking his nose.

The saving grace was that Baker also happened to be the finest rock drummer of his generation. With Cream he helped to invent heavy rock and became the first drummer outside of jazz to be revered as a virtuoso musician. For better or for worse, he introduced the extended drum solo into popular music, creating percussive storms of rhythm that sometimes lasted up to half an hour in concert while his fellow musicians left the stage.

His kit featured two bass drums, so that he could play with both feet, while his hands attacked the snares, tom-toms and cymbals, so that at times all four limbs were playing different cross-rhythms. It was a formidable display of technique that he combined with ferocious physical strength, creating the template for several generations of rock drummers who followed in his wake, from John Bonham of Led Zeppelin to Nirvana's Dave Grohl.

In full flight Baker was an arresting sight, feral, agitated and bug-eyed, arms flailing and his head shaking under a wild shock of red hair that made him look like a Celtic warlord or a disgruntled wizard. One of life's incorrigible extroverts, he didn't do modesty any more than he did bourgeois good manners and he characteristically titled his autobiography *Hellraiser: the Autobiography of the World's Greatest Drummer.*

Unfortunately those who played with the world's greatest drummer found that the privilege came with a price attached. There were ill-tempered fights, bitter feuds and rancorous fissions. On one occasion he pulled a knife on Jack Bruce, a bass player whose crime had been to play too loudly while Baker was executing a drum solo. Over the years Baker and Bruce played in four bands together and reconvened one last time in a Cream reunion in 2005, so the creative tension must have worked after a fashion. But the drummer sustained the feud until Bruce's death in 2014.

It wasn't only Bruce who rubbed him up the wrong way, for Baker regarded most other rock musicians with contempt. Asked about the Beatles, he would belligerently roar, "They weren't musicians!" George Harrison was denounced as "a musical moron" after they had worked together. The Rolling Stones were dismissed as "a load of little kids trying to play Black blues music and playing it very badly, naive and banal". To mention Led Zeppelin in his presence was to risk injury to life and limb. His bile was partly rooted in professional pride, for he had learnt his trade playing in serious jazz combos and could sight-read music, something that most rock musicians were unable to do. Nor could they play in the complex jazz time signatures he regarded as second nature and he despised the simplistic 4/4 beats of pop music. What few words of praise he had were reserved for virtuoso jazz drummers such as Elvin Jones, Max Roach, Phil Seamen and Art Blakey, who he regarded as his peers.

His abrasiveness was heightened by an addictive personality and chronic drug abuse. He started using heroin and cocaine in the 1950s in imitation of his jazz heroes, and spent decades as an addict.

He claimed to have kicked his habit 29 times and to have relapsed again 28 times. "Several times I've thrown a large amount down the toilet, then, two hours later, I'm saying, 'I wish I hadn't done that,'" he said.

Baker lived his life on the edge and for a while it seemed unlikely that he would survive; he enjoyed joking ghoulishly about a 1970s magazine article that tipped him soon to be drumming in heaven with a superstar "dead band" featuring Janis Joplin on vocals and Jimi Hendrix on guitar. In the end the drum stool in the "live fast, die young" line-up went to Keith Moon and John Bonham, both of whom – perhaps to Baker's surprise – he outlasted by about four decades.

"I was reported dead several times, including once when I was driving a Shelby Cobra with three tasty chicks, and the radio station announced I'd been found dead in my hotel room from a heroin overdose," he recalled, cackling maniacally at the memory.

He rejected conventional drug rehabilitation, which he dismissed as "a bloody con to make money and take advantage" and had his own favoured "cures". One of the most effective – at least in the short term – was to take himself off to remote parts of Africa where the drug was simply unavailable; on one occasion he decided to drive across the Sahara Desert as a way of getting away from the drug dealers and the inner demons that forced him to seek them out.

He finally kicked his habit in Italy in the 1980s. "I moved to a little village in the middle of nowhere, where nobody spoke English. I got into olive farming. It was hard work, but very good therapy," he said.

His other passions included fast cars and fast women, and among many dalliances he slept with the 30-year-old Germaine Greer after a 1969 concert. "She wasn't kinky at all," he reported. "She's a really nice girl, Germaine. I've always thought the world of her." Another story involved him and Jimi Hendrix sharing two groupies in a four-in-the-bed romp.

Despite a string of casual girlfriends and one-night stands, like so many things in his life marriage too became an addiction. He married his first wife, Liz Finch, in 1959, when they were 20. They had two daughters, Ginette and Leda, and a son, Kofi, who became a drummer. Liz left him when the children were teenagers and she discovered that he was sleeping with one of their daughters' friends. Interviewed many years later, she said: "If a plane went down and there was one survivor, it would be Ginger. The Devil takes care of his own."

He married his second wife, Sarah, in 1983, having eloped to Italy with her when she was 18. He divorced her when he discovered that she was having an affair, a curious application of a moral code that he never applied to his own behaviour.

He met and married his third wife, Karen Loucks, while living in California. She was a pretty young blonde who was introduced to him by his hairdresser; the marriage was short-lived and when he refused to agree to a divorce settlement she kept his gold discs.

In 2010 he married for a fourth time to the Zimbabwean-born Kudzai Machokoto, a nurse he met in an internet chatroom, who was 42 years his junior. At the time he was living in South Africa, where he ran a ranch on which he kept 38 polo ponies, having developed a passion for the sport in the 1970s. He lost the farm after being embezzled by his South African accountant.

Although he won the court battle that ensued, he did not get his money back and was forced to return to Britain with Machokoto and her teenage daughter, Lisa, who had been born after her mother was raped at 16, and was adopted by Baker. They lived in a rented house in Kent on money lent to him by Clapton and, despite being in his mid-70s and suffering from a chronic lung condition, osteoarthritis of the spine and various other ailments, Baker went back on the road in 2013 with a new band, the Ginger Baker Jazz Confusion.

"With all my disabilities it's a miracle I can play at all," he said. "If I'm enjoying the music, that overrides everything and the pain goes away. But after a gig, having played an hour and a half, I'm exhausted."

Peter Edward Baker was born in 1939 in Lewisham, southeast

London. He barely knew his father, Frederick, who was killed in the Second World War when his son was four. "He died because of that stupid sod Churchill," Baker opined with characteristic bluntness. A letter from his father, delivered from beyond the grave, told him that his fists would be his "best pals". It was advice that he never forgot.

His mother worked in a tobacco shop and he was brought up in poverty. As a teenager he stole records, joined a gang, got into fights with razors and set his heart on becoming a racing cyclist, until a smash-up on his way to work in the art department of a London advertising agency wrote off his bike and left him badly injured.

He took up the drums and blagged his way into a jazz band after answering an advertisement in *Melody Maker*. "I didn't have a drum kit so I bought a toy kit and worked on it," he said.

"I cut up a tent to put a head on the bass drum, added a biscuit tin to one of the tom-toms, and told them I'd been playing professionally for three years, and my normal kit was busted."

In 1962 Baker joined Alexis Korner's Blues Incorporated, with whom Mick Jagger sometimes sang prior to the formation of the Rolling Stones. Baker took an instant and lifelong dislike to the singer. "We played complicated time things to throw Mick off the beat. He would lose it completely," he recalled with satisfaction half a century later.

A year later he joined the Graham Bond Organisation and began his highly combustible relationship with Bruce. When it became obvious they could not appear on the same stage together without a fight breaking out, one of them had to go. To Baker's glee it was Bruce who got the bullet.

Although the Graham Bond Organisation was one of the seminal British R&B acts of the era, a lack of commercial success persuaded him to quit and form his own group. In search of a guitarist he approached Clapton, who at the time was playing in John Mayall & the Bluesbreakers. Unaware of the violent history between Baker and Bruce, he agreed to join, but on the condition that Bruce should be the bass player. Baker reluctantly agreed and Cream was born, bursting on to the scene in autumn 1966, about the same time as the Jimi Hendrix Experience.

Both groups were power trios with bass and drums backing the two most acclaimed electric guitarists of the day; both fused blues riffs and psychedelic rock, shared outrageous fashion sense and played at extreme volume. Between them they changed the face of British rock, rivals but with a shared camaraderie. Cream's second album, *Disraeli Gears*, became a classic of the era, with Baker's inventive drumming heard to fine effect on songs such as *Strange Brew* and *Sunshine of Your Love*.

Cream broke up in 1968, with Baker and Bruce at each other's throats again. Clapton teamed up with Traffic's Steve Winwood to form Blind Faith. According to Clapton, Baker showed up one day and announced that he was going to be the drummer. A reluctant Clapton agreed against his better judgment, scared of Baker's reaction if he refused.

Blind Faith soon disbanded and Baker formed Ginger Baker's Air Force, a sprawling big band that featured three drummers, before he moved lock, stock and drumsticks to Lagos in Nigeria. There he studied African percussion, learnt to play polo, drummed with Fela Kuti and built a recording studio.

When a dispute with local drug dealers turned nasty, he sold the studio for a fraction of its worth and moved on. It set a chaotic pattern for the next 40 years. After another confrontation, drug deal gone wrong or failed marriage, Baker would sell up, pick a new location and start making enemies all over again.

In Italy he butted heads with the local mafia. In South Africa he fell out with the white denizens of the local polo club when he allowed black squatters to live on his property. When they painted a warning in red on his fence that read: "Beware, Mr Baker" he amended it to: "Beware of Mr Baker".

Whatever life threw at him, he threw it back with twice as much force. "It's been an amazing rollercoaster ride," he said. "I've lost everything many times. A lot of people would have just given up." On a point of principle he never did.

Ginger Baker, drummer, was born on August 19, 1939. He died of undisclosed causes on October 6, 2019, aged 80

JANIS JOPLIN

*Hard-living, rebellious Texan who became the foremost
female blues singer of her generation*

The Times, October 5, 1970

Janis Joplin, who died in Hollywood early yesterday at the age
of 27, was the foremost female blues singer of her generation.

Born in Port Arthur, Texas, she heard the blues at an early age,
and began singing when a student at Austin University.

For several years she drifted in and out of music and various
other jobs all over America until in 1966 she moved to San Francisco,
where she joined the resident band at the Avalon Ballroom, an easy
"psychedelic" dance hall which spawned many top groups. Her
band, Big Brother and the Holding Company, rapidly rose to fame
and really broke through with a stunning performance at the
Monterey Pop Festival in 1967.

Inevitably she was given the star treatment and broke away from
the group the following year to form her own outfit. After a

disastrous debut in Memphis she triumphed in New York early in 1969 and visited Britain in April of that year to play at the Royal Albert Hall to an enraptured audience. A few months later she was voted World's Top Female Singer by the readers of *Melody Maker*, but since then her career had gone quiet until, a month before her death, she began recording with a new band. Her harsh delivery and sensual stage act put her in a direct line of descent from Bessie Smith, the greatest of all female blues singers, and she cultivated the outrageous image by seldom being seen without a bottle of Southern Comfort whiskey near to hand. This quickly became her trademark, as did the tough, hard-boiled exterior which hides the tensions and fears inside all women who choose to sing the blues for a living.

Janis Joplin, singer, was born on January 19, 1943. She died of a suspected accidental overdose on October 4, 1970, aged 27

PHIL MAY

———————●———————

*Wild and hairy frontman of the Pretty Things who was considered
a rival by Mick Jagger and was "stalked" by the teenage David Bowie*

The Times, May 22, 2020

In the days when anxious parents were locking up their daughters whenever Mick Jagger and his group of long-haired libertines hit town, there was only one band that was shaggier, wilder, lewder and more degenerate than the Rolling Stones.

That band was the Pretty Things, led by Phil May, who rivalled Jagger as a lascivious, hip-wiggling lead singer and was dubbed "the longest-haired man in Britain".

The marketing campaign behind May and his band was crude but effective and could simply be paraphrased as "If you thought the Stones were a bunch of scruffy yobs, wait until you see this lot."

For a while the carefully promoted sense of outrage worked well and the Pretty Things' first two rambunctious singles, *Rosalyn* and *Don't Bring Me Down*, featuring May's yowling vocals, were as ferociously potent as anything recorded during the 1960s British beat boom.

"He's just too fucking pretty. ... He's dangerous," Jagger was reported to have said after May had made a spectacular TV debut with the Pretty Things on *Ready Steady Go!* in 1964. Andrew Loog Oldham, the Stones' manager, was dispatched to tell the show's producer, Vicki Wickham, that if she put May and his reprobates on again, *Ready Steady Go!* should forget about getting the Stones back.

The rivalry was given an added piquancy by the fact that the guitarist in May's group was Dick Taylor, who had been at Dartford Grammar School with Jagger and had briefly played in the Stones' pre-fame line-up.

The Pretty Things' most enthusiastic uberfan was a teenager named David Jones, who hung around the stage door at so many of the band's gigs that they took to calling him "the Stalker". When he got to know May he entered his number in his phone book under the name "GOD". Jones later changed his name to David Bowie, and recorded deferential versions of *Rosalyn* and *Don't Bring Me Down* on his 1973 album *Pin Ups*.

Bowie also namechecked the band in the song *Oh! You Pretty Things* and borrowed aspects of May's androgynous appeal. From the outset May had hinted at bisexuality in songs in which he interchanged the pronouns "he" and "she". May claimed on one occasion to have ended up with Brian Jones, Judy Garland and Rudolf Nureyev in the same bed at the Dorchester Hotel.

He was married for 30 years to Electra Nemon, the sister-in-law of the former Conservative MP Sir George Young and daughter of the sculptor Oscar Nemon, whose bronze statue of Churchill stands in the members' lobby in the House of Commons. He divorced her in the 1990s and entered a long-term relationship with Colin Graham, with whom he lived in Norfolk. Graham survives him, along with two children from his marriage: a son, Paris, and daughter, Sorrel, a TV producer.

Phil May was born Philip Dennis Arthur Wadey in Dartford, Kent, in 1944 and was brought up in his early years by his mother Daphne's sister, Flo, and her husband, Charlie May, whom he considered to be his real parents and whose name he took. When he was ten he returned to live with his mother and stepfather.

On leaving school he studied graphic design at Sidcup Art College, where Keith Richards was a student in the year above him. He formed the Pretty Things with Taylor, another fellow art student, in 1963.

After the Pretty Things' early flush of success the group was bedevilled by poor decision-making, bad luck and a reputation that preceded them.

In 1965, at the height of their British success, they were invited to tour by Sid Bernstein, the New York-based promoter who had introduced the Beatles to the United States. As one of the most exciting acts to emerge from the British beat boom, they should have been more or less guaranteed to follow the Beatles and the Stones in the "British invasion" of the American charts but Bryan

Morrison, the Pretty Things' manager, turned down the invitation on the grounds that the fee was too low and sent the band to New Zealand instead. The quiet country wasn't ready for the Pretty Things and the tour was a disaster. May and his bandmates provoked so much outrage, including starting a fire on an aircraft at 30,000ft, that their antics were debated by the New Zealand parliament and there were calls for them to be banned from the country for life.

Like the Sex Pistols a decade later, everywhere the Pretty Things went there were drug busts, fights and riots. It was claimed that members of the group made 27 court appearances in 1965 alone.

Even the indefatigably transgressive May grew tired of the chaos and considered a return to art school. "We'd had the screaming girls, we'd be chased down the streets and locked in hotel rooms. We couldn't get out because of the screamers. So I went back to my tutor and said, 'Look, I want to come back and paint,'" he recalled.

"Why sit in a life class in London when you can travel the world?" came the sage reply. "Fill your life up with experiences, go back on the road, carry on playing and see in three or four years' time."

May carried on, although one by one his bandmates dropped by the wayside. Viv Prince, the drummer, who was so wild that he made Keith Moon appear sane and sober, was fired because it was impossible to know if he was going to turn up.

Brian Pendleton, the guitarist, disappeared in 1966 on the way to a gig in Leeds by train. "When we got to the other end, he wasn't on the train any more. We never saw him again for a year and a half," May said. He was later found working in a bank. Over the years the band went through 33 members with May as the only constant.

After switching his drug of choice from Purple Hearts to LSD, May reinvented the Pretty Things in the 1967 "summer of love" as psychedelic rock pioneers. He deserved the credit for writing the first "rock opera" with *SF Sorrow* in 1968, a story chronicling a life from birth through childhood, love and old age.

Today the album is regarded as a landmark but at the time the group's record company, EMI, was unimpressed and failed to promote it. Six months later The Who released *Tommy* and Pete Townshend got the plaudits.

When May suggested that The Who's rock opera had been influenced by *SF Sorrow*, Townshend wrote him a letter instructing him to desist with his claim and implying legal action could follow if he did not. May was deeply hurt and described the letter as "a kick in the bollocks".

After *SF Sorrow* had flopped, the remains of the Pretty Things were reduced to recording low-budget film soundtracks with an embarrassed May hiding the group's identity under the name Electric Banana. They appeared as such in the 1969 Norman Wisdom comedy *What's Good for the Goose*. Needless to say, one night May managed to get Wisdom stoned for the first and probably only time in the comedian's life.

With a new line-up, the Pretty Things' next album, *Parachute* (1970) was voted record of the year by *Rolling Stone*. Typically, for the band, it became the only album of the year in the magazine's history not to sell a million copies.

There was one further tilt at superstardom in the mid-1970s when Led Zeppelin signed May and the Pretty Things to their label, Swan Song. According to Zeppelin's manager, Peter Grant, within three months May and his colleagues had spent their entire advance of $150,000 on cocaine. The two albums that they recorded for the label flopped.

May carried on regardless until lung disease caused by years of heavy drinking and smoking forced him to retire from the stage. He played his final concert with the Pretty Things in 2018, when he was joined onstage by his old friends David Gilmour and Van Morrison.

"You could have surfed on the warmth that was coming out of that audience," May said after the show. "The power of people expressing their gratitude for the music you made was quite thrilling."

Phil May, rock singer, was born on November 9, 1944. He died of complications following hip surgery on May 15, 2020, aged 75

FATS DOMINO

———————•———————

Rock'n'roll pioneer with a beaming smile who was labelled
the "King" by Elvis

The Times, October 25, 2017

When a journalist at a press conference in 1969 referred to Elvis Presley as "the king", Presley shook his head and gestured instead towards Fats Domino, who was sitting across the room. "No," he said, in refusing the crown, "there's the real king of rock'n'roll."

Between 1950 and 1963, Domino made the American Billboard pop chart 63 times and scored more hits than Chuck Berry, Little Richard and Buddy Holly put together. Among the first generation of rock'n'roll stars, his record sales were exceeded only by Presley. But Domino got there first; his debut hit made the charts four years before Presley, who admitted that he had been heavily influenced by the singer known universally as "The Fat Man".

With his broad, beaming smile, inherent shyness and uncomplicated approach to life, Domino cut an improbable figure as the first significant star of the rock'n'roll age. Barely 5ft 4in tall and weighing 15 stone, he was nobody's idea of a conventional matinee pop idol and there was no hip-wiggling or flamboyant showmanship.

"I didn't need none of that. The beat was enough," he said. He came up with a seemingly endless production line of classic songs such as *Ain't That a Shame, Blueberry Hill, Blue Monday* and *I'm Walkin'*, many of which he wrote or co-wrote. They were sung in a warm and vibrant baritone, accompanied by his uniquely rhythmic piano-playing in the rolling style of his native New Orleans.

It was an approach that made a virtue of simplicity and earned him a huge youthful following, spanning the racial divide at a time when American music was heavily segregated, with a "pop" chart for predominantly White acts and a "race" chart (later renamed the "R'n'B" chart) for Black music. Domino was one of the first artists to top both.

"Teens always heard my music with their hearts," he said.

"The beat was just happy. It didn't have colour or hidden meaning. I was just playing and singing about life."

Musicologists continue to argue about who invented rock'n'roll, but Domino had a better claim than almost anyone. His first hit, *The Fat Man* in 1949, established the rudiments, his piano pounding out a steady bank of triplets with three notes to every beat, the drummer hitting the second and fourth beats to create the backbeat and the horns playing "call and response" bass riffs. Mixing elements of boogie-woogie, R&B, blues, Dixieland, zydeco and the swing of a Mardi Gras marching band, he created a thrilling hybrid sound that the world did not yet know as rock'n'roll, but soon would.

By the mid-1950s he was at the height of his commercial success and a dominant figure in the charts, although he still suffered the indignity that afflicted all Black performers of the era as White crooners stole their songs and had bigger hits with anodyne covers. When Domino made No 10 in the American pop charts in 1955 with *Ain't That a Shame*, for example, Pat Boone immediately copied the song and took it to No 1.

At least he had the compensation of the songwriting royalties. A short while later Domino found himself sharing a stage with Boone. He flashed a huge gold ring at the audience and told them: "Pat bought me this."

Appearances in the teen films *Shake, Rattle & Rock!* and *The Girl Can't Help It* raised his profile further and he made his first visit to Europe in 1962, when he was introduced to the Beatles, who were among his most ardent fans. Ironically, it was "Beatlemania" that brought about his decline.

The new wave of beat groups effected a fundamental change in popular tastes, and Domino and the stars of the 1950s suddenly found themselves regarded as yesterday's heroes. The hits dried up, although he remained a revered and influential figure. When an album of covers of his songs was recorded to mark his 80th birthday, those queuing to pay tribute included Paul McCartney, Robert Plant, Norah Jones, Neil Young, Randy Newman, Elton John, Tom Petty, BB King and Willie Nelson.

He enjoyed the trappings of his success and developed a passion for expensive cars and a taste for ostentatious jewellery. Yet in many ways he was a reluctant star, who preferred staying at home in New Orleans to touring the world and playing the celebrity game. "He always hated interviews," his biographer, Rick Coleman, noted. "And he didn't want to go on television unless he absolutely had to. He didn't care and he turned down million-dollar offers."

His love of down-home cooking meant that he took his own food, pots and pans on the road even when he was one of the biggest-selling stars in America, instructing his manager to book him into motel rooms with a kitchenette. If one wasn't available, he'd cook his favourite New Orleans recipes, such as seafood gumbo, on a hot plate that he carried with him. "A lot of the stuff I like I can't find when I travel," he said.

In the 1960s a series of residencies in Las Vegas, where he met Presley, resulted in him spending more time away from home than he liked. He also played several concerts in London, where many people recall him using his tummy to bump the piano off stage at the same time as he was playing.

Although he continued to tour, he seldom left New Orleans for long after 1970, living contentedly on the royalties from his earlier hits in a sprawling pink and white mansion that he had built in the same poor Lower Ninth neighbourhood in which he was born.

"People wanted to know: why would you build an expensive house in that neighbourhood and why didn't I move with the well-to-do, with the people who've got money? Well, I was satisfied right there," he explained. Even into old age he liked to sleep at night outside on the porch in a hammock.

Next door to the big house he built an annexe, which he used as a clubhouse to entertain his friends. Painted black and gold – the colours of the New Orleans Saints football team – and with "FD" emblazoned on the façade, the annexe housed a home cinema, a kitchen to cook gumbo and the rear of a 1959 Cadillac, which he used as a couch.

He lived in the house for more than 50 years until it was destroyed by Hurricane Katrina in 2005. As the flood waters rose he tried to ride out the storm at home, as his family had done in Hurricane

Betsy 40 years earlier. National Guard helicopters hovered over the neighbourhood rescuing residents who had clambered on to their roofs. When there was no sign of Domino, his manager and a niece reported him missing.

By the time the waters had risen to 8ft and he was forced to take refuge on a second-floor balcony, he bowed to the inevitable and reluctantly summoned a Harbor Police boat, which rescued him and members of three generations of his extended family. They were taken to the safety of the Superdome, with 19,000 other homeless people.

In the end he lost everything, including his grand piano and most of his gold discs, but he remained stoical. "I ain't missed nothing, to tell you the truth, and I was able to replace what I lost," he said after he had moved to a new home in a gated suburb. President George W Bush paid him a visit and replaced the National Medal of Arts that had been awarded to him by Bill Clinton.

After the flood waters had subsided, his home became an attraction on the disaster-sightseeing tours that cruised the neighbourhood. Somebody must have thought he hadn't made it because spray-painted on his house was the message: "RIP Fats. You will be missed."

Among those rescued with him were his wife, Rosemary Hall, who had been his former school sweetheart when they married in 1947, several of his eight children – whom he whimsically named Antoinette, Andrea, Adonica, Antonio, Anatole, Anola, Andre and Antoine III – and his numerous grandchildren.

When asked how many members of his extended family lived with him, he was vague to the point of carelessness. "I never count 'em. I got a lot of them," he replied. His wife died in 2008.

Antoine Domino Jr was born in 1928 in New Orleans, the youngest of nine children. He was brought up speaking Creole and English, and the city's piano bars and street marching bands provided his musical education.

When he was ten the family inherited a battered piano with keys so worn that the ivory had become almost translucent. A brother-in-law, who had once played banjo in Kid Ory's famous jazz band, taught him to play. He was soon skipping school and performing in clubs and bars.

He was fond of New Orleans's rich cuisine, which resulted in an expanding waistline and the band leader Billy Diamond nicknaming him "Fats". Domino was offended, but pragmatic enough to keep it as a stage name, noting that it hadn't done Fats Waller any harm.

By the age of 12 he had stopped attending school and was working by day delivering ice – few homes in New Orleans had refrigerators at the time – and later in a factory that made bed springs. By night he was playing in clubs such as the Hideaway. His growing reputation around town brought him to the attention of the bandleader Dave Bartholomew, who had been hired as a talent scout for the recently formed Imperial Records.

Bartholomew was to become his soul brother, producing and co-writing Domino's hits from his first 1949 recording until 1963. He was also one of the few who called him Antoine, which cemented their friendship. "Fats and I didn't have a formal way of working on those songs," Bartholomew recalled. "We would just jam and we'd jot down words and music. Then I'd hum what I wanted the horns to play. Fats knew exactly what to do from there."

New Orleans had a reputation for being the South's most relaxed city when it came to racial intermingling, and Domino showed little interest in the civil rights struggle. "I knew what they had going on so it was no use me trying to do anything about it," he said. "You did what you were supposed to do according to what the law was. I just went about my business."

He didn't raise an objection when, during an appearance on *The Ed Sullivan Show* in 1956, his backing band were hidden behind a curtain so there weren't too many Black faces.

When his hit-making days were over he showed little appetite for remaining in the limelight. If there was a lack of ambition – allegedly a common New Orleans trait, hence the city's nickname "The Big Easy" – he was content that by his mid-thirties he had already made enough money to remain comfortable for the rest of his life.

He described himself as "lucky" that music had given him a living. There were no tales of wild drinking, drug use and womanising. His family and his religion were the twin pillars that sustained him.

"Nobody lives for ever," he noted in one of this final interviews, when he was well into his eighties. "Stay as close as you can to the Bible. That's the main thing."

Fats Domino, singer and songwriter, was born on February 26, 1928. He died on October 25, 2017, aged 89

MARC BOLAN

$\bullet$

*Enigmatic pioneer of the glam-rock movement in the early 1970s
with his band T Rex*

The Times, September 20, 1977

Marc Bolan was one of pop music's more enigmatic figures
and had reached a critical point in his career. After shrewdly
adapting his early folk style to the needs of "heavy metal" rock in
the early 1970s, and achieving considerable commercial success
with his band, T Rex, Bolan's star had declined. He was attempting

to retrieve his position this year, hosting a children's pop programme on ITV, *Marc*, among other activities.

Born Mark Feld in 1947, he came from a family of Soho costermongers and was an early entrant into the pop world. He learnt the guitar and sang in local London shows while still at school.

After modelling and acting, he made his early recordings for Decca as a solo artist in 1965 when he was 17. At this time, his lyrics were described by George Melly as "rather like Walter de la Mare", and he was indeed a child of that time. He sang about wizards and woodlands, sea beasts and satyrs – a reflection of the gentle "flower children" period.

This powerful folk music flavouring was sustained when, with Steve Peregrin Took, he founded in 1967 the duo called Tyrannosaurus Rex. Bolan wrote all the words and music, and played acoustic guitar; Took joined him in the singing, and played exotic percussion and other instruments, including bongos, African talking drums, Chinese gongs and "pixiephones". Typical titles of the period were *Warlord of the Royal Crocodiles*, *The Seal of Seasons* and *Cat Black (The Wizard's Hat)*.

After two years, during which he won a modest but loyal following, Bolan's music began to change. He took to amplification and a harder rock sound, and when Mickey Finn replaced Took in September 1969, the moment was ripe for a transformation towards the "heavy metal" rock which was increasingly the vogue. Within a few months they had a hit album, *A Beard of Stars*.

Within a year, their single, *Hot Love*, held top position in the British charts for six consecutive weeks. For over three years from October 1970 – by which time the duo's name had been shortened to T Rex – Bolan and Finn, sometimes augmented by other musicians, enjoyed consistent success in the British (and, less often, the American) rock charts.

Among their best-known singles were *Ride a White Swan* (1970), *Get It On* (1971), *Telegram Sam* and *Metal Guru* (1972), and *20th Century Boy* (1973). Their albums, including *Electric Warrior*, *Bolan Boogie* and *Best of T Rex*, were consistently in the charts.

After 1973, however, T Rex records achieved only lowly positions in the charts and the band lost its charisma. Not long before his death, Bolan had publicly described his efforts successfully to overcome drug addiction and alcoholism. He had prepared rigorously for his television comeback, and the show was accounted a success, with young audiences in excess of ten million. He had plans to tour in Germany and the US, and to make more recordings.

Marc Bolan, pop star, was born on September 30, 1947. He died in a car crash on September 16, 1977, aged 29

TOM PETTY

———————— • ————————

Musician whose high cheekbones, "heartland" sound and 80 million
record sales made him the quintessential American rock star

The Times, October 3, 2017

One hot and steamy day in July 1961, Tom Petty was sitting by
the pond in the back yard of his parents' home in Florida when his
aunt came by and asked if he would like to meet Elvis Presley.

The singer was in town to shoot a scene for the movie *Follow
That Dream* and Petty's uncle had been employed by the film crew as
a local gofer.

The ten-year-old boy's audience with Presley was brief, but it
was enough to determine the course of his life. "He didn't have
much to say to us. He sort of grunted in my way," Petty recalled.
"But for a kid at an impressionable age, he was an incredible sight."

The next day he traded his catapult for a pile of Elvis singles
that his childhood friend Keith Harben had inherited from an older

sister. "And that was the end of doing anything other than music with my life," he said. "I didn't want anything to fall back on because I was not going to fall back."

Four years later he formed his first band, although it would be another 12 years before Petty achieved rock'n'roll fame when his first hit, *Breakdown*, charted in 1977, the year that Presley died. True to his word, there was no going back and he spent the next 40 years as one of the world's most quintessential rock stars, selling more than 80 million records and scoring memorable hits with songs such as *Don't Come Around Here No More, Free Fallin'* and *I Won't Back Down.*

His high-profile performance at Live Aid in 1985, seen by a television audience estimated at 1.9 billion in 150 countries around the world, was one of the highlights of the star-studded show.

Bob Dylan, who was on the same bill, was so impressed that he employed Petty and his band the Heartbreakers as his support act and backing band on his next world tour. By then his star had risen so high that Dylan admitted that more people were turning up to see Petty than to see him.

"It's a strange [thing] to say out loud, but I always felt destined to do this," he said in 2009. "From a very young age I felt this was going to happen to me."

One knew what he meant. With his long, straight blond hair and high cheekbones, everything about Petty suggested that he was born to be a star, while his music seemed to synthesise all of the best elements of rock'n'roll into a single package.

His sound wasn't startlingly original. The jangling guitars were borrowed from the Byrds, and the harmonies from the Beatles and the Beach Boys. His riffs owed much to the swagger of the Rolling Stones, and he drew energy from punk and garage rock. He added an American roots flavour derived from the Band, the Eagles and the like, and as a songwriter he was the first to acknowledge his debt to Dylan.

Yet he welded all of these elemental forms into an everyman style of "heartland rock", which was rejuvenating and utterly distinctive. When a new Tom Petty record came on the radio, nobody was ever in any doubt about who it was.

He was driven by an all-consuming passion. Apart from his family and watching a little basketball in later years when Jack Nicholson gave him a ticket to the Los Angeles Lakers, he admitted that there was not much else in his life besides music. "It's like I caught a disease. I've never been able to get it out of my blood for a minute. I'm over-obsessed," he confessed.

It meant that unlike so many rock stars, he was celebrated principally for his music rather than his lifestyle. There was a vigorous rock'n'roll purity about his records that seemed to reduce the normal trappings of celebrity to an irrelevant side issue.

He had a reputation for being stubborn, a trait he captured on *I Won't Back Down*, the autobiographical 1989 hit on which he sang, "You can stand me up at the gates of hell/But I won't back down." But he mostly kept his head beneath the parapet and concentrated on expressing himself through his songs.

He famously fought a principled battle in which he threatened to go on strike when his record label hiked the price of his album *Hard Promises*. When they backed down his victory cast him as a champion of the people against corporate greed. On another occasion he punched a wall in frustration over a song's arrangement, breaking his left hand.

Yet outside such incidents his self-confessed "obsession" with what he did on stage seemed to offer thin gruel as tabloid fodder.

The reality was very different, for his private life was as turbulent and tempestuous as that of any wayward rock'n'roll star. Unbeknown to many, his backstory ranged from a tormented childhood to heroin addiction, and depression and a volatile marriage involving mental illness and threats of suicide.

When Petty and members of his closest family collaborated on a biography in 2015, his fans were genuinely shocked by the lurid detail when he told the writer Warren Zanes, "I was used to living in hell. I lived through being terribly abused as a kid and then I found myself in an abusive marriage. I spent a month not getting out of bed, just waking up and going, 'Oh, fuck.' The only thing that stopped the pain was drugs."

He had kept so much of his inner torment to himself that even

Fleetwood Mac's Stevie Nicks, his best friend in the music business for almost 40 years with whom he duetted on the 1981 hit *Stop Draggin' My Heart Around*, had no idea that he had been addicted to heroin. "We used to sit around and drink, and we did coke and smoked pot – and that was hard enough on us," she said. "But if you'd said to me that Tom Petty was doing that, I wouldn't have believed you for a second."

His addiction had its roots in a troubled marriage to Jane Benyo, whom he had met when they were 17 and he was an unknown aspiring musician in the boondocks of Florida. They began living together and married in 1974, before they moved – together with his band – to California in search of the big time. When success arrived, it meant Petty was hardly ever at home, and his wife turned to alcohol and drugs to ease her loneliness and isolation.

By then she had given birth to their first daughter, Adria, now a director of music videos. A second daughter, Annakim, who is an artist, followed.

On returning home one night from a recording session, Petty found his wife passed out in the hallway from a drink and drugs overdose. Concerned that she was fighting a losing battle with mental illness, he considered cancelling his 1986 tour with Dylan, but was persuaded to go ahead by Nicks, who joined him on the trip. When the tour was over he moved out of the family home and his wife became verbally abusive, phoning him obsessively and threatening suicide if he said he was hanging up.

Racked by guilt, he turned to heroin. His therapist told him: "People with your level of depression don't live. They kill themselves or someone else."

His friendship with Nicks provided a rock, although whether there was an affair is unclear. It was the only subject on which Petty was coy with his biographer. When asked if they had been a couple, he merely replied, "We had our times."

Petty's problems deepened when his home in the San Fernando Valley burnt down in 1987. Arson was suspected and he claimed to have "suspicions" as to who was responsible. Firefighters saved musical tapes and a guitar stored in his basement studio, but the rest of his possessions and all of his career memorabilia – including the signature "Mad Hatter" top hat he regularly sported on stage and in videos – were destroyed. "It felt like a death in the family," he said.

Yet he turned up for rehearsals with his band the next day and later claimed the disaster had been "really therapeutic". He subsequently built a new house on the same spot with his second wife Dana York, whose son from an earlier marriage, Dylan, he adopted.

Initially he kept his heroin addiction secret from her, but she stood by him after he was hospitalised. "They shoot this drug into you that literally drives the heroin out and your body goes into spasms. It forces the detox process," he said. When he woke up two days later, she was there and continued to support him while he received treatment at home. "I'd stepped on to a fast-moving train, but we were having moments of tremendous happiness. Chaos and darkness and all this happiness at the same time," she said.

He was born Thomas Earl Petty in 1950 in Gainesville, Florida, the first child of Earl and Kitty Petty. The family had a colourful history: his paternal grandfather was a logger from Georgia who married a Cherokee woman and killed a man with an axe after getting into a fight in a logging camp over interracial marriage. He fled across the state line to Florida, where Petty's father was raised.

An insurance salesman who had been in the air force, Earl Petty was a violent drunk. "I learnt to absolutely disappear and got the fuck away when he was around," Petty said. Once, when he was five years old, his father "beat me so bad that I was covered in raised welts, from my head to my toes," Petty recalled. On another occasion, he smashed his son's record collection to smithereens. "Dad, if you'll just leave me alone, I'll be a millionaire by the time I'm 35," his son told him.

He credited his mother with keeping "an element of civilisation in the house to show us there was more to life than rednecks". After meeting Presley, he persuaded her to buy him a guitar; with the violence and abuse all around him music was his "safe place".

By the early Seventies, he had formed the band Mudcrutch with Mike Campbell and Benmont Tench, who would work with him for the rest of his life in the Heartbreakers, the band he formed in Los Angeles in 1976.

In the 1980s, as rock music became increasingly corporate and manufactured, Petty's stripped-down, passionate take on the genre marked him out, along with Bruce Springsteen, as a standard bearer for authenticity in a sea of schlock. It led to him joining Dylan, George Harrison, Roy Orbison and Jeff Lynne as the youngest member of the short-lived ad hoc supergroup the Traveling Wilburys.

He was still touring with the Heartbreakers in 2017 and played his final show at the Hollywood Bowl a week before his death. When he announced the tour he had hinted that he was contemplating retirement. By its conclusion he had changed his mind and declared, "Why would we quit? The band is playing better than ever."

Tom Petty, musician, was born on October 20, 1950. He died following a cardiac arrest on October 2, 2017, aged 66

STEVE STRANGE

———•———

"New romantics" poster boy and singer whose life spiralled
into a tale of drug addiction and therapy

The Times, February 14, 2015

As the head boy of the "new romantics", Steve Strange was the flamboyant scene-maker of a colourful subculture that dominated early 1980s British pop music as a showily garish counter-reaction to the stylistic austerity of punk.

If punks were the roundheads in pop's civil war, the "new romantics" were the cavaliers, ushering in a restoration of glitz and glamour, with a delectably decadent flourish. Other acts associated with the scene included Strange's close friend Boy George and his group Culture Club, Duran Duran and Spandau Ballet.

The music Strange made with his band Visage – best exemplified by their eerie 1980 Top 10 hit *Fade to Grey* – pioneered the use of synthesisers and chilly, robotic vocals. However, the aesthetic of "new romanticism" was about style and fashion as much as music, and Strange and his camp followers were nicknamed "the Blitz Kids", a reference to the club in Covent Garden at the epicentre of the scene. Here, Strange acted as gatekeeper and style guru, imposing a strict door policy of admitting only "the weird and wonderful".

In practice, this meant a gender-bending look which drew its inspiration from glam-rockers such as David Bowie, but took pop exhibitionism to new levels of faux sophistication, with high-camp costumes that spanned sartorial history from Beau Brummell to Busby Berkeley, via anything that might be raided from the dressing-up box in grandma's attic. All that mattered was that the clothes were striking, colourful and outlandish.

"It was about showing your creative side, and about showing that you'd taken time and effort in what you had created," Strange said. "It was about classic style and being outrageous, but done with an element of taste."

Strange dressed variously as a pierrot, a porcelain-faced manikin, a sailor, Robin Hood, a Russian tsar, a Regency dandy and a lounge lizard, frequently mixing the styles together and crowning the theatrical look by teasing his hair into the most extravagantly shaped quiffs. Tourists gawped as lines of similarly attired exotic peacocks queued around the block in Covent Garden to gain admittance to the Blitz and the dance nights which Strange grandiloquently named "Club for Heroes".

Strange and his partner Rusty Egan later moved the venue to the Camden Palace, where the club ran for a further two years. By then he had become a ubiquitous 1980s pop fashion icon, who had appeared in a video with Bowie, been photographed by Helmut Newton and modelled for Jean Paul Gaultier.

However, fame exacted a heavy price. Regular use of cocaine – "just to keep me going" – developed into a heroin addiction that, at its height, he calculated was costing £150 per day.

For a while be believed that the drug "pushed aside all the problems and made them disappear". The reality, of course, was very different. By 1985, Visage had broken up, the "new romantics" scene was over and Strange was yesterday's news. "When all the limousines are there, you're staying in the top hotels, and your first cheque comes in for £250,000, you think this is going to go on forever," he recalled. "But when your album isn't going Top 5 and you're not having a number one worldwide, it's quite degrading because the limousine isn't a limousine anymore. You're lucky if it's a taxi."

Disillusioned, he left Britain for Ibiza, where he played a key part in the emergence of the island's house music scene and set up the Double Bass club, which hosted parties for celebrities including Sylvester Stallone.

Back in Britain, he became embroiled in controversy when the *News of the World* accused him of supplying drugs to Paula Yates and he was left devastated in 1997 by the suicide of her lover and his close friend, the INXS singer Michael Hutchence.

Within 24 hours, Strange's London home was mysteriously destroyed in a fire. He was not insured and, with his few remaining worldly belongings in a carrier bag, he retreated to South Wales to live with his mother and younger sister Tanya, in a house he had bought for them at the height of his fame.

A nervous breakdown and a spell in a psychiatric hospital followed. Heavily medicated on prescription drugs, including Prozac, he took to shoplifting and in 2000 was given a three-month suspended sentence for stealing a Teletubby toy for his nephew's birthday from Marks & Spencer. Labelled "a persistent thief" by the magistrate for what was his third offence, he avoided a custodial sentence only after his solicitor presented evidence that there was "a substantial risk of self-harm".

Strange later said: "When you're on that amount of medication you're really not responsible for your actions. I was thinking I was invincible, invisible, superhuman. Sometimes I'd be a different person, laughing hysterically like a nutcase to myself."

Attendance at a holistic healing centre weaned him off the medication and, living on benefits with his probation officer effectively operating as his manager, he began to rebuild his life and to make media appearances to talk about his fall from grace. As if to illustrate the extent of his decline, at least one interview was capped by the request for a £20 note "to cover the taxi home".

He published a candid autobiography, *Blitzed!*, in 2002, in which he addressed his ambiguous sexuality and confirmed that he had enjoyed relationships with both men and women. He never had children. He also returned to music and in 2013 released the first new Visage album in 29 years. He was admitted to hospital in late 2014 complaining of breathing difficulties and died of a heart attack while on holiday in Egypt.

Born Steven John Harrington in 1959 in Newbridge, Monmouthshire, his desire to be outrageous was evident from an early age. At 13, he made the papers when he was suspended from school for dyeing his hair orange and wearing a nose chain. It was, perhaps, a way of escaping an unhappy home life; after his mother walked out on his bullying father he was brought up in financially straitened circumstances. His father soon committed suicide. "It didn't affect me at all. I realised what he had put Mum through. I was the only one at the funeral who didn't cry," he said.

He cited attending a Sex Pistols gig in Caerphilly in 1976 as a life-changing moment and within a year he had moved to London, where he threw himself eagerly into the burgeoning punk scene. The Pistols' manager, Malcolm McLaren, employed him as a willing gofer and he joined the provocatively titled punk band the Moors Murderers.

He also briefly joined the Photon but Strange – as he had now named himself – was finding punk an increasingly drab straitjacket. In 1979 he formed Visage with members of Magazine and Ultravox, and the "new romantic" movement was born. For the next six years he was one of pop music's most high-profile faces, quaffing champagne with bangers and mash on the party circuit. He later came to look back on fame and the temptations that accompanied it with some bitterness: "It was the era of excess, the whole 'greed is good' thing. It was pure stupidity. It was a bit like being on a sinking ship and not realising it."

Steve Strange, singer, was born on May 28, 1959. He died of a heart attack on February 12, 2015, aged 55

EDDIE VAN HALEN

—————•—————

Virtuosic, bouffant-haired guitarist who played as fast as he lived and whose band, Van Halen, was so loud it went "all the way up to 15"

The Times, October 7, 2020

At the height of his reign as the fastest guitar-slinger in the west, Eddie Van Halen guested on Michael Jackson's *Beat It*, playing a typically razzle-dazzle solo and rearranging the song. The single went to No 1 and *Thriller*, on which the song featured, became the biggest-selling album of all time, but Van Halen waived his fee and told Jackson to regard it as a favour.

Van Halen could afford to be so generous because the band that carried his name was at the time the most successful heavy-rock act in the world. A month after Jackson's song had gone to No 1, Van Halen and his group were paid $1 million for a show in San Bernardino, California, the largest sum ever paid for a single concert performance at the time. The group then followed Jackson to the top of the singles chart with their own No 1, *Jump*, and the album *1984*, which sold 10 million copies.

The fastest and flashiest lead guitarist in the rock firmament, Van Halen was also one of the loudest. "I'm always pushing things past where they're supposed to be," he said. "When Spinal Tap was going to 11, I was going to 15."

The comment was apposite, for his band were said to have been one of the models for the spoof group immortalised in the 1984 film *This Is Spinal Tap*. Together with the flamboyant lead singer David Lee Roth, Van Halen formed a wild, hyperkinetic and sometimes preposterous partnership that rivalled Mick Jagger and Keith Richards, or Jimmy Page and Robert Plant.

As Roth high-kicked in leather chaps with a bare backside and the drummer and older brother Alex Van Halen flailed at a kit that included a flaming gong, Eddie would soar over the cacophony and then dive-bomb with pyrotechnic effects and a wide grin.

The bouffant locks sported by Van Halen and Roth inspired a new name for their style of screaming, pummelling heavy-riffing rock: hair metal. It was a look made for MTV and the group won best stage performance at the channel's first video awards. MTV was soon awash with Van Halen lookalike bands.

The virtuosity of Van Halen's guitar playing was beyond compare and at the height of his success he topped polls for best guitarist, above his own heroes and role models such as Page and Eric Clapton. He also developed a taste for hedonistic excess to match his success. Alongside the obligatory industrial quantities of booze, contract riders stipulated the dressing-room provision of packets of M&M's with all the brown sweets removed. On the road in Aberdeen, when the band heard that their debut album had gone gold, hotel rooms were trashed, in time-honoured rock'n'roll style, in the wild party that followed.

The chaotic scenes at concerts often made it seem as though the entire audience had been invited to the group's backstage parties, and lurid stories of drug taking and debauchery followed the band everywhere. When the *Spinal Tap* film opened in 1984, the group was not going to allow fiction to outdo reality and they organised a "win a lost weekend with Van Halen" competition. More than one million fans entered.

Inevitably such a lifestyle took its toll. There were fights within the band that led to Roth's acrimonious departure for a solo career in 1985 and a feud that carried on for 20 years. Van Halen's relationship with Roth's replacement, Sammy Hagar, went the same way. Van Halen's health suffered too, and his alcoholism grew so chronic that he admitted that he would wake up in the morning and "have to drink a six-pack of beer just to feel normal". He also struggled with cocaine addiction.

His stage antics led to chronic joint pain and a hip replacement in 1999. The next year he had part of his tongue removed due to cancer. He was declared clear but the disease later returned. His addictions contributed to the break-up of his first marriage to the actress Valerie Bertinelli, whom he had met at a Van Halen concert in Louisiana. They married in 1981, separated 20 years later, and their divorce was finalised in 2007. Their relationship was not improved when, against his wife's wishes, Van Halen took their son, Wolfgang, known as Wolfie, out of school at the age of 15 to become the bass player in his band.

His son survives him along with his second wife, Janie Liszewski. They met when she was working as a PR for a film production company for which he had been composing a soundtrack. She became the band's publicist and helped him finally overcome his substance abuse after several failed attempts at rehab. They married in 2009 with his son as his best man.

Edward Lodewijk Van Halen was born in Amsterdam in 1955, the younger son of Jan van Halen and Eugenia (née van Beers). His father was a classical musician who played clarinet, saxophone and piano and met his Java-born wife while on tour in Indonesia.

In 1962 the family moved to California, living in one room in a house shared with two other families. His mother worked as a maid and his father took a job as a janitor while seeking work as a musician. Both boys had piano lessons and Eddie won several competitions despite never learning to read music. He played by ear and was good enough to fool his tutor for years that he was sight-reading.

He was a nervous performer in front of an audience and claimed that when he was 12 his father gave him a shot of vodka and a cigarette to ease his nerves. It did the trick and started him on a lifetime of taking the stage in a state of inebriation. "I'd get so damn nervous and for so long it really did work," Eddie said. "I certainly didn't do it to party. I would do blow and I would drink, and then I would go to my room and write music."

When the two brothers discovered rock'n'roll, Eddie initially played drums and Alex the guitar, but they soon swapped instruments. "I never wanted to play guitar," Eddie insisted. "But my brother was a better drummer than me, so I said, 'Go ahead, take my drums. I'll play your damn guitar.'"

While still at school the brothers formed a band, known first as the Broken Combs and later as Mammoth. Roth was invited to join the group less for his voice and more for the fact that he had his own PA system, which saved them having to hire one.

It proved to be a teaming of inspiration as well as convenience and Mammoth soon built a reputation as the loudest, noisiest live act in Los Angeles. Gene Simmons of Kiss was impressed enough to produce a demo tape that included such future Van Halen classics as *Runnin' with the Devil* and *House of Pain*, but it was rejected by every label in town. A further blow came when they learnt that the name Mammoth was already registered to another band.

Without a record deal they appeared to be going nowhere. Looking for a new name, they toyed with Rat Salade, but settled on Van Halen at the suggestion of an uncharacteristically modest Roth. They were eventually signed by Warner Bros. and the group's 1978 debut album flew a defiant flag for traditional, bone-crunching hard rock at a time when the charts were dominated by punk and disco.

With Jimi Hendrix dead and the likes of Clapton and Page dismissed as dinosaurs by the punk insurgency, the world was ready for a new guitar hero and "flash Eddie" with his unique homemade guitar, which fans nicknamed Frankenstrat, fitted the bill to perfection. "All we're trying to do is put excitement back into rock'n'roll," he told *Rolling Stone* at the time. "A lot of people seem like they forgot what rock'n'roll is about. We're very energetic. We get up there and blaze."

The group's debut album eventually topped 10 million sales. Further multiplatinum albums followed with *Van Halen II, Women and Children First, Fair Warning* and *1984*.

The latter was the final album with Roth and the relationship between the two men was as complex and twisted as the dynamics between lead guitarist and lead singer often are. "I don't think the guy was ever real. I never felt any connection," Van Halen complained. Yet, after one of their periodic rapprochements, Van Halen claimed: "We never really hated each other. I think the press blew that out of proportion."

The group did not seem to miss Roth. The first album with Hagar as Roth's replacement, *5150*, released in 1986, went to No 1 in the Billboard chart. The band's next three albums featuring Hagar all followed suit, including *For Unlawful Carnal Knowledge* (1991), which generated some controversy over the acronym formed from its title. Despite the fuss the album won a Grammy award, although a hapless teenager in Arkansas was less fortunate when he was arrested for wearing a promotional T-shirt bearing the album's title. Van Halen did the decent thing and paid his fine.

In later years the role of lead singer in the group became a revolving door. After a falling out with Hagar, Roth was invited back. Inevitably they fell out again and Van Halen hired Gary Cherone of the metal band Extreme. The sole album he recorded with the band was poorly received, which led to the brief return of Hagar before another bust-up. Finally Roth resurfaced in 2012 on *A Different Kind of Truth*, his first album with the band in 28 years. The album reached No 2 and several successful tours followed.

Van Halen carried on playing until declining health finally forced him off the road. "I'm just a guitarist in a kick-ass rock'n'roll band," he said. "What more could I have asked for?"

Eddie Van Halen, guitarist, was born on January 26, 1955. He died of throat cancer on October 6, 2020, aged 65

CILLA BLACK

*Liverpudlian pop singer who rose to stardom with the Beatles
in the 1960s and became a national favourite on television*

The Times, August 3, 2015

As the undisputed queen of Saturday night television, Cilla Black joked that it was an unlikely role for someone who grew up in a house without a TV set and whose early screen appearances were, to say the least, unpromising. However, Black's winsome Scouse charm – punctuated by catchphrases such as "Lorra, lorra laughs" and "Ta-ra luv" – had become so bankable in the Eighties when she hosted primetime shows such as *Surprise, Surprise* and *Blind Date* on ITV, that she was disconcerted to find that her success as a television presenter eclipsed her earlier career as a singer. She had emerged from the Merseybeat scene in Liverpool in the early Sixties to become a star and the first woman to record two consecutive No 1 hits in the British charts with *Anyone Who Had a Heart* and *You're My World*.

As a gawky buck-toothed teenager, she was a determined wannabe bestriding Liverpool's febrile music scene, which centred on the Cavern Club. Brian Epstein managed her, while Paul McCartney and John Lennon, who wrote songs for her, treated her like their kid sister. Only Dusty Springfield and Lulu rivalled her among pop music's favourite "dolly birds" of the swinging 1960s.

Her early television appearances were far from smooth, but there was something about her effervescent, if accident-prone, character that producers found irresistible and, in 1968, BBC One commissioned her to present her own show, *Cilla*. With its theme song, *Step Inside Love*, written for her by McCartney, the show drew an audience of 22 million at its peak and ran for eight years.

Only a handful of celebrities have come to be known predominantly by their first name – Kylie Minogue is perhaps the best contemporary example – but Black's approachable, giggling girl-next-door style made the familiarity seem entirely natural. Unapologetically working-class, later referring to herself as "dead common", she was not to everybody's taste on the showbusiness circuit. After appearing with her at a variety performance, Noël Coward described her as "ghastly beyond belief".

She shrugged off such sneers, enjoying the riches that came her way as she was proclaimed to be the "Scousewife Superstar" at the height of her television fame. "You need a personality," she asserted. "You need to be able to join in. Live TV can sniff fakery a long way off, so you have to be real." If her achievements in popular culture were not particularly profound or thought-provoking, she was always "real" and was widely and genuinely loved for it.

She was born Priscilla Maria Veronica White in 1943 into a Catholic family with Irish and Welsh ancestry in Liverpool's run-down Scotland Road district, where sectarian brawling in the nearby pubs was common. Her father was a docker and her mother ran a market stall selling stockings and trinkets. They lived in a council flat above a barber's shop. There was no indoor lavatory and the family used a tin tub in the kitchen as a bath. The family had to make their own entertainment and Black's music-loving parents led by example.

Her father, John, who was known to his fellow dockworkers as

"Shiner" on account of his well-polished boots, would often bring friends back to the house after the pub on a Friday night with a takeaway of pig's trotters and chips for musical entertainment. He would play the mouth organ and his wife, also called Priscilla, would lead the singing in music-hall favourites. One evening he caught his daughter listening on the stairs. He lifted her up on to a table and said: "All right, queen, you sing something." She sang *Mammy* by Al Jolson. "From that moment on, I wanted to be a film star," she recalled.

At secondary school she adopted the red hair that was to become a trademark. "I would buy a dress and wear it back to front. I just wanted to be different, even when I was 13," she recalled. "I was mousey-blonde and I bought a Camilatone rinse from Woolie's, and I turned up bright red the next day. My headmistress sat me by a window with the sun blazing, to make an example of me." Undeterred, she would continue to touch up her red hair with a toothbrush every Friday night.

Swept along by the arrival of rock'n'roll, she took a part-time job as a cloakroom attendant at the Cavern Club, where she got to know the Beatles. Having left school at 15 with a report that declared "Priscilla is suitable for office work", she also took a secretarial course and landed a job in the typing pool at the construction company BICC.

At night, she would often slip out after her parents had gone to bed to sing and dance at local clubs. One of her earliest gigs came in 1960 when the Beatles were playing at the Iron Door club. She recalled: "My friends said, 'Give Cilla a go,' so John said, 'OK, Cyril, gerrup and sing.'" She sang *Summertime* and was soon performing with other local groups, including the Big Three at the Zodiac Club. A write-up in the local music paper *Mersey Beat* mistakenly referred to her as Cilla Black, rather than White. She decided that she preferred the new name and adopted it. John Lennon continued to call her "Swinging Cyril". She regularly permed Ringo Starr's mother's hair. On one occasion, smoke started rising from Mrs Starkey's perm, and Ringo exclaimed mournfully, "Me mam's on fire."

It was at the Zodiac Club in the early 1960s that she met Bobby Willis, an aspiring singer and songwriter whom she married in 1969 and who took over the management of her career from the time of Brian Epstein's death in 1967 until his own from lung cancer in 1999. It was a tempestuous relationship in the early days. She prevented Epstein from signing Bobby as a singer because she thought it would affect her career, and she admitted that her husband resented her early success.

However, they settled down to a happy marriage and she came to rely on him as the one person who would tell her the truth in a showbusiness world built on sycophancy. She also insisted that he sat in on all her interviews after one journalist in the 1960s had invited her "to stroke his war wound".

They had three sons: Robert, who was born in 1970 and took over as her manager when his father died; Ben, who was born in 1974; and Jack in 1980. A daughter, Ellen, was born prematurely in 1975 and lived for only two hours.

Black made an inauspicious start to her singing career. In 1961 John Lennon persuaded Epstein to audition her at the Majestic Ballroom in Birkenhead, where she was backed by the Beatles. Unfortunately, the group played the song in their own male vocal key, a register which she could not manage. "I was dreadful and I walked off the stage and got the next ferry home," she confessed. It was another year before Epstein heard her again, singing with a jazz band at the Blue Angel. Afterwards he approached her and asked why she had not sung like that at the Majestic. She replied that this time she was singing "with proper musicians and in the right key".

When Epstein agreed to take her on, her father – who was required to sign the contract because she was under 21 – told him he wanted her name changed back to White, otherwise his fellow dockers would not believe she was his daughter. Epstein declined and, according to Cilla, her father's workmates then nicknamed him The Frustrated Minstrel "because he didn't know if he was Black or White".

Her first single, *Love of the Loved,* was only a minor hit even though it was written by Lennon and McCartney, but the follow-up, *Anyone Who Had a Heart,* written by Burt Bacharach and Hal David for Dionne Warwick, was a million-seller that took her to No 1 in 1964. She and Epstein had to fight for her to be able to sing it after the record producer George Martin announced that he wanted Shirley Bassey to record the song instead. Black's version eclipsed Warwick's recording, to the chagrin of the American singer, who was still complaining bitterly about the "theft" of the song decades later. "Dionne was dead choked and she's never forgiven me to this day," Black admitted.

You're My World gave her another million-seller. It was followed into the charts by *It's for You*, which was written by Lennon and McCartney and also featured McCartney on piano. She then went head to head with the Righteous Brothers with a cover of *You've Lost That Lovin' Feelin'*, reaching No 2.

The Bacharach-David songbook provided her with another Top Ten hit with *Alfie* in 1966, but Epstein foresaw that changing tastes would not be good for her career and already had plans to reinvent her as a television star. After launching her first TV series, the young mother stopped touring. "I couldn't go back to travelling all over the country, singing, and have babies at the same time. So television was great for me, cos it meant one day a week I'd rehearse, do the show, then I was back at home."

Television exposure reinvigorated her chart career as *Step Inside Love, Conversations, Surround Yourself with Sorrow, If I Thought You'd Ever Change Your Mind* and *Something Tells Me (Something's Gonna Happen Tonight)* all gave her Top 20 hits in the 1970s.

Her place on the A-list seemed over until, in 1984, John Birt, head of LWT, saw her being interviewed and instantly knew she would make the perfect game-show host. He invited her to present *Surprise, Surprise,* a down-market magazine-format programme that featured emotional reunions of long-lost relatives and "Cillagrams", in which she turned up unannounced to mark special events with a song. The script did not always go according to plan; on one occasion while she was singing *Hooray for Holyhead* in the town's main street, the entire staff of the local branch of Woolworths came out to hear her. By the time they returned to work, the store had been looted.

In 1985 she took on another primetime show, *Blind Date*, which paired off couples who had never met. Black came up with the idea herself, urging LWT to make it after seeing a version in Australia. The nudging innuendo was inevitable but Black kept it all just within the realms of decency. She later revealed that the producer, Alan Boyd, had told her that when he was trying to come up with the right presenter for the show he had tried to think of the most sexless person on TV: "He said it was me."

By the mid-1980s Black had overtaken Esther Rantzen as the highest-paid woman in television, enabling her to laugh off critics who accused her of dumbing down the medium. "I didn't choose television. Television chose me," she said. "I was a bit of fun and a bit of Scouse rough and everybody liked me. I was normal. I could have been the kid next door. And then I turned into the auntie next door. And now I'm the granny next door."

She announced her retirement from *Blind Date* live on air in 2003. By then, there had been at least three marriages to have come out of the show and Black attended all of them.

A strong supporter of the Conservative party, she claimed that Margaret Thatcher had "put the great into Great Britain" and during the 1992 general election she appeared at a Conservative party rally with John Major. She was appointed OBE in 1997.

She maintained a ten-bedroomed house with a 17-acre garden in Denham, Buckinghamshire, which she bought in 1965 for £40,000. She also had a home in Marbella, Spain.

Praised for collaborating fully with a highly acclaimed "warts and all" dramatisation of her life on ITV in 2014, starring Sheridan Smith, Black marvelled at how the actress "sang so well with those false teeth in". She appeared on television only rarely in recent years because of crippling arthritis and deafness, which she said was brought on by having spent too much time in small, cacophonous nightclubs.

Although she was proud of her success as a TV presenter, she wanted to be known as a singer. "That's what I want on my gravestone. 'Here lies Cilla Black, singer, not TV presenter.'"

Cilla Black, OBE, singer, was born on May 27, 1943. She died on August 2, 2015, aged 72

GERRY RAFFERTY

Singer and songwriter whose hit Baker Street *made him a fortune, but who fell out with his colleagues and battled with alcohol*

Gerry Rafferty (right) with bandmate Joe Egan (left)

The Times, January 5, 2011

Gerry Rafferty made some of the most appealing folk-tinged pop of the late 1960s and 1970s, including *Stuck in the Middle with You* and *Baker Street*, both of which remain radio staples to this day.

After beginning his recording career as a duo with Billy Connolly in the Humblebums, he tasted success with the group Stealers Wheel before enjoying further hits as a solo singer. He was also a songwriter of considerable sensitivity with an enviable melodic flair, which at its best recalled Paul McCartney.

But it was *Baker Street* in particular with which he achieved renown and it provided him with an endless supply of royalty cheques, reportedly logging more than four million radio plays since its release in 1978.

In later years he became something of a recluse and disappeared from the music scene. His rare forays back into the limelight tended to involve drunken incidents that were salaciously reported by the tabloid press, invariably quoting back at him the lyrics of *Baker Street*, which told of an unsuccessful attempt to "give up the booze and the one-night stands". He received treatment for alcoholism and a drink-related liver problem.

Born Gerald Rafferty in Paisley, Renfrewshire, into an Irish-Scottish family, his father was deaf but refused to allow the impediment to stop him singing Irish rebel songs. These fed into the young Gerald's early musical experience – alongside Catholic hymns, traditional Scottish folk music, skiffle and other 1950s pop styles.

By the age of 21 he was singing and playing guitar in Scottish folk clubs by night while working in the shipyards by day. On the folk circuit he met Billy Connolly, who was at the time in a duet with the guitarist Tam Harvey called the Humblebums, combining folk-styled songs with a joke-filled stage patter that would lead to his future career as a stand-up comedian. The duo had already recorded an album for Nat Joseph's Transatlantic Records, one of Britain's leading folk labels of the era, and when Rafferty played Connolly some of his songs, he was immediately invited to join.

The Humblebums were a trio for only a few short months. Harvey, who was not a songwriter and felt rather eclipsed by Rafferty, soon left and Rafferty and Connolly went on to record two albums of great charm, *The Humblebums* (1969) and *Open Up the Door* (1970). Both showed that if Connolly was the dominant personality on stage, Rafferty was by far the better singer and infinitely the superior songwriter.

He wrote 13 of the songs on the two albums, compared with Connolly's ten, and his compositions numbered most of the finest moments, including *I Can't Stop Now*, *All the Best People Do It*, and *Her Father Didn't Like Me Anyway*.

It was evident to both men that their futures lay in very different directions and the Humblebums broke up in 1971. While Connolly pursued a new career as a comedian, Rafferty reaffirmed his songwriting class on the solo album *Can I Have My Money Back?* which featured distinctive cover art by John Patrick Byrne, with whom he would forge an enduring working relationship. Among those playing and singing on the album was the session man and songwriter Joe Egan, who had been at school with Rafferty in Paisley.

Soon after the album's release the pair combined to form Stealers Wheel. Accompanied by a backing group of constantly changing personnel, Egan was musically a better match for Rafferty's skills than Connolly.

Stealers Wheel were also more rock-orientated than the Humblebums, their close harmonies leading them to being dubbed Britain's answer to Crosby, Stills and Nash, and the American producers Jerry Leiber and Mike Stoller, who had written *Hound Dog* and *Jailhouse Rock* for Elvis Presley, were brought in to produce.

With another eye-catching cover design by Byrne (who went on to create the artwork for all three Stealers Wheel albums), their self-titled debut included *Stuck in the Middle with You*, an infectious song with an irresistible hook co-written by Rafferty and Egan, which made the Top Ten in both Britain and America in 1973.

However, the relationship between the two men was volatile and Rafferty walked out of the group before the album could reach the shops. He was temporarily replaced by Luther Grosvenor of Spooky Tooth, only to be coaxed back a few months later by the group's management, which recognised that his songwriting skills were critical to Stealers Wheel's success.

Leiber and Stoller returned to produce a second album, *Ferguslie Park*, in 1974. Named after a district of the Stealers Wheel duo's home town of Paisley, it was another wonderfully inventive and melodic record, but despite including such minor hit singles as *Everyone's Agreed That Everything Will Turn Out Fine* and *Star*, the album sold disappointingly.

The tension between Rafferty and Egan grew increasingly poisonous and an 18-month delay ensued before Stealers Wheel's third and final album, *Right or Wrong*. By the time that was eventually released in 1975, the group had already ceased to exist.

Worse, the acrimony between the two was so bad that their respective management entered into a legal dispute that prevented either man from recording.

The impasse was not resolved until 1978, when Rafferty was finally able to release the album *City to City*, which included the hit *Baker Street* that reached No 3 in Britain and No 2 in the US. The album, which also featured such fine songs as *Home and Dry* and *Right Down the Line*, went on to sell almost six million copies, and in the summer of 1978 toppled the *Saturday Night Fever* soundtrack from the top of the American charts.

The follow-up album, *Night Owl*, also sold well and included three hit singles in the title track, *Days Gone Down* and *Get It Right Next Time*. However, *Snakes and Ladders* (1980), *Sleepwalking* (1982) and *North and South* (1988) had poor sales and included no further hits, although Rafferty did co-produce *Letter from America*, the Proclaimers' chart-topping single in 1987.

Somewhat surprisingly, Rafferty was reunited with Egan in 1992 when his old friend and foe sang on several tracks on his solo album, *On a Wing and a Prayer*. That same year, the use of *Stuck in the Middle with You* in Quentin Tarantino's film *Reservoir Dogs* revived interest in Stealers Wheel, although fans hoping for a full-scale reunion were disappointed.

A solo album, *Another World*, appeared in 2000 but Rafferty, who had emigrated to California in the 1980s, declined to tour in support of it.

He was seldom seen in public in later years and rumours circulated of his increasingly eccentric behaviour. He was said to be paranoid and depressed and he entered into a bizarre feud with his elder brother, Jim, who became so exasperated that he set up a website in which he launched virulent attacks on his brother, calling him "the Great Gutsby" and "my psychotic sibling".

In 2006 he was taken by police to a drying-out clinic after they had been called to escort him from an aircraft on a flight to Scotland. He was reportedly so drunk that a wheelchair was required to move him from the plane. In August 2008, he was committed to St Thomas' Hospital in London after police had again been summoned when he wrecked a hotel room in the capital after a whisky binge.

A few days later he absconded from the hospital leaving his belongings behind. A missing person's report was filed, but he turned up some months later, issuing a press release in which he claimed that he was living in Italy and announcing a "new" album entitled *Life Goes On.*

It was another attempt to throw everyone off his scent. He was actually living in Dorset and the album was hardly new at all, but contained remastered versions of songs from old albums and a brace of well-known Christmas carols. It was his final release and marked a sad end to the derailed career of a consummate songwriter who at one time had the pop world at his feet.

Gerry Rafferty, singer and songwriter, was born on April 16, 1947. He died on January 4, 2011, aged 63

GLENN FREY

———————•———————

Drug-fuelled hedonist who was a founding member of the Eagles,
becoming the chief architect of their country-rock sound

Glenn Frey (second from left) with bandmates Bernie Leadon, Don Henley,
Randy Meisner and Don Felder

The Times, January 18, 2016

Their immaculate harmonies and perfectly sculpted soft-rock songs evoked a carefree lifestyle rooted in the hippy dream: Glenn Frey and the Eagles epitomised the laid-back cool of 1970s California. The combination of highly polished songcraft and outlaw chic made them one of the biggest-selling groups in rock history. Yet there was a dark underbelly to their success – the product of different egos within the band battling for creative control.

As the group's celebrity grew, breezily innocent songs with titles such as *Take It Easy* and *Peaceful Easy Feelin'* gave way to *Take It to the Limit* and *Life in the Fast Lane.* Enjoying the fruits of their labours to the hilt, they took to drinking, drugging and fighting like debauched champions. "Led Zeppelin might argue with us, but I think we had the greatest travelling party of the 1970s," Frey boasted. "The wine was the best, the drugs were good and the women were beautiful."

As Frey and his bandmates made the transition from scuffling on the fringes of the Los Angeles music scene to revelling in riches, the journey from innocence to decadence was reflected in their songs. Frey's yearning melody on *Lyin' Eyes* disguised an account of sleazy marital cheating; *Hotel California*, with its "mirrors on the ceiling, pink champagne on ice", was given a burnished tune that turned an enigmatic tale of disenchantment into one of rock music's most uplifting anthems. The contradictions were delicious: "This could be Heaven or this could be Hell," they sang.

Don Henley, with whom Frey founded the group in 1971, credited the guitarist, singer and songwriter as the chief architect of the Eagles' sound. "We gave Glenn a nickname, the Lone Arranger," he said. "He had a vision about how our voices could blend." Frey also had a hard-nosed, go-getting attitude that belied the mellifluous arrangements – one that he had learnt growing up on the mean streets of Detroit. Even the loyal Henley, who remained a lifelong friend, described him as "bull-headed".

The discordant notes offstage failed to dent their popularity. An executive at their record company once remarked: "These guys could sing a chorus of 'shit stinks on shinola' and still sell a million copies." Frey and the Eagles scored four consecutive chart-topping albums and five No 1 singles; their greatest hits album sold 32 million certified copies. Until Michael Jackson's *Thriller*, it was the bestselling album of all time. *Hotel California* sold a further 22 million, making the Eagles the only act to appear twice in the sales chart of the world's Top 10 albums.

When the group eventually crash-landed, it was in spectacular fashion – and Frey was at the controls. The implosion came after a benefit concert in 1980 for the Democratic senator Alan Cranston at Long Beach. Frey's relationship with the lead guitarist Don Felder had hit a low point, and he was infuriated when – at a press conference before the show – Felder said he did not really care about Cranston and that to him it was just another gig. By the time the

Eagles took the stage, Frey had worked himself into a rage. After the first song, he walked over to Felder and told him, "When this show is done, I'm going to kick your ass." The sound technicians cut Frey's microphone to prevent the audience from hearing his threat. Throughout the performance, he walked over to Felder between every number, informing him how many songs were left before he got his ass kicked.

After *Best of My Love* had brought the crowd to its feet and the group had left the stage, Frey cornered Felder on a stairway and charged at him. Felder wielded an acoustic guitar in self-defence, which in the mêlée smashed into a wall – with the breaking strings and splintering wood sending a clang through the arena. The rest of the band joined in the scuffle and, according to producer Bill Szymczyk, gave a bravura display of "the fine art of turning acoustic guitars into kindling wood". It took a dozen roadies to pull the warring factions apart. The next day, Frey rang the Eagles' manager, Irving Azoff, and told him he would never play with the group again. (It came as no surprise to Azoff, who once said: "The Eagles talked about breaking up from the day I met them.") The incident was known as the "Long Night at Wrong Beach". In an interview more than 30 years later, Frey admitted: "I could have handled some things a lot better. We were young and I had a temper."

The bust-up led to Henley's infamous comment that the band would only reunite "when hell freezes over". Frey added that fans should "rule out any possibility of putting the Eagles back together for a Lost Youth and Greed tour", and flew to Hawaii for a holiday to recover from, as he described it, "a nine-year fame and fortune bender".

Fourteen years later, Frey, Henley and Felder – plus guitarist Joe Walsh and bassist Timothy B. Schmit – reunited for a series of concerts. The baby boomers who had bought the Eagles' records in the 1970s were now bankers, captains of industry and corporate titans, and they eagerly snapped up the tickets. The sold-out tour grossed $75 million; the live album that followed topped the charts and sold more than 10 million copies. They could hardly have called it the "Lost Youth and Greed Tour". Instead, both the concerts and the album commemorating the reunion were titled *Hell Freezes Over*.

Glenn Lewis Frey was born in 1948 in Detroit, where his father worked on a car production line and his mother was a cook in the canteen at General Motors. He took piano lessons from the age of five –"That alone could get you beat up after school in suburban Detroit," he said – but switched to guitar after seeing the Beatles perform when he was 15. Frey later said that it was the sight of the girls in the audience going wild that made him hungry for fame.

Frey eventually got married in 1983 – to the Texan heiress Janie Beggs – and announced his conversion to monogamy by declaring, "The best feeling in the world is when you love somebody, not that you've got eight or nine girls who would walk in front of a freight train for you." After they divorced, he often dedicated the song *Lyin' Eyes* to his first wife, whom he called "the Plaintiff". He married for a second time, in 1990, to the dancer and choreographer Cindy Millican. They had a daughter and two sons.

During the early days of his career, in 1968, Frey left his native city and headed to Los Angeles. He began hanging out at the Troubadour – a well-known musicians' haunt on Sunset Strip. It was there that he met JD Souther, with whom he formed the band Longbranch Pennywhistle; Jackson Browne, with whom he would later write *Take It Easy*; and Linda Ronstadt. The original line-up of the Eagles – Frey, Henley, Randy Meisner and Bernie Leadon – first came together as Ronstadt's backing group. The four then decided to form their own band, initially calling themselves Teen King and the Emergencies.

By the time the Eagles released their fourth album, *One of These Nights*, in 1975, they were accustomed to wealth, fame and excess. "Glenn and I were living in a house that had belonged to Dorothy Lamour, up in the hills with a 360-degree view," Henley recalled. "We were the odd couple. I was sort of the housekeeper, the tidy one. He was the loveable slob." Their nights were spent out on the town – "dudes on the rampage", as Henley put it.

To amuse themselves on tour, the group invented their own high-rolling game called "Eagle Poker". Like most other things they dabbled in, it became addictive: at one point they took a break mid-tour to fly to the Bahamas for no other purpose than to hold a non-stop two-day card game. Frey also developed a cocaine habit, regularly snorting what he called an "eight ball" – a massive eighth of a gram, which he hoovered up in seconds. It reportedly resulted in him needing to have the inside of his nose surgically rebuilt.

While the Eagles were hors de combat in the 1980s, Frey launched a successful solo career and had a hit with *The Heat Is On*, used as the main theme in the film *Beverly Hills Cop*. After the group re-formed, he continued to record and tour with the Eagles until intestinal surgery forced him off the road in 2015. Two years earlier, the band had raked in an estimated $100 million in 12 months with their "History of the Eagles" tour.

Throughout their years of hedonism, the Eagles remained sticklers for detail in the studio. While recording the opening line of *Lyin' Eyes* ("City girls just seem to find out early how to open doors with just a smile"), Frey took three days getting the word "city" just right. "It would either be a little early, or a little late, or the 'T' would be too sharp," Felder said of his bandmate's efforts. "It took a long time, but every time that word goes by now and I hear it, I can appreciate the time and dedication and perseverance that it took to get it perfect."

Glenn Frey, guitarist, was born on November 6, 1948. He died of pneumonia on January 18, 2016, aged 67

IAN DURY

———————•———————

Acceptable face of punk rock, who enjoyed brief chart success before branching out into acting

The Times, March 29, 2000

Short, stocky and afflicted with polio in childhood, which left him with a limp, Ian Dury was never anyone's idea of a conventional pop star. His music was similarly nonconformist, but with his band the Blockheads, his lyrical and often risqué wit gave him a string of hit singles in the late 1970s, including the chart-topping *Hit Me with Your Rhythm Stick*, and made him an unlikely cult figure on the punk scene.

Although he continued to be regarded with affection by the music industry, the hits dried up in the 1980s and Dury turned to other forms of expression, including acting. He wrote a play, and his Cockney vowels were much in demand for television voiceovers, yet music remained close to his heart. He made an acclaimed comeback album after a diagnosis of colonic cancer in 1998, and continued to work, making light of living with a terminal condition.

Ian Dury was an Essex lad, born into a working-class family in Upminster during the Second World War. His father was a bus driver and his mother a health visitor, but they separated when he was young. At the age of seven he contracted polio and spent two years in hospital before he was sent to a special school.

At hospital he discovered the harsh realities of death, disability and sickness, and claimed he once joined two other patients trying to hang another from a tree. "We knew he wouldn't mind. He went a horrible colour and then we let him down," he said. He hated school and kept running away, but he was bright and despite the gap in his education he eventually made it to grammar school and then to the Royal College of Art.

He abandoned the idea of a career as an artist when he realised he was not good enough to compete with the very best. "I was a good draughtsman but I wasn't a very good painter. I got good enough as an artist to know I would never be happy. I'd always be frustrated because I'd never be that good," he said years later.

He lectured briefly at Canterbury College of Art and formed his first band, Kilburn and the High Roads, in 1970, initially on a part-time basis. They turned professional as part of the so-called pub-rock scene of the early 1970s, when they played regularly on the London circuit alongside bands such as Brinsley Schwarz, Ducks Deluxe and Bees Make Honey. Few of them ever made the transition from bar-room to concert hall, and Dury and his band had their share of ill-luck. An album recorded for Warner Bros. was not released, while an album for Pye made little impact. Eventually the band split in 1976, mainly because Dury's doctor had ordered him off the road for health reasons.

He spent a year writing songs with his old friend Chas Jankel and was in the right place at the right time when Dave Robinson, who had managed Kilburn and the High Roads, set up his own label, Stiff Records, as a bridge between the pub-rock scene and the exploding punk movement. Dury signed as a solo artist and formed the Blockheads as a backing band. His first solo single, the anthemic *Sex & Drugs & Rock & Roll*, became his calling card but was not a hit; it was enlisted for AIDS education in 1987 with his approval: "Two of these just became more dangerous," he said. The follow-up, *Sweet Gene Vincent*, was no more successful although he finally reached the Top Ten at the third attempt with *What a Waste*.

His first solo album *New Boots and Panties!!* was, of its kind, an instant classic, full of songs inhabited by outrageous characters such as Clever Trevor, Plaistow Patricia and Billericay Dickie, as well as Nina, who, as rhyme would have it, was obscener than a seasoned-up hyena and enjoyed sex in the back of a Ford Cortina.

Dury's scatological poetry and rhyming slang were a more knowing take on the anarchy of punk, with references far wider than teenage rebellion, and musically his hybrid sound was considerably more accomplished than the usual three-chord thrash.

He toured with the legendary comedian Max Wall, writing a song for him, *England's Glory*, and over Christmas 1978 he had his biggest success with *Hit Me with Your Rhythm Stick*, which reached No 1 and was to be a minor hit twice more in subsequent years in remixed versions.

A further single, *Reasons to be Cheerful, Part 3*, reached No 3, appropriately enough, and his second solo album, *Do It Yourself*, was kept from the top slot only by Abba; but by the end of 1980 Dury's days in the charts were largely behind him.

There were a number of reasons, including a backlash against punk and because he was in some ways unfairly seen as a novelty act. Despite a tour supporting Lou Reed, his career had failed to take off in America: his songs were too Anglo-centric and ironic for mass tastes. Nor did he help his cause with the single *Spasticus Autisticus*, a criticism of the United Nations Year of the Disabled in 1981. Most radio stations refused to play it and his record label Polydor withdrew it after a month.

A further album, *Lord Upminster*, was recorded in the Bahamas with the Jamaican rhythm section Sly and Robbie replacing the

Blockheads, but there were more problems with Polydor in 1984 over 4,000 *Weeks' Holiday*. The album was delayed for six months because the company demanded the removal of an obscenely titled song and another about Billy Butlin. A censored version finally appeared, but it was to be his last solo album for eight years.

Dury meanwhile looked in new directions. He wrote the theme songs for two series of ITV's *Adrian Mole*, worked for UNICEF and made his acting debut opposite Bob Geldof in *Number One*. Further parts followed in Roman Polanski's *Pirates* and with Bob Dylan in the ill-fated, unfettered *Hearts of Fire*.

He appeared in the BBC series *King of the Ghetto* and toured in repertory in *Talk of the Devil*. He also wrote a musical, *Apples*, which was staged at the Royal Court (rather a disaster, he later confessed), and turned down the chance to write the lyrics for Andrew Lloyd Webber's *Cats*. During the 1990s he appeared in the movie *Split Second* and began hosting ITV's *Metro* series. He made occasional live musical appearances, but his 1992 comeback album *The Bus Driver's Prayer and Other Short Stories* was largely ignored. His 1998 album *Mr Love Pants* was better received, partly because interest in him had been grimly revived by the news that he had terminal cancer. Typically he chose to break the story in the *Mirror* under the headline "I am dying of cancer – but I've still got reasons to be cheerful".

He said: "You don't have cancer; it has you. The 'chemo' won't get rid of it. But it's another lease of – well, however long it is. You just don't know, but it's better than being hit by a bus tomorrow; you have time to sort yourself out."

A strong advocate of disability awareness, he travelled with the star of the moment Robbie Williams into the Sri Lankan war zone to highlight efforts to vaccinate children against polio.

He had lost his first wife, Betty, to cancer, and he amazed everyone around him by the fortitude and good humour with which he bore his illness, performing as recently as last month.

Ian Dury, singer, songwriter and actor, was born on May 12, 1942. He died on March 27, 2000, aged 57

---•---

Flamboyant pioneer of rock'n'roll who revolutionised music with hits such as Tutti Frutti *and influenced everyone from Jimi Hendrix to the Beatles*

The Times, May 11, 2020

No word in the dictionary summed up the uninhibited frenzy of rock'n'roll better than Little Richard's "A-wop-bop-a-loo-bop-a-wop-bam-boom".

He kicked off his first big hit, *Tutti Frutti,* with the feral cry in 1955, and pounding his piano and singing in a high, explosive voice that seemed to be permanently on the edge of hysteria, he made other early rock'n'rollers such as Bill Haley and Elvis Presley sound tame by comparison.

He followed it with a string of equally wild hits including *Long Tall Sally, Rip It Up* and *Good Golly Miss Molly.* "A-wop-bop-a-loo-bop-a-wop-bam-boom" ended up in *Webster's Dictionary* as a synonym for rock'n'roll.

Little Richard's singing style owed much to the gospel music he heard as a child.

It is impossible to overstate his importance in the history of popular music. When he was placed eighth in a list of the greatest performers of all time by *Rolling Stone* magazine, all of the seven ranked above him had been heavily influenced by him.

To Paul McCartney, who chose *Tutti Frutti* as one of his eight records on BBC Radio 4's *Desert Island Discs,* he was simply "the king of rock'n'roll". Keith Richards of the Rolling Stones said appearing on stage with him in 1963 was the greatest moment of his life. David Bowie went out and bought a saxophone after hearing one of Little Richard's records and Jimi Hendrix, who cut his teeth playing in Little Richard's backing band, said that his ambition was to do with a guitar what Little Richard had done with his voice.

His theatrical and impassioned style owed much to gospel and the rabble-rousing of the southern evangelists that he grew up hearing as a boy. However, he invested the preaching style with an almost demonic edge, singing with a lack of inhibition that took rock'n'roll to places it had never been before.

Like many of the early rock'n'rollers, the hits soon dried up, but he was not so much a victim of changing musical fashions as torn apart by his own internal struggles. As a boy he had hoped to become a preacher and, at the height of his success, he became convinced that he was heading for damnation. At the same time as Chuck Berry was lost to rock'n'roll while he served a jail sentence, Little Richard went missing in action by enrolling at a theological college and abandoning secular music to tour with an evangelical show.

By the time he returned, in the early 1960s, popular music was changing rapidly, but the beat groups who were about to eclipse the first generation of rock'n'roll stars were all in awe of him. The Beatles took second place to him on the bill when he toured Britain in October 1962 and the following year the Rolling Stones supported him. Mick Jagger admitted he could not compete. "I heard so much about the audience reaction, I thought there must be some exaggeration," he said. "But it was all true. He drove the whole house into a complete frenzy."

Little Richard never recovered the chart dominance he enjoyed in the 1950s but he continued to tour endlessly, singing his old hits, a revered figure who found an accommodation between evangelism and rock'n'roll by distributing biblical literature to his audiences. When he appeared at a "Legends of Rock'n'Roll" show at Wembley in 1998 with Chuck Berry and Jerry Lee Lewis, the *Times* review of the concert reported that he had spent much of his appearance fee on paying for a Bible to be placed on every seat in the arena.

He finally retired from touring in 2013. "I think my legacy should be that when I started in showbusiness, there wasn't no such thing as rock'n'roll," he said. "When I started with *Tutti Frutti*, that's when rock really started rocking." He was not boasting. It was simply a statement of fact.

He is survived by a son, Danny Jones, who worked for him as a bodyguard and was adopted by Richard and his wife, Ernestine Harvin, whom he met at an evangelical rally in 1957. They married two years later and divorced in 1964. He claimed the marriage failed because he was gay. He never remarried. He later told a biographer that he was "omnisexual" but also denounced homosexuality as "against the way God wants you to live".

Richard Wayne Penniman was born in 1932 in Macon, Georgia, the third of 12 children. His parents Leva Mae (née Stewart) and Charles "Bud" Penniman were God-fearing Baptists. His father, a stonemason and a church deacon, supplemented his income by bootlegging, and owned a nightclub called the Tip in Inn. There were frequent police raids on the family home in search of illicit liquor, but the trade enabled Richard to grow up a level above the abject poverty that he saw all around him in the Deep South.

The family had a gospel group called the Penniman Singers, who performed in local churches, and at an early age Richard displayed a loud, screaming voice that earned him the family nickname "War Hawk".

By the age of 10 he had became a child "healer" and was soon preaching as well as singing gospel songs. At 14 he ran away from home and sang with itinerant gospel groups, and in a more secular style in the Black segregated dance halls of Atlanta, as well as in the city's homosexual red-light district, where he became known as Little Richard.

Tragedy struck the family in 1951 when his father was murdered, and he returned to Macon to help support his mother and siblings by washing dishes. He had not given up on music, though, and at 18 made his first recording for RCA Victor.

In 1954, the same year that Elvis Presley made his first recordings for Sun Records in Memphis, Richard cut a demo tape that landed on the desk of Art Rupe, the owner of Specialty Records. Rupe was sufficiently impressed to put him in the studio with the producer Robert "Bumps" Blackwell, who had helped to set Ray Charles on the path to stardom.

At their first recording in New Orleans in early 1955, they were recording a slow blues number when Richard began pounding out an irrepressible boogie-woogie rhythm over which he screamed a lewd lyric he had picked up when singing in the red-light district.

The song was *Tutti Frutti* and "A-wop-bop-a-loo-bop-a-wop-bam-boom!" was about to explode.

There was still a racial divide in American music, however, and although Richard's version of *Tutti Frutti* reached No 17 in the charts, the White singer Pat Boone had a bigger hit with an anodyne cover version in which all of the original's sexual exuberance was removed.

Richard's follow-up, *Long Tall Sally*, was characterised by the same speeded-up boogie-woogie piano and a saxophone solo by Lee Allen that screamed as maniacally as Richard's voice. Once again the song was covered by Boone, although this time Richard's original fared better than the sanitised White copy, making No 6 in the American charts, two places higher than his imitator.

It was a significant breakthrough in the desegregation of pop music and by the time of his third hit, *Rip It Up*, Richard easily outperformed the White copy, this time by Bill Haley. After that, he had the field to himself, as the practice of bland Caucasian copies of Black records was dropped.

Over the next two years Richard had an unstoppable string of hits in the same sexually charged style, including *Lucille, Slippin' and Slidin', Jenny, Jenny, Good Golly, Miss Molly, Keep A-Knockin'* and *The Girl Can't Help It*, the title track from a 1956 film in which he also appeared.

On stage he was wild and flamboyant. Flashily dressed, he did not so much play his piano as assault it, and the sexual energy he generated produced an extraordinary reaction. It all came to an abrupt end in late 1957 when he announced, during a tour of Australia, that he was quitting rock'n'roll in order to train for the ministry.

One story has it that he had been scared half to death on a rough flight across the wild Australian outback and had prayed to God for deliverance. When his plane landed safely in Sydney, he supposedly threw his expensive jewellery into the harbour and cancelled the rest of the tour.

Back home, he enrolled at a college run by the Church of God of the Ten Commandments in Alabama. For the next few years Specialty Records was reduced to putting out old material recorded before his "retirement", while Richard himself recorded gospel songs for another label.

Yet he did not settle easily into life as a minister and by 1962 he was back and as wild as ever. Two years later, a young guitarist known at the time as Maurice James joined his band. The world later got to know him as Jimi Hendrix and much of his showmanship was derived from observing Richard at close quarters. Richard also had a profound influence on Otis Redding and James Brown, both of whom admitted that when they started out they were attempting to sound like him.

Although he continued recording, in 1977, following the death of a much-loved nephew in a violent fight over a drug deal, Richard once more repented of his rock'n'roll lifestyle and returned full-time to evangelism, proclaiming that it was not possible to sing the Devil's music and serve God at the same time.

Yet he was soon back again. The struggle between his religion and his rock'n'roll lifestyle, which included copious drug abuse and promiscuity, was later graphically chronicled in Charles White's authorised biography *The Life and Times of Little Richard: The Quasar of Rock*.

After accepting a role in the film *Down and Out in Beverly Hills*, he wrote the song *Great Gosh A'Mighty* for its soundtrack, which returned him to the charts. Further acting roles followed, including an appearance in *Miami Vice*, and he was a prolific guest performer on other artists' records, such as the U2/BB King hit *When Love Comes to Town*. As a minister he also officiated at the funerals of several old friends from the music industry, including Wilson Pickett and Ike Turner.

For the rest of his life he was torn between the stage and the pulpit. "Although I sing rock'n'roll, God still loves me," he said in 2009. "I'm a rock'n'roll singer, but I'm still a Christian." In one of his more reflective moments, he observed: "I did what I felt, and I felt what I did, at all costs."

Little Richard, musician, was born on December 5, 1932. He died of bone cancer on May 9, 2020, aged 87

TERRY HALL

Frontman of ska band whose hits such as Ghost Town *perfectly captured a period of social decay and disillusion in Britain*

Terry Hall (centre) with Fun Boy Three bandmates Lynval Golding and Neville Staple

The Times, December 20, 2022

In the middle of the Specials' hit *Ghost Town,* the lead singer Terry Hall let out a cry of anguish that said every bit as much as the song's doom-laden lyrics.

Released in 1981 at a time when Britain was in the grip of recession, unemployment was at its highest levels since the 1930s and there was rioting on the streets, the song seemed to echo a moment of crisis in the national psyche – and Hall's mournful, deadpan delivery as he sang "can't go on no more" captured the sense of decay and disillusion.

Yet the song's success made the singer deeply uneasy. "*Ghost Town* was No 1 for weeks when all the riots were going on," he later recalled. "All this money and all these gold discs were floating in from this record about how terrible everything was. Something about it just wasn't right."

Backstage as they prepared to perform the song on *Top of the Pops*, Hall announced that he was leaving the band, seemingly traumatised not only by the highly charged politics of the divisive times but equally by the spotlight into which the rapid rise of the Specials had unexpectedly thrust him.

Formed in Coventry in 1979, the Specials went on to score six consecutive Top Ten hits in little more than 18 months, including *Gangsters*, *A Message to You Rudy*, *Rat Race* and *Stereotype*. In doing so they had launched a musical genre and an entire youth movement known as 2-Tone, a fusion of Jamaican ska and punk elements.

The name referenced both a fashion style and the multiracial nature of the group. For a time, the Specials' 2 Tone Records became Britain's most successful label, as they signed similar-sounding groups including Madness, the Beat and the Selecter, all of whom followed them into the charts.

However, the intensity of their sudden success took its toll. Aligning with the Rock Against Racism movement, the Specials found themselves in the eye of a storm as their highly politicised stance made them a target for National Front thugs. The group's Black guitarist Lynval Golding was badly injured in a racist attack in south London, and Specials gigs became a magnet for trouble. Fighting regularly broke out in the audience and at a gig in Cambridge in 1980 Hall and Jerry Dammers, the keyboard player, were arrested, charged with incitement to riot and fined after intervening in a fracas between fans and security staff.

When not battling with neo-Nazis in the audience, Hall also found it difficult to deal with his "own side" as the Specials garnered a young following that was fervent in its devotion to all things 2-Tone.

"Everything was a drama," Hall complained. "You couldn't get any space, not even for an hour or two, because wherever you went there were these lads who'd travelled miles to see you play and didn't have anywhere to stay, so you had to put them up in your room and then you had to sit up all night with them, talking about the fucking Specials."

The pressure took its toll on Hall's already fragile mental health. On the group's early hit *Nite Klub*, he sang the line "Is this the place to be? What am I doing here?" with such existential angst that it seemed to be far more than simply an expression of feeling uncomfortable on the dancefloor.

On TV and in photoshoots his demeanour was so lugubrious that a rumour gained traction that he had a rare medical condition affecting the muscles in his face which left him physically unable to smile.

It later emerged that his problems dated back to a traumatic incident of sexual abuse. At the age of 12 he was abducted by one of his schoolteachers and delivered into the clutches of a paedophile ring in France.

He was found abandoned by a roadside and rescued, but he was so scarred by the episode that he was unable to cope with going to school and spent much of his adolescence sedated on Valium. "I didn't do anything. I just sat on my bed rocking," he said.

He made a brave attempt to forgive his abuser. "You can let it eat away at you but you know paedophilia is just part of life," he said. Yet he spent years trying to come to terms with what had happened. "The only way I could deal with the experience was to write about it in a song. It was difficult for me to write, but I wanted to communicate my feelings."

The song was *Well Fancy That!*, which he recorded in 1983 with Fun Boy Three, the band he formed after leaving the Specials. It included the harrowing lyric: "The hedge that you dragged me through led to a nervous breakdown/ If I could have read what was going on inside your head/ I would have said, that I was blind to your devious mind/ There's no excuse, but your abuse, and the scars that it leaves."

The effect of the abuse led to increasingly erratic behaviour, including one incident in which he tried to break into Hamleys toy store "because I saw a teddy bear and decided that I wanted to spend the rest of my life with him".

Eventually he was diagnosed with bipolar disorder after an attempt to take his own life when he was in his forties. He was again put on anti-psychotic drugs and to the end was still talking about the decades of mental turmoil that the abuse caused.

"It sort of switched something in my head and that's when I started not listening to anyone," he said in a 2019 podcast. "But you can't just let it destroy your life." He worked hard to ensure that it did not, and music was his escape, albeit a restless one. There were further hits in the 1980s with Fun Boy Three on *It Ain't What You Do* (featuring Bananarama) and with The Colour Field on *Thinking of You*.

He later recorded with Dave Stewart of Eurythmics as Vegas, and with Damon Albarn and Dub Pistols. After years of "putting as much distance between myself and the Specials as I could", he relented and at his instigation the band reunited for a tour in 2009. The reunion became permanent and the esteem in which the original group was still held was evident when their 2019 album *Encore* topped the UK chart.

"Without wanting to sound arrogant, I think we made some important music and there's a timelessness about it, so I hope new generations of fans can continue to latch on to it," he said.

It was followed last year by *Protest Songs 1924–2012*, a collection of cover versions of politically charged songs from different eras of struggle that showed Hall had lost none of his political militancy. It went to No 2 in the UK album chart.

Hall is survived by his second wife, Lindy Heymann, a film director, and their nine-year-old son Orson. He is also survived by two adult sons, Felix and Leo, from his first marriage to Jeanette Hall, which ended in divorce.

Another relationship was with Jane Wiedlin of the American band the Go-Gos, whom he met in a club in Los Angeles in 1980. They co-wrote the song *Our Lips Are Sealed* about their romance, which became a Top Ten hit for Hall with Fun Boy Three.

Terence Edward Hall was born in Coventry in 1959. His upbringing was so dominated by what happened to him at the age of 12 that he seldom talked about other aspects of his childhood, other than to describe his family as "gypsy-spirited … and everyone used to sing in pubs".

He left school before his 15th birthday and drifted through a series of dead-end jobs, including as a bricklayer and a trainee hairdresser. His weekends were spent watching football, supporting Manchester United rather than his local club Coventry City.

He was inspired to try his hand at singing by hearing David Bowie's 1975 album *Young Americans* and later joined a punk band named Squad. When the band supported an early incarnation of the Specials, then known as the Automatics, Dammers invited Hall to join them, impressed by his transgressive approach to performing by singing with his back to the audience. At the time Hall was working in a stamp shop and Dammers claimed to have told him: "Philately will get you nowhere."

By 1979 the Specials had their first Top Ten hit with *Gangsters*. Less than two years later Hall quit, taking his fellow Specials Neville Staple and Golding with him to form Fun Boy Three (the name was thought to be an ironic reference to Hall's demeanour).

Despite his mental health struggles, he professed to be looking forward to growing old. "A lot of people think that 60 is part of the downward spiral, which it is if you allow it to be, but you can fight it. I always thought I'd make my best music in the years between 60 and 70."

Terry Hall, singer, was born on March 19, 1959. He died after a short illness on December 18, 2022, aged 63

POLY STYRENE

———————•———————

*Lead singer of X-Ray Spex whose unconventional style made her
an inspirational figure to generations of female pop singers*

The Times, April 27, 2011

It was on her 19th birthday, at a Sex Pistols concert in the normally reserved surroundings of the Pier Pavilion in the seaside town of Hastings, that Marianne Elliot Said experienced her epiphany. During the broiling summer of 1976 the Pistols were refining the new musical style known as punk that would soon make them famous and notorious in equal measure. Their concerts were largely word-of-mouth affairs in small venues attended by a mixture of the curious and unconventional teenagers in search of something new and different.

As the daughter of a marriage between an English legal secretary and a displaced Somali aristocrat, Said certainly belonged in the latter category. What she saw and heard that night changed her life and, in time, the future direction of female pop performers.

In the manner of other punk artists she changed her name to something suitably unconventional and became Poly Styrene, lead singer of the band X-Ray Spex, whose short and meteoric career was, in many respects, a perfect microcosm of punk.

They made just one album, *Germfree Adolescents*, in 1978, and became best known for the single *Oh Bondage Up Yours!*, which began with the spoken lines that amounted to Poly Styrene's mission statement, "Some people think little girls should be seen and not heard. But I think, Oh bondage, up yours." What followed was a typically frenetic and chaotic punk song which – in less than three minutes – was one of the pieces of music that captured the spirit of the times for a substantial section of British youth.

Marianne Joan Elliot Said was born in 1957 after her mother, a legal secretary from Hastings, met her father, who had recently arrived from Somalia, in London. The family moved from Bromley,

Kent, which her mother considered too judgmental of her daughter's interracial background, to Brixton, where she enjoyed a happy if restless childhood in a relaxed interracial environment.

She left home at the age of 15, touring pop festivals in a manner that was more hippy than punk, and on returning to London formed a band and set up a boutique in Beaufort Market on the King's Road, Chelsea. Elsewhere on the same fashionable London road, Malcolm McLaren and his then girlfriend Vivienne Westwood had opened the shop Sex, where the future Pistols bass player Glen Matlock worked and other members of the band were frequent visitors. The punk style and attitude – so crucial to its success – was being honed before the groups that would spread the gospel were well known.

X-Ray Spex provided a counterpoint to the earnestness of much of the punk movement. Although there was plenty of anti-establishment anger in their songs – *Plastic Bag*, *Warrior in Woolworths* and *I Live Off You* were three of their titles and, in *Identity*, Poly Styrene explored her interracial background – they set out to strike a lighter note. In this their lead singer was crucial.

Unconventionally attractive, with wild hair (often topped by military headgear), eccentric clothes and braces on her teeth, Poly Styrene was far from what was expected of a female pop singer.

But it was a look and vocal style that proved instantly inspirational for hundreds of young women aspiring to a career in pop music and was enduringly appealing for successive generations of female performers. Poly Styrene has subsequently been cited by many successful artists for the impact she had on their development.

X-Ray Spex also left a strong musical legacy with *Germfree Adolescents* regularly featuring in polls of the leading punk albums.

She left the band soon after its early success and released an album of experimental music, *Translucence*, in 1980. Later in the decade she was sectioned after schizophrenia was wrongly diagnosed; she was later found to have bipolar disorder. She lived for a time in a Hare Krishna temple and in the mid-1990s X-Ray Spex re-formed, but she was injured after being hit by a fire engine in London soon after the band's relaunch.

She released a solo album, *Generation Indigo*, last month and gave interviews to promote it from a hospice bed in St Leonards-on-Sea.

She is survived by her daughter, Celeste Bell-Dos Santos, who fronts the group Debutant Disco.

Poly Styrene, pop singer, was born on July 3, 1957. She died of cancer on April 25, 2011, aged 53

DENNIS WILSON

●

Wild-living drummer and founder member of the Beach Boys

Dennis Wilson (front left) with bandmates Brian Wilson, Al Jardine, Carl Wilson and Mike Love

The Times, December 30, 1983

Dennis Wilson, a founder member of the Beach Boys, the American pop group, died on December 28 after diving into the water from a boat at Marina del Rey, Los Angeles. He was 39.

Temperamentally the most volatile of the three brothers at the core of a group whose internal harmony rarely matched the celebrated blend of its singers, Dennis Wilson was at first a drummer, later he also sang, composed and played keyboards.

Born in Hawthorne, California in 1944, his adolescent prowess as a surfboarder inspired his older brother, Brian to write the group's first hit song, *Surfin'* in 1961, quickly followed by several successful variations on the theme and by the establishment of a specifically Californian style of pop known as "surf music".

The arrival of the Beatles threatened the pre-eminence of American pop music, and that of the Beach Boys in particular. Brian, Dennis and Carl, the youngest, responded by achieving in such songs as *Good Vibrations* and *Heroes and Villains* a musical richness and sophistication rare in pop and sometimes exceeding that of their British rivals.

Brian Wilson's various illnesses were subsequently to hinder the Beach Boys' development, but their popularity on records and in concert has been maintained for more than 20 years. Earlier this year they performed in Washington for President and Mrs Reagan, thus confirming their stature as a contemporary American institution.

Dennis Wilson's contributions to the group included a series of sombre compositions, notable for imaginative musical settings and suited to his slightly hoarse delivery. An LP under his own name, titled *Pacific Ocean Blue*, was issued in the late 1970s.

Dennis Wilson, musician, was born on December 4, 1944. He died on December 28, 1983, aged 39

JEFF BECK

◆

Influential "guitarist's guitarist" who came to prominence in the Sixties
with the Yardbirds before later fronting his own group

The Times, January 11, 2023

Eric Clapton once joked that there must have been something in the water in the English home counties in the 1950s, when the Thames basin came to resemble Britain's equivalent of the Mississippi Delta in its capacity to produce high-class musicians who looked to the blues for their inspiration.

The holy trinity of British blues-rock guitarists – Clapton, Jimmy Page and Jeff Beck – emerged simultaneously from the leafy, middle-class suburbs of outer London.

All three at one time or another plied their trade in the Yardbirds and there are many who claim that, in terms of technique and the sheer range of sounds he coaxed from his guitar, Beck was the most gifted of the three.

Geoffrey Arnold Beck was born in 1944 in Wallington, Surrey, to

Ethel and Arnold Beck, an accountant. His mother "forced" him to play piano two hours a day when he was a boy and as a ten-year-old he sang in the local church choir.

He attended Sutton Manor School (now Sutton Grammar) and, as well as classical music, he was exposed to jazz and blues on the radio. What he heard soon persuaded him to leave the piano behind and pick up a guitar.

By the time he went to Wimbledon College of Art – the customary training ground for aspiring British rock musicians in the 1960s – he was already an accomplished virtuoso on the instrument.

His stay at college was a brief one, for he soon left to work full-time as an in-demand session guitarist on the London recording scene. He played with Screaming Lord Sutch and the Tridents and built a formidable reputation, which made him a natural choice to replace Clapton as the Yardbirds' lead guitarist in 1965.

Clapton had left the group because he wanted to play a purer form of the blues than was available to him in the Yardbirds. Beck had no such qualms and slotted perfectly into the group's hybrid style that combined pop, rock, blues and psychedelia.

He became one of the first guitarists to experiment with feedback and distortion, most notably on the Yardbirds' 1966 album *Roger the Engineer*, anticipating the techniques that Jimi Hendrix was about to make his own.

Beck played on hits such as *Heart Full of Soul*, *Evil Hearted You*, *Shapes of Things* and *Over Under Sideways Down*, and toured America with the group in 1966, sharing a bill with the Rolling Stones.

By then Page had joined the group, which for a brief period had an enviable twin-guitar attack. However, Beck soon left owing to various personal problems and differences with the other members, walking out without notice in the middle of an American tour.

The Yardbirds enjoyed no further Top Ten hits after his departure. Having initially claimed that he was retiring, Beck signed a solo deal with EMI's Columbia subsidiary and put together his own band, including the then-unknown Rod Stewart and the future Rolling Stones guitarist Ron Wood on bass.

The Jeff Beck Group's first release, *Hi Ho Silver Lining*, was a novelty pop song, produced by the Tin Pan Alley svengali Mickie Most, who bizarrely believed that Beck was a better singer than Stewart and insisted that he took the lead vocal.

Tallyman followed, again with Beck singing lead. Even odder was *Love Is Blue*, the group's third single, an instrumental based on a Eurovision Song Contest entry for which the far superior *I've Been Drinking*, with Stewart taking the lead vocal, was relegated to the B-side.

Such ultra-commercial singles could hardly have been more different from the Jeff Beck Group's 1968 debut album *Truth*, a groundbreaking release that came to rival Led Zeppelin's debut album for its seminal influence on the plethora of blues-rock and heavy-metal bands that were to emerge in the late 1960s and early 1970s.

Beck-Ola, the album that followed in 1969, was in a similar style, but by then the group had self-destructed. Beck himself had developed a notorious reputation for unreliability, frequently cancelling gigs at short notice.

Stewart and Wood quit to form the Faces and, to cap it all, Beck, whose other passion alongside his guitars was fast cars, suffered a serious road accident, resulting in an 18-month layoff.

He returned in 1971 with a new line-up that produced the album *Rough and Ready*. The self-titled album *Jeff Beck Group* was released the following year, but the seemingly ever-restless Beck was ready to move on again and in 1973 he teamed up with the former rhythm section of the American group Vanilla Fudge to form the thunderous power-rock trio Beck, Bogert & Appice. Like so many of his attempts to work collaboratively, it proved short-lived and in little more than a year he had dissolved the group to embark on a solo career.

He would never again submerge his musical personality in a group, but his decision to embark on a solo project immediately led to some of the most innovative and satisfying music of his career. With George Martin, the Beatles' former éminence grise, in the producer's chair, Beck recorded the groundbreaking jazz-rock fusion album and career highlight *Blow by Blow* in 1975.

The record re-established his reputation as one of the most

inventive and experimental guitarists of his generation and restored him to the upper echelons of the charts. It was followed by further equally adventurous recordings backed by the Jan Hammer Group, including *Wired* (1976), a live album the following year and *There & Back* (1980).

Then, in a stop-go pattern that typified his career, he retired for half a decade, restricting his appearances to guest spots on albums by Tina Turner and Robert Plant while working on his cars and hot rods.

He finally returned in 1985 with *Flash*, a pop-rock album featuring a variety of vocalists, including Stewart, who sang on a version of Curtis Mayfield's *People Get Ready*. Surprisingly, the album sold poorly, although the vocal-free track *Escape* won a Grammy as best rock instrumental performance of the year.

Over the next two decades he continued recording sporadically, releasing albums every few years that displayed a total disregard, if not downright contempt, for whatever was happening and trendy in popular music at the time, before disappearing again to play with racing cars.

He played on Mick Jagger's debut solo album and released albums at irregular intervals, including *Jeff Beck's Guitar Shop* (1989), *Frankie's House* (1992) and a covers album of Gene Vincent songs, *Crazy Legs* (1993), on which he paid tribute to one of his early guitar heroes, Cliff Gallup, who had played in Vincent's backing band, the Blue Caps. He also played guitar on Spinal Tap's second album.

Such projects suggested a band leader with little sense of direction, although his guitar playing was clearly still impeccable. A late and, by his standards, prolific flurry of releases, including *Who Else!* (1999), *You Had It Coming* (2000) and *Jeff* (2003) found him fusing guitar pyrotechnics and electronic and techno elements.

His 2010 album *Emotion & Commotion* even included versions of *Over the Rainbow* and *Nessun Dorma* played as guitar instrumentals: the latter won a Grammy award, the eighth of his career. To blues-rock purists, it confirmed a lack of direction. A kinder interpretation would be that it reflected a restless musical curiosity that had led him to explore genres far beyond his rock'n'roll roots and was the reason he never stuck with any one band or style for very long.

If the chopping and changing and the curveballs that characterised his career meant he didn't quite attain the high-profile celebrity of Clapton or Page, he minded not one jot. "I've never made the big time, mercifully," he told *Rolling Stone* in 2018. "When you look around and see who has made it huge, it's a really rotten place to be."

There was another unexpected twist in 2020 when he teamed up with Johnny Depp to release a cover of John Lennon's *Isolation*. According to Beck, the pair bonded over "cars and guitars" and a mutually dry sense of humour. It was followed by live concerts and an album *18*, so titled because they claimed that was the age playing together made them feel.

While in some ways he led the hedonistic lifestyle expected of rock stars, he was never especially wild when it came to sex, drugs and drink. He was briefly married to Patricia Brown in the 1960s and in 2005 married Sandra Cash, who was 20 years his junior and remained his partner for the rest of his life. They had no children.

In between there were a string of girlfriends, including Sable Starr, known as the "queen of the groupies" and who claimed Iggy Pop, David Bowie and Jimmy Page among her other conquests; the Hollywood starlet Mary Hughes; the model and animal rights campaigner Celia Hammond; and Heather Taylor, who later married Roger Daltrey, The Who's singer.

Despite his patchy output of later years, his early work with the Yardbirds, his blistering power trio of the late 1960s and his startlingly inventive jazz-rock fusion albums of the mid-1970s secured his reputation as one of Britain's most revered guitar heroes, constantly seeking to expand the repertoire of sounds associated with the electric instrument.

"I don't care about the rules," he once said. "In fact, if I don't break the rules at least ten times in every song, then I'm not doing my job properly."

Jeff Beck, guitarist, was born on June 24, 1944. He died of bacterial meningitis on January 10, 2023, aged 78

MIKE NESMITH

———————— • ————————

Bobble hat-wearing singer and guitarist with the Monkees who fought
against the band's "manufactured" image before striking out alone

The *Times*, December 10, 2021

On a visit to Britain in 1967 the Monkees' Mike Nesmith met
the Beatles at Abbey Road Studios, where the Fab Four were
recording *A Day in the Life*. Coming straight to the point, he asked
John Lennon: "Do you think we're a cheap imitation of the Beatles?"
In reply Lennon, being quite polite by his standards, likened the
group's comic talent to the Marx Brothers.

The Monkees, a manufactured American group, were propelled to the top of the charts in the 1960s by the success of the zany TV series of the same name. At the peak of their popularity they generated scenes reminiscent of Beatlemania, with screaming girls mobbing their public appearances.

Often known as "the prefab four", each of the Monkees was assigned a "character" in the TV series and Mike Nesmith played the part of the "serious one". The term was relative, of course; the audition advert to which he had responded had appealed for "four insane boys" and Nesmith cultivated an endearing eccentricity, symbolised by the bobble hat he wore in every episode.

On the back of their TV fame, between 1966 and 1970 the Monkees sold an estimated 65 million records and enjoyed numerous hits, including *Last Train to Clarksville, I'm a Believer, Pleasant Valley Sunday, Daydream Believer* and *A Little Bit Me, a Little Bit You.* None was written by the group and once the Monkees found success, Nesmith became a vocal critic of the group's "bubblegum" music and "teenybop" image, complaining that they were being manipulated. He denounced the group's second LP as "probably the worst record in the history of the world" and led a campaign for its four members to loosen the shackles of their contract and take charge of their own destiny.

He succeeded in wresting greater control, and later records were more experimental and adventurous. But nobody was much interested in a former "teenybop" group parading as serious musicians. The revelation that they had not played on their early records created a credibility deficit from which they were never able fully to recover. In 1970, with record sales declining, Nesmith left the Monkees to form the First National Band. The Monkees made one more album with only two of the original quartet remaining, before the name was put to rest.

Of the group's members, Nesmith enjoyed by far the most successful post-Monkees career, releasing a series of pioneering country-rock albums characterised by a strong songwriting ability. He also became a novelist and film producer, creating music videos for Michael Jackson and Lionel Richie.

Robert Michael Nesmith was born in 1942 in Houston, Texas. His parents, Warren, a soldier, and Bette, a secretary, divorced when he was four. He was brought up by his mother, who went on to build up a remarkable business career after she invented a typewriter correction fluid. She turned it into a business called the Liquid Paper Corporation and sold the enterprise in 1980 for $48 million. Nesmith inherited the fortune on her death.

At Thomas Jefferson High School in Dallas he showed an interest in amateur dramatics, but at the age of 18 he enlisted in the US Air Force. On his discharge in 1962 he returned to college in Texas, where he met his first wife, Phyllis Barbour, and began writing songs. In 1963 the couple moved to Los Angeles for Nesmith to pursue a career as a singer and songwriter.

He recorded a few commercially unsuccessful singles under his own name and as Michael Blessing, played the folk clubs and landed a job as a staff songwriter with a music publishing house run by Randy Sparks of New Christy Minstrels fame. This placed his compositions with the Paul Butterfield Blues Band, Frankie Laine and Linda Ronstadt, who recorded one of his best-known works, *Different Drum*.

In 1965 he responded to an advert in *The Hollywood Reporter* placed by Bob Rafelson and Bert Schneider, aspiring film-makers who had been inspired by the Beatles' films *A Hard Day's Night* and *Help!* to create a TV series about a fictitious pop group, with the twist that the group would also release "real" records. Nesmith arrived at the audition on a motorcycle, wearing a woollen hat to keep his hair out of his eyes and carrying his laundry in a plastic bag. His insouciance was just what the producers were looking for, and alongside Davy Jones, Micky Dolenz and Peter Tork he landed a role in the pilot for *The Monkees* TV series.

The Monkees' first single *Last Train to Clarksville* was released in August 1966, immediately before the TV series started. The first LP, *The Monkees*, was released a month later and shot to the top of the charts, selling three million copies in its first three months. It was followed to No 1 in America and Britain by the single *I'm a Believer*. With an audience heavily dominated by screaming girls, by 1967 the

Monkees were being hailed, perhaps a little ironically, as "America's answer to the Beatles".

On stage the group played their own instruments, with Nesmith on lead guitar, but then came the revelation that session men were responsible for their early recordings. That had been the decision of the group's producer, Don Kirshner, and, as an accomplished musician, Nesmith railed against it.

The issue reached boiling point with the second album, *More of the Monkees*; the first Nesmith knew of the album's release in early 1967 was when he saw a copy in a record shop. He forced a showdown, which Kirshner sought to head off by summoning the group to a meeting and presenting them with large royalty cheques and a set of gold discs. Nesmith accepted the money but then punched a hole through the office partition wall and told Kirshner: "That could have been your face."

Kirshner was forced out and the Monkees' third album, *Headquarters* (1967), featured them playing their own instruments for the first time and included songs written by Nesmith. It gave the Monkees their third No 1 album and was followed to the top of the charts at the end of the same year by *Pisces, Aquarius, Capricorn & Jones Ltd.*

By the time of the fifth album, *The Birds, The Bees & The Monkees* (1968), the TV series had finished and the record became the first Monkees album not to hit No 1. Freed of TV duties, the group worked on the feature film *Head*, co-written and co-produced by Bob Rafelson and the then unknown Jack Nicholson. The film and accompanying album were not a commercial success, which suited Nesmith, who saw it as an opportunity to kill off the group's teenybopper image. Over the years the anarchic film has developed a cult following and the soundtrack, with its more adventurous, psychedelic influences, was described by Nesmith as the band's finest musical achievement.

It was the beginning of the end for the Monkees, though. During 1968, Nesmith enrolled at the University of California, Los Angeles, on a part-time course in American history. By 1970 he had bought himself out of the three years remaining on his Monkees contract at a cost of $450,000 to launch a new project, Michael Nesmith and the First National Band. At the time the Byrds and Bob Dylan were experimenting with the fusion of country music and rock, and today Nesmith's records from the period are regarded as landmarks in the development of the newly emerging country-rock genre.

With his first wife, Phyllis, he had three children before divorcing in 1972. He also had a son with Nurit Wilde, whom he met while working on *The Monkees*. In 1976 he married his second wife, Kathryn Bild, and in 2000 his third, Victoria Kennedy. After 11 years that marriage also ended.

Nesmith made sporadic returns to music in later years but did not participate in the Monkees' 20th anniversary reunion in 1986. He did agree to take part in the 30th anniversary in 1996, helping to record *Justus*, the first Monkees album to include all four original members since 1968. After that they never got back together again.

More recently he described how he felt about being one of the Monkees as "old timey and kind of like watching Fred-and-Ginger movies, although not quite that good", adding: "You can't really get your arms around what the thing was – is. It persists, even though all of us are old men now or dead."

Mike Nesmith, musician, was born on December 30, 1942. He died of undisclosed causes on December 10, 2021, aged 78

LORETTA LYNN

———————•———————

*Coalminer's daughter who married at 15 before becoming a country star
to rival Dolly Parton and Tammy Wynette*

The Times, October 6, 2022

When Loretta Lynn was growing up in the backwoods of Kentucky, there was no electricity or paved roads and when her family needed to visit the nearest town, they walked three miles there and three miles back.

Her dresses were made by her mother from old flour sacks and she was 13 when she encountered a lavatory with running water for the first time. It scared her half to death.

It sounds like the plot of a movie and it became one when Lynn's life story was put on the screen in the 1980 film *Coal Miner's Daughter*, in which she was memorably played in an Oscar-winning performance by Sissy Spacek. But it was also all true, the authentic realisation of the "rags-to-riches" mythology that lies at the core of so much in American popular culture – and in country music in particular.

From the gritty mining community of Butcher Hollow, which she always pronounced "Holler", Lynn transcended her impoverished childhood to become an international star who rivalled Dolly Parton and Tammy Wynette as the first lady of country music.

Married at 15 and a mother of two by 18, she was an indomitable woman who never ducked a challenge. She led her life with great personal dignity and professional integrity, somehow remaining above the shallow glitz of the Nashville star-making machinery and addressing subjects in her songs often far removed from the saccharine, sentimental banalities of much country music. Drunken and abusive husbands (*Don't Come Home A-Drinkin' (With Lovin' on Your Mind)*), the forgotten wives whose husbands were sent to fight in Vietnam (*Dear Uncle Sam*), the liberation of reliable birth control (*The Pill*), the double standards faced by divorced women (*Rated X*) and the loss of teenage virginity (*Wings Upon Your Horns*) were unlikely subjects for hit songs but she addressed them all to become something of a feminist heroine, a rare achievement in country music with its traditional, chauvinistic "redneck" attitudes. Minnie Pearl, one of country music's earliest female stars, who was denied such latitude in her career, observed in old age with admiration and perhaps a little envy: "Loretta sang what women were thinking."

Her sound remained deeply rooted in rural tradition, the strong, clear, confident Kentucky twang of her voice and her grassroots arrangements for the most part eschewing the slick urbanisation that has come to characterise modern country music. She racked up more than 70 American chart hits between 1962 and 1985, either solo or in duets with Ernest Tubb, Conway Twitty and others.

She largely disappeared from view in the late 1980s and spent several years taking care of her sick husband, who died in 1996. But it was a measure of her standing that, in her seventies, Jack White – one of the hippest young gunslingers in rock music – with his band the White Stripes, offered to produce a comeback album. The resulting record in 2004, *Van Lear Rose*, allowed her to reach a new audience of rock fans who had previously paid her work scant attention. It received rave reviews and won her two Grammy awards.

Four of her six children survive her: Ernie, Cissie and the twins Peggy Jean and Patsy Eileen, who enjoyed some musical success in the 1990s as the country duo The Lynns.

Born Loretta Webb in 1932, she was the second of eight children to Melvin "Ted" Webb, a coalminer, and his wife, "Clary" Marie. However, for years it was thought her year of birth was two or three years later than it really was. Music was in her veins from an early age and as a girl she sang in church and at local barn dances and picnics. One of her younger sisters also found fame as the country singer Crystal Gayle.

She had little formal education and at 15 she married Oliver Lynn, whom she always called "Dolittle" or "Doo". At the time their union was perfectly legal in Kentucky and they were married for 48 years, until his death, although it was a stormy relationship with numerous incidents of infidelity on his part and frequent fights.

Lynn claimed she always hit him back with twice the ferocity.

At 16 she was pregnant with her first child and before she was 18, she had produced two children. By then her young family had moved to Custer, Washington, where her husband, determined not to become a coalminer like his father and father-in-law, found employment in a logging camp.

Having sung to her children around the house, she began singing with local country groups the Penn Brothers and the Trailblazers, after her husband bought her a guitar. In 1960 she was spotted by the Canadian businessman Norm Burley, who signed her to his Zero Records label and took her to Los Angeles to make her first recordings. Her debut single was *I'm a Honky Tonk Girl*. Unusually for the time, she wrote the song herself and it marked her out as an independent woman who wanted to be in control of her own destiny.

She was equally determined in promoting the record, mailing records to disc jockeys around the country and touring radio stations to play the song live. Her hard work paid off and when the song became a minor hit, she headed with her husband for the country music capital of Nashville, in search of greater things. Writing her own songs first landed her a publishing deal with the Wilburn brothers, Doyle and Teddy, who then helped her sign with Decca, with which she recorded her first Top 10 hit in the country chart in 1962.

The Wilburns, who were performers in their own right, could legitimately lay claim to having launched her career and she appeared on the Grand Ole Opry with them and on their television show. But it was at a high price: she signed over her publishing rights to them and, despite a lengthy legal battle, never regained control of her own songs.

A more benign mentor was the singer Patsy Cline, who befriended her. Lynn set out to emulate her and was devastated when Cline died in a plane crash in 1963, writing *This Haunted House* as a tribute to her.

For the next two decades, Lynn was seldom out of the Billboard charts. A series of duets with the country legend Ernest Tubb was a good start but songs such as *Before I'm Over You, Blue Kentucky Girl*, later covered by Emmylou Harris, and *You Ain't Woman Enough* gave her Top Ten solo hits.

Initially she worked in a traditional honky-tonk style but gradually her records grew more personal and adventurous, musically and lyrically. Her 1966 hit *Dear Uncle Sam* was one of the first songs about the human cost of the Vietnam War, written from the perspective of the unhappy women left at home. Her first country No 1 came in 1967 with the defiant *Don't Come Home A-Drinkin' (With Lovin' on Your Mind)*, although the kind of unreconstructed attitudes she was up against were abundantly displayed when her brother, Jay Lee Webb, immediately recorded an "answer" song titled *I Come Home A-Drinkin' (To a Worn-Out Wife Like You)*. *You Ain't Woman Enough (To Take My Man)*, a 1966 hit, was allegedly written about a woman with whom Lynn's errant husband was having an affair and the hits continued with the similarly-themed 1969 country chart-topper *Woman of the World (Leave My World Alone)*. The autobiographical *Coal Miner's Daughter* followed it to the No 1 slot in 1970, and would provide the title for her autobiography as well as the film about her life.

Throughout the 1970s she duetted regularly with Conway Twitty, and the pair scored five country No 1 songs, including *Louisiana Woman, Mississippi Man* and the sentimental *As Soon as I Hang Up the Phone*. Her solo success continued simultaneously with *One's on the Way* (1971), *Here I Am Again* (1972), *Rated 'X'* and *Hey Loretta* (both 1973) and 1975's controversial *The Pill*.

She also recorded an album of covers of songs by Cline, a move taken in part as a protest against the Wilburns, who still owned her publishing rights and earned money on every song she wrote.

The hits continued into the 1980s with *Pregnant Again, Naked in the Rain* and *I Lie* but by the middle of the decade the successes were drying up as a new generation of female country stars took over. The failing health of her husband also kept her out of the limelight as she put her career on hold to care for him, although she teamed up with Dolly Parton and Tammy Wynette for a 1993 summit of country queens on the album *Honky Tonk Angels*.

Despite his frequent infidelities, the death of her husband in

1996 hit her hard. He had been her "security and safety net", she said. "I'm explainin', not excusin'. ... Doo was a good man and a hard worker. But he was an alcoholic and it affected our marriage all the way through."

She did not return to the recording studio until 2000, when she recorded the album *Still Country*, which included *I Can't Hear the Music*, a touching tribute to her husband and to her former singing partner Conway Twitty, who had died in 1993.

She looked to be settling gently into retirement but Jack White, more than 40 years her junior, had other ideas. Having cited Lynn as his all-time favourite singer and having covered her song *Rated 'X'* with his band the White Stripes, he offered to produce a comeback record for her. It led to a late-career resurgence as she returned to the concert stage and duetted on records with the likes of Elvis Costello and Willie Nelson. As she entered her 90th year in 2021, she released her 50th album, *Still Woman Enough*, which was also the title of her second autobiography.

"Being on stage is the only time I feel grown-up and in control of things," she once said. "I don't know what I'd do with myself if I retired. Wash dishes?"

Loretta Lynn, singer, was born on April 14, 1932. She died on October 4, 2022, aged 90

CAPTAIN BEEFHEART

───────●───────

Acclaimed musician and painter who pioneered an avant-garde
fusion of rock, blues and jazz

The Times, December 20, 2010

Seldom has any artist enjoyed a cultural influence quite so disproportionate to his sales as Captain Beefheart. Most of the dozen albums he made between 1967 and 1981 stubbornly refused to fly out of the shops.

But his avant-garde rock, blues and jazz stylings had an immeasurable effect upon other musicians and when he abandoned music to concentrate on painting, his mystique grew along with his silence. The special place he occupied in the rock pantheon was captured by the music magazine *Mojo*, which, many years after he had played his last note, described him as an "Eco-freak, control freak, visionary, charlatan, band leader, painter, avant-garde hero, would-be pop star, genre originator and mutator, the original high-voltage man".

Born Don Van Vliet in Glendale, California, in 1941, Captain Beefheart was all of those things and more. He was a child prodigy as a clay sculptor who regularly appeared on television but by his teens his first love was R&B music, which he discovered via the circuitous route of the British beat groups of the time.

Frank Zappa was a high-school friend in a teenage band called the Soots, and their career paths were to cross at regular intervals over the coming years. Adopting the name he was to be known by throughout his recording career, Beefheart put together the first Magic Band in 1964. They did not secure a recording contract until 1966, making two singles, *Diddy Wah Diddy* and *Frying Pan* for the A&M label, produced improbably by David Gates, who was later to find middle-of-the-road fame with Bread. The records failed to sell, and Beefheart was swiftly dropped. It was to be the first of many such experiences.

Signed to a new label, his first album *Safe as Milk* appeared in April 1967 and it remains an avant-garde masterpiece. The strange and wonderful music it contained was not even hinted at by the cover, which depicted a bunch of clean-cut college kids in suits and ties. Inside lay another world: warped, hard-rocking blues driven by Ry Cooder's slide guitar and Beefheart's own growling, Howlin' Wolf-like vocals. It was too far outside the mainstream to reach the charts, even in that psychedelic summer of love.

Yet songs such as *Electricity* and *Dropout Boogie* became classics of their kind and, thanks to the ceaseless championing of a young John Peel, the album became a cult object in Britain. Many years later the DJ remained a devoted fan, saying "If ever there has been such a thing as a genius in the history of popular music it is Beefheart."

Strictly Personal, his second album (on his third record label) followed in 1968, an extreme version of the same distorted sound with some of the heaviest phasing ever committed to record. But it was *Trout Mask Replica* (1969) which was to take Beefheart to the pinnacle of inspired weirdness. Produced by Zappa, who seemed intent on promoting his friend as an oddball freak, it took his bizarre lyrics to their surreal limit, mixing in asides and quirky non-sequiturs in an early example of audio vérité. The 28-track odyssey, which sprawled across a double album, sounded dissonant and random but in fact was the result of complex charts and eight months of rehearsals.

Many regard it as the height of Beefheart's art, others as one of the most audacious musical jokes of all time. Both views are probably correct.

Apparently recorded with the band in one studio with Beefheart adding his vocals out of earshot in another, at times it resembled the free-form jazz of artists such as Ornette Coleman. As throughout his career, it proved more popular in Europe than in America and reached No 21 in the British album charts, a remarkable achievement for such a wilfully uncommercial record.

He made a notable contribution to Zappa's 1969 solo album *Hot Rats*, singing the vocal on *Willie the Pimp*, and followed up *Trout Mask*

Replica with *Lick My Decals Off, Baby*, which continued the experiment with atonality and non-conventional structures.

Yet if it was clear that Beefheart was a rare musical genius, no one had worked out how to make money from his talent. "For my whole life they repeated to me that I was a genius. But in the meantime they've also taught the public that my music is difficult to listen to," he once complained.

Away from the archly self-conscious weirdness of Zappa, his new label Reprise tried a more commercial pop sound on *The Spotlight Kid* in 1972 and *Clear Spot* the following year. The approach was more linear if not exactly mainstream, but the effect was merely to dilute his unique genius. Two 1974 albums for Virgin, *Unconditionally Guaranteed* and *Blue Jeans for Moonbeams* were equally unsatisfying.

The Magic Band had by now split from their founder to set up Mallard, complaining that he was tyrannical and impossible to work with, and Beefheart teamed up once again with his old friend Zappa on *Bongo Fury* (1975), a live album recorded in Austin, Texas. Then he announced that he was retiring to the Mojave Desert to paint.

It was not quite the end of his recording career: there was a comeback in 1978 with *Shiny Beast (Bat Chain Puller)*, followed by *Doc at the Radar Station* (1980) and finally in 1982 came the well-received *Ice Cream for Crow*. It struggled to No 90 in the British charts but once again did nothing in America, despite a rare television appearance by Beefheart on the *Late Night with Letterman* show.

Beefheart returned once again to the desert to paint, reverted to his original name and eventually announced that there would be no more music. His early vivid oils bore the influence of Francis Bacon but he later adopted a rural expressionist style and left the desert and moved with his wife Jan to the Pacific coast of Trinidad, northern California, where he had a house and studio by the ocean.

He exhibited widely in the 1980s, and his paintings came to command high prices in London and at the San Francisco Museum of Modern Art. By in the 1990s his work was exhibited less often and in 1993 it was said that he had multiple sclerosis, although he continued to paint. In 1995 Anton Corbijn made the film *Some Yoyo*

Stuff about him and Beefheart's musical influence is still apparent today in the work of artists such as Tom Waits, PJ Harvey and Beck.

Captain Beefheart, musician and painter, was born on January 15, 1941. He died of complications related to multiple sclerosis on December 17, 2010, aged 69

DON EVERLY

One half of the country-rock duo the Everly Brothers whose close-knit harmonies influenced the Beatles and Simon and Garfunkel

The Times, August 22, 2021

As the elder of two singing brothers, Don Everly was part of the most successful duo in pop chart history. With their roots in country music, the Everly Brothers brought close harmonies and sweet melodies into the rambunctious world of 1950s rock'n'roll, creating a string of hits that included *Bye Bye Love, Wake Up Little Susie, All I Have to Do Is Dream, When Will I Be Loved* and *Cathy's Clown*.

Their lyrics often dealt with teenage angst and their songs had a strong backbeat, but it was the two-part vocal harmonies of Don and his younger brother Phil that made the Everly Brothers stand out from the rest of the rock'n'roll crowd.

With Don generally singing the lower harmony and taking most of the solo lines, together their voices were simple and honest with a natural twang, delicately interwoven and exquisitely phrased.

Without the Everly Brothers the course of popular music would surely have been different and the profundity of their influence was readily acknowledged by Paul McCartney and John Lennon, and Simon and Garfunkel. "When John and I first started to write songs, I was Phil and he was Don," McCartney once said.

Most of the brothers' Top Ten hits were sandwiched into a thrilling period between 1957 and 1962. By the mid-1960s their star was waning, eclipsed first by the Beatles and the British beat boom and then further sidelined by psychedelic and progressive rock. Yet they regained credibility towards the end of the 1960s when their music returned to its country roots and they were recognised as pioneers of the burgeoning country-rock movement among whose adherents were the Byrds, Bob Dylan and Gram Parsons.

Despite the sweetness of their harmonies, offstage relations between the two brothers were notoriously inharmonious. There were fights, tantrums and, eventually, an inability even to share the same room except when they were on stage.

They continued to perform live and to record together until 1973. After that they spent a decade communicating only through managers and lawyers and did not even speak to each other at their father's funeral. Neither enjoyed significant success as a solo artist and in 1983 they agreed to bury the hatchet and reunited, recording a trio of well-received albums. After 1989 they concentrated solely on live performances, playing their old hits to nostalgic audiences of baby boomers.

In addition to his difficult relationship with his brother, Don Everly's life was full of other seemingly endless troubles. There were divorces, lengthy periods of drug addiction and alcohol abuse, two attempted suicides and a spell in a mental hospital, where he underwent electroshock therapy.

He was born Isaac Donald Everly in 1937, in Brownie, Kentucky. His parents, Ike and Margaret Everly, were both musicians who had their own show on country radio in Shenandoah, Iowa. By the age of eight Don had joined the show and had his own spot, in which he was given three or four songs and required to read a commercial. Phil was soon brought into the act too, and they sang with their parents as the Everly Family, both on radio and at live shows across the Midwest.

Despite their two-year age gap the brothers were treated almost like twins. They were dressed alike and shared birthday parties. Don had to wait for his first sports jacket until Phil was also old enough to have one. Once they had shot to fame, fans often had difficulty telling them apart, though Don had darker hair and a deeper voice.

In 1954 the Everly family moved to Nashville and the brothers were ready to perform on their own. Under the mentorship of the guitarist and talent scout Chet Atkins, Don started to make headway as a songwriter and Kitty Wells recorded his composition *Thou Shalt Not Steal*. Two years later, in 1956, the brothers cut a single for Columbia called *Keep a-Lovin' Me*. It failed to sell but the Everlys found a new patron in Wesley Rose, the president of Acuff-Rose, one of the biggest music publishing companies in Nashville. He promised he would get them a record deal if they signed with Acuff-Rose as songwriters and duly introduced them to Archie Bleyer, the owner of Cadence Records.

The label was looking to branch out into country music and Bleyer saw the Everly Brothers primarily as a country act, hence his decision to make their first Cadence single *Bye Bye Love*, by the established country songwriting team Felice and Boudleaux Bryant.

Their recording of the song featured the cream of Nashville's country session players, but the Everly Brothers invested it with the urgency of rock'n'roll and it became a huge crossover hit, making No 2 in the pop charts and only kept from the top by Elvis Presley.

Bye Bye Love was followed with another Bryant composition, *Wake Up Little Susie*, which despite being banned in conservative parts of America for being too suggestive gave them another hit. In fact, the song was entirely innocent, with lyrics describing two teenagers falling asleep at a drive-in movie and fearing unwarranted parental suspicions about the broken curfew.

Over the next three years the Everlys poured out hits on the Cadence label, including *All I Have to Do Is Dream, Bird Dog, Problems, Poor Jenny* and the Don Everly composition *(Till) I Kissed You*. Most of their singles were aimed at a teenage pop audience rather than a country fan base, but they had not forgotten their musical origins. The 1958 album *Songs Our Daddy Taught Us* dug deep into country music's roots and is regarded as one of their finest collections.

In 1960 they left Cadence and signed with Warner Bros., then just branching out from the film industry into the recording business. Their debut for Warner – and the label's first release – was the self-composed *Cathy's Clown*, which became the biggest single of the duo's career, selling eight million copies. It was followed by *So Sad (To Watch Good Love Go Bad)* (1960), *Walk Right Back* (1961) and *Crying in the Rain* (1962), while Cadence continued to release singles from their back catalogue.

There were a number of reasons for their commercial decline. The drafting of both brothers into the Marines for a six-month spell in 1961 at the height of their success did not help. Then on a 1962 "comeback" tour of Britain, Don was unable to perform because of a drug overdose and a suicide attempt. It was diplomatically reported that he had been forced to abandon the tour because of "food poisoning" and Phil completed the shows with their bass player, Joey Page, singing Don's parts.

Just as seriously, in 1961 the brothers fell out with Acuff-Rose, which denied them access to the source of some of their strongest material, including their own compositions, as they were still contracted to the company, and those of Felice and Boudleaux Bryant.

The advent of Beatlemania and the changes it wrought upon teenage musical tastes also had an effect upon their chart fortunes, even though the Beatles had been deeply influenced by the Everlys and McCartney subsequently confessed that the vocals on the Beatles' first No 1, *Please Please Me*, had been loosely based on the harmonies of *Cathy's Clown*. By the time the dispute with Acuff-Rose was settled in 1964 and they were once again able to record their own material and work with the Bryants, the Everly Brothers' signature sound was beginning to seem as out of date as the title of their 1962 hit, *That's Old Fashioned*. The artistic highlight of the otherwise dispiriting period that followed was the 1968 album *Roots*. The record failed to sell particularly well but came to be regarded as a landmark in the birth of country rock.

Meanwhile, Don Everly's personal problems were again catching up with him; addicted to amphetamines and Ritalin, he was admitted to hospital. The strong sibling rivalry was also getting out of hand and in 1973 the brothers went their separate ways. The final break came on stage: Don was so drunk that a show had to be stopped halfway through and Phil stormed off, smashing his guitar in disgust. Don declared that the Everly Brothers had "really died ten years ago" and the pair did not speak for another ten years.

Don Everly released a few solo records backed by his band Dead Cowboys before reuniting with his brother in 1983, a rapprochement engineered by the British guitarist Albert Lee, who acted as musical director of their comeback concert at the Royal Albert Hall. The brothers also returned to the studio, recording the albums *EB 84* (which included *Wings of a Nightingale*, written for them by McCartney); *Born Yesterday* (1985); and *Some Hearts* (1988).

Speaking about their clashes in 1999, Don said: "Everything is different about us, except when we sing together. I'm a liberal Democrat, he's pretty conservative. We give each other a lot of space [on reunion tours]. We say hello, we sometimes have a meal together. Wherever I go, it's 'Are you still mad at each other?' I say, 'Do you have a family? Do you have a brother?'"

Yet he could not deny their musical chemistry. "That's one part where being brothers makes a difference. It's just instinct," he said. "That's the charm of what the Everly Brothers are: two guys singing as one."

His first marriage, to Mary Sue Ingraham, was short-lived. They had eloped in 1957 when she was pregnant, but the baby died shortly after birth and they divorced in 1961. The next year he married Venetia Stevenson, an actress whom he had met on *The Ed Sullivan Show*, and they divorced in 1970.

Phil died of lung disease, aged 74. Don is survived by his wife of 24 years, Adela (née Garza), his son, Edan Everly, a musician with whom he would often play concerts, and three daughters, Venetia, Stacy and Erin Everly, who was briefly married to the Guns N' Roses singer Axl Rose and who inspired *Sweet Child of Mine*.

The Everly Brothers were inducted into the Rock & Roll Hall of Fame in 1986, its inaugural year, and into the Country Music Hall of Fame in 2001. They received a lifetime achievement award at the Grammys in 1997. All were fitting tributes to a pair hailed by *Rolling Stone* magazine as "the most important vocal duo in rock". Or, as Bob Dylan said of the brothers: "We owe these guys everything. They started it all."

Don Everly, singer, was born on February 1, 1937. He died of undisclosed causes on August 21, 2021, aged 84

Don Everly (left) with brother Phil Everly

FRANK ZAPPA

●

Uncompromising, experimental and blunt rock musician
and satirist who called his audiences pigs

The Times, December 7, 1993

An obstreperous and delightfully barking-mad spirit, Frank Zappa was one of rock music's innovatory forces. But, though a talented musician, his penchant for bizarre humour and his gift of waspish satire were a combined insurance policy against his taking either himself or the rock ethos too seriously. California's Sixties counter-culture and its Flower Children were no more proof against his barbs than a conservative Eighties housewives' pressure group which wanted cinema-style ratings for pop records to alert the public to their content. "The whole hippie scene is wishful thinking,"

Zappa said in 1968. "They wish they could love but ... it's easier to make someone mad than to make somebody love." The content of much Sixties music he felt was "pitiful".

In this he displayed sharper critical acumen than was at that time to be had from much of an adoring press (even *The Times* music critic described the Beatles as "the greatest song-writers since Schubert"). Zappa took a different view of pop music's icons. His 1967 album *We're Only in It for the Money*, mercilessly parodied in both content and cover artwork the Beatles' reverentially received *Sergeant Pepper's Lonely Hearts Club Band*. The Fab Four, at that stage accustomed to plaudits for whatever they did, were not amused.

Zappa was too intelligent to be part of an ambience which accepted the half-baked and the second-rate as "culture". (So were a number of other rock musicians – but they were making far too much money to say so). He was familiar with classical music, particularly the works of 20th-century masters such as Stravinsky and Edgar Varese. And he was one of the first rock musicians to inject elements of jazz and classical music into his work.

Zappa also had a refreshing lack of desire to be idolised by his fans. "Hello, pigs," he would snarl by way of greeting to his audiences, thus putting them neatly in the place of the police they themselves loved to hate. Allied to his talent for verbal satire was a love of theatrical outrage, which he employed in a ceaseless search for new ways to cause offence to his fellow-Americans.

At the Garrick Theatre in New York's Greenwich Village in 1968, he incited a party of US marines in the audience to get up on stage and demonstrate their bayoneting skills on some baby dolls. Over the years his songs poked fun at Jews, Catholics, politicians, the police and homosexuals. He once described the trade of rock journalism as "people who can't write interviewing people who can't talk for people who can't read."

Frank Vincent Zappa Jr was born in Baltimore, Maryland, in 1940 of Sicilian-Greek parentage. When he was nine, the family moved to California, eventually settling in Lancaster, a small town in the Mojave Desert. There, at Antelope Valley High School, he started a school band called the Blackouts. After high school Zappa began playing with local groups. In 1959 he enrolled in Chaffee Junior College, where he studied harmony for a while before dropping out. In that year he married a girl called Kay. The marriage was dissolved in 1964.

For a time he scraped a living playing in cocktail bars and then, with the money earned from writing the soundtracks for a couple of B-movies, he set up a recording studio in Cucumonga, San Bernardino. Studio Z, as he named it, was closed down in 1964, after Zappa made a pornographic recording, commissioned by a used-car salesman who turned out to be a detective from the San Bernardino Vice Squad. Zappa was jailed for ten days for the offence.

He moved to Los Angeles, where he joined the singer Ray Collins in a band called the Soul Giants. The Giants became the Mothers and were eventually spotted by Bob Dylan's producer Tom Wilson, playing at the Whiskey-A-Go-Go club. Wilson got them a contract with Verve records, a subsidiary of MGM intended primarily as an outlet for jazz and rhythm and blues. The group, now called the Mothers of Invention at the insistence of the record company, released its debut album, *Freak Out*, in 1966. This was followed in 1967 by *Absolutely Free*. It was *We're Only in It for the Money*, which cemented the Mothers' international reputation. A frenetic patchwork of styles from hardcore rock to doo-wop pastiche, it mocked everything held dear by the Flower Power generation. They lapped it up nevertheless.

Zappa disbanded the Mothers in 1969, proclaiming himself to be "tired of playing for people who clap for all the wrong reasons", and embarked on a solo career. Later the same year he married Gail Sloatman; they had two sons, Dweezil and Ahmet, and two daughters, Moon Unit and Diva.

The commercial appeal of Zappa's recordings was circumscribed by their unpredictability and their often outrageous content. America, in particular, tended to be rather squeamish about his lyrics. Either their scatological content as in: "Watch out where the huskies go/And don't eat all that yellow snow" offended the American housewife, or the wildly politically incorrect "He's So Gay" and "Jewish Princess" had their respective pressure groups apoplectic with rage. Zappa did not much like England, which he thought of as a Third World country and its people as being in thrall to notions of regality and pecking order: "Until you change yourself from subjects to citizens, you are going to be eating shit, aren't you?" But Britain liked him, and his most impressive album, *Hot Rats* (1969), was a success here though it barely registered on the other side of the Atlantic. His work was popular, too, in Germany and the Netherlands, where earthy, straight-speaking lyrics have never been a bar to success. In samizdat recordings, he was also popular in many Soviet bloc countries, notably Czechoslovakia.

His work continued to provoke controversy. In 1971 he was forced to cancel a concert performance of 200 *Motels* with the Royal Philharmonic Orchestra due to be held at London's Royal Albert Hall, after the venue's representatives declared the libretto obscene. Later that same year, at a concert at London's Rainbow Theatre, Zappa was attacked and pushed off the stage by a fan's jealous husband. Badly injured, he spent several weeks in hospital and most of the ensuing year in a wheelchair. For some time afterwards he tried to avoid England. Nevertheless he returned to this country in 1988, bringing a breathtaking two-and-a-half-hour show which mixed his latest work of tortuous musical intricacy with a leavening of the old favourites.

Besides music Zappa also spent time and energy opposing the Parents Music Resource Center, a pressure group of Washington women dedicated to "cleaning up" rock lyrics, through censorship if necessary. Zappa dismissed the PMRC's leaders – Vice-President Al Gore's wife Tipper and former Secretary of State James Baker's wife Susan – as "bored housewives" and, before a congressional panel, derided the notion that his lyrics could influence behaviour: "I wrote a song about dental floss but did anyone's teeth get cleaner?"

Another activity was Why Not? – an international "licensing, consulting and social engineering company", which he founded in 1989. One of its first clients was the Czechoslovak government, whose leader Václav Havel regarded Zappa as one of the great influences on his life. On their first meeting in 1990 Havel was so taken with Zappa that he appointed him his consultant for trade, culture and tourism. James Baker thereupon advised Havel that he could do business with either the US or Zappa, but not both.

Cancer of the prostate was eventually diagnosed in 1991, but Zappa continued to work until physical strength failed him completely.

His wife Gail and the four children of what Zappa always called "marriage as a Dada concept" survive him.

Frank Zappa, musician, was born on December 21, 1940. He died of prostate cancer in Los Angeles on December 4, 1993, aged 52

KURT COBAIN

———————•———————

Implacable, innovative and enigmatic leader of the seminal
grunge-rock band Nirvana

The Times, April 11, 1994

Success may have been too much for Kurt Cobain. As the lead singer, guitarist and songwriter of Nirvana, he had become the high priest of "grunge rock", the sound which has come to dominate the popular music scene over the past four years. Raw and uncompromising, backed by a sound that combined the nihilistic fury of punk rock with some of the tunefulness of the Beatles, Cobain's lyrics for a generation coming of age in an era of unemployment and frustration.

It was ironic that as he raged against the material and synthetic trappings of pop music, Cobain was inevitably swallowed up by those same excesses. Born in a small rain-soaked timber town on America's northwest coast where young men became lumberjacks, not singers, Kurt Cobain showed his independence at an early age by learning to play the guitar. Actually, he was given lessons in order to keep him out of trouble after his parents had divorced when he was seven.

Cobain went on to drop out of high school and, with his friend Krist Novoselic, left Aberdeen to head for the relatively bright lights of Seattle. Together with drummer Dave Grohl, the pair founded Nirvana in 1986.

The group made a slow start, performing mainly in small clubs in the Seattle area, and it was 1990 before they produced their first album, *Bleach*, which was made for $606 and initially sold 30,000 copies. This was tiny by commercial standards, but respectable for an independent label, and it helped Nirvana to establish a strong cult following on the American college circuit.

In a series of deafening live shows, the group began to smash more than the icons of pop music, they frequently smashed the equipment as well. In 1991, with the album *Nevermind*, Cobain put grunge rock into the mainstream with a vengeance. The record sold nearly ten million copies worldwide, and knocked Michael Jackson off the top of the popular music charts.

One of the songs, *Smells Like Teen Spirit*, became an anthem for a generation. But success did not sit easily with Kurt Cobain. "I do not want to have a long career if I have to put up with some of the stuff that I'm putting up with," he told *The New York Times* last November. "I'm trying it one last time, and if it's more of a pleasant year for us, then fine, we'll have a career. But I'm not going to subject myself to being stuck in an apartment building for the next ten years and being afraid to go outside of my house. It's not worth it."

In some of his last songs on the album *In Utero*, released last year to critical acclaim, Cobain reproached his own fame. "I do not want what I have got," he sang, and "What's wrong with me?" One thing wrong with him was an addiction to heroin, said to have been brought about in part by a persistent and unexplained stomach ailment, but also for psychological reasons. Cobain was, according to his biographer Michael Azzerad, "a very sensitive person, sweet and bright, which are not the best qualities to have if you are a rock star".

In Rome last month he was taken to hospital in a coma brought on by a combination of drugs and alcohol, and the group was forced to cut short its European tour. Cobain's drug habit, together with squabbles over royalties, almost caused the group to break up. They also brought family problems when Cobain and his wife, the singer Courtney Love, temporarily lost custody of their baby daughter after Ms Love admitted taking heroin during her pregnancy.

As news of Cobain's suicide spread, hundreds of young fans stood outside his home in the pouring rain, and wept. His mother, on being told of his death, recalled other rock stars who died young after using drugs. "Now," she said, "he's gone and joined that stupid club."

Kurt Cobain, frontman of Nirvana, was born on February 20, 1967. He died of an apparently self-inflicted gunshot wound on April 8, 1994, aged 27

Kurt Cobain (front) with bandmates Krist Novoselic and Dave Grohl

JERRY GARCIA

*Hirsute and chemically challenged lead guitarist and vocalist of
the rock group the Grateful Dead*

The Times, August 11, 1995

Discursive, diffuse and often seemingly interminable in live performance, the Grateful Dead and Jerry Garcia were exemplars *par excellence* of the counterculture of the Sixties. Nevertheless, they turned out to have a shelf life that far exceeded that of most of their West Coast contemporaries.

When the fragile optimism of the Haight-Ashbury hippy ethos that had spawned them collapsed towards the end of the decade, their survival as a group did not seem likely. While other bands, notably their close San Francisco competitors, Jefferson Airplane, seemed ready to play the marketing game, re-creating themselves on record with little apparent effort, the Grateful Dead remained a recording studio executive's nightmare. Although they had been rated one of the best acts at the Monterey festival of 1967, they appeared simply incapable of transposing the qualities that infused their live performances onto disc.

Yet their army of fans, known as the Deadheads, remained loyal to them, following them avidly from concert to concert. And, in spite of a pharmaceutically challenged lifestyle that caused casualties to its individual members, which were heavy even by rock'n'roll standards, the Grateful Dead retained some sort of cohesion as the Seventies rolled by. In the Eighties their ageing hippy devotees were augmented by a rash of teenaged neo-hippies to whom Sixties flower power and love-ins were things of hearsay, if not of history. And in the last few years the Grateful Dead suddenly struck a vein of recording success that brought them a hit single and hit albums, forms of acknowledgment that would have seemed unthinkable to them in the Sixties.

Garcia himself remained disarmingly bemused by these developments (the title of the band's only Top Ten single, *A Touch of Gray*, was a wry acknowledgment of the advance of years). To the end he confessed to having to overcome this thing of "feeling like a fool, singing in front of a bunch of people".

Jerome John Garcia was born in 1942 and grew up in San Francisco's Bay Area. At school in the 1950s he played rock'n'roll but later switched to folk. He made an extensive study of blues, country music and bluegrass and made a reputation as one of the finest guitarists on the West Coast.

Moving to Palo Alto, California, in 1964, he set up a group called Mother McCree's Uptown Jug Champions with a number of other young musicians, including Bob Weir and Ron McKernan. In the following year the group renamed itself the Warlocks, playing an increasingly psychedelic form of rock at ear-splitting decibel levels, in small clubs. At this time the band's name achieved its final form, the Grateful Dead, popularly – though almost certainly apocryphally – supposed to have been alighted on by Garcia in the pages of the the *Oxford English Dictionary* as he opened it at random.

By now their performances were heavily influenced by copious indulgence in LSD and they became acquainted with one of the leading exponents of the drug, the author Ken Kesey. Jam sessions and the dropping of LSD at the La Honda club, often orchestrated by Kesey, were known as Acid Tests. Tom Wolfe, who immortalised these events in his cult book of the period, *The Electric Kool-Aid Acid Test*, described the Grateful Dead as "weird".

The band's first album *The Grateful Dead*, which included psychedelic rock versions of established blues and bluegrass numbers, was not a success. It somehow failed to capture the excitement of their live performances. The second, *Anthem of the Sun*, suffered from an innate dislike of the studio ethos on the part of the band, in spite of the fact that Warner had sent recording crews into the field to tape some of their material live. Their immediate successors also had a patchy reception.

The death in 1973 of McKernan from alcohol abuse placed some check on the band's progress (another member, Ken Godchaux, was to be killed in a car accident, and the keyboard player, Brent Mydland, died of a drug overdose) but the band continued to record, under its own name. It also toured Europe as well as the US. Sustained by its loyal army of followers, it survived the decade of the Seventies, in which it never really seemed to reap the financial rewards of its efforts.

Then, halfway through the Eighties, Garcia and his men suddenly found an unexpected batch of new recruits for their unreconstructed bohemian idealism. A generation to whom Monterey, Woodstock and Altamont were events almost as distant as Anzio or the Normandy landings learned to love the free-wheeling four-hour ramblings of this hirsute but no longer svelte crew of rockers. And their forays into the conventional heartland of Middle America, pursued by hordes of adoring teenagers, had every small-town sheriff and local police department on standby.

They began, too, to make considerably more money than they ever had before (business had never been their strong suit). They began to cut platinum albums and when something so awfully conventional as a Top Ten single came their way, Garcia permitted himself a snort of disbelief.

Not long ago Garcia himself acknowledged the march of time.

At one point he had had to plead with the Grateful Dead's increasingly manic young fans to "cool it". As for himself, shaggily bearded and corpulent: "When I was 23 I used to jump around a bit on stage, but gravity works on me too much now. These days I'm too busy trying to play that darned guitar."

Jerry Garcia, musician, was born on August 1, 1942. He died of a heart attack in a Californian drug treatment centre on August 9, 1995, aged 53

MICHAEL HUTCHENCE

*Hard-living, hell-raising and sultry-looking lead singer of
the Australian rock band INXS*

The Times, November 24, 1997

Michael Hutchence was the closest Australia has come to having an equivalent of rock rebels such as Mick Jagger and Jim Morrison. A hard-living hell-raiser who often boasted of his copious intake of drugs, he did his swaggering best to live up to the danger implicit in the name of his band, INXS ("in excess"). He marked his birthday this year by claiming that he was "never going to live my life in a way that's deemed appropriate", but actually lived, and apparently died, in the antic manner now virtually de rigueur for rock's hard men.

In recent years he became a more regular fixture in the gossip columns than in the music press, which had come to regard the uncomplicated funk-rock played by INXS as unfashionable. Yet for several years Hutchence led one of the best-selling stadium rock bands in the world, selling more than 20 million albums. He relished the part, considering himself "bloody good at being a rock star", and was once described as "surfing on the irony of it all".

Hutchence was born in Sydney to a suburban middle-class family, but led a peripatetic childhood, living in Hong Kong, where he picked up his English accent, and Los Angeles. He always believed that his upbringing influenced the restlessness and bohemianism that came to characterise his adult life.

Back in Sydney in 1977, he became lead singer with a band known as the Farriss Brothers, which became INXS the following year when it moved to Perth. The band's original six-strong line-up was to remain unchanged throughout. They developed a driving sound that combined rock, dance and soul, and spent the next four years travelling across Australia, playing up to 300 dates a year, mostly in small and seedy venues. Some of these had separate bars for men and women, with gutters running between so that the lager and vomit could be hosed away.

The band's first album appeared in 1980, and there were several minor Australian hits before they were signed to a major label in 1982. The deal took them to America and Britain, where they traded successfully on the sultry good looks and bad boy charisma of Hutchence, who was also rapidly developing as a songwriter.

Touring incessantly, they also became one of the first bands to benefit from the emergence of MTV, with a series of striking videos. In 1986 Hutchence made his film debut in *Dogs in Space*, playing a heroin-addicted punk. Shortly afterwards, the single *What You Need* reached the Top Five in America and, aided by a satellite appearance in Bob Geldof's Live Aid and sell-out shows supporting Queen, *Listen Like Thieves* became the band's first million-selling album. Some of the proceeds were invested in the film *Crocodile Dundee*, initially as a tax loss.

Kick, INXS's best album, occupied the British charts for more than two years at the end of the 1980s, and was followed by the successful *X* and the hit singles *Need You Tonight*, a No 1 in America, and *Suicide Blonde*. By 1990 Hutchence was at his peak, an all-round celebrity as well as a senior member of the rock aristocracy, starring as Shelley in Roger Corman's *Frankenstein Unbound* and winning a Brit award as best international artist.

INXS were to top the British album charts once more, in 1993 with *Welcome to Wherever You Are*, but by then the dual influences of Britpop and house were about to change musical fashions. Sales began to decline outside Australia and last year Liam Gallagher of Oasis denounced Hutchence as a "has-been". The last album, *Elegantly Wasted*, received a critical mauling for repeating the same old rock clichés, although Hutchence enjoyed some success singing on the soundtracks of the hit films *Batman Forever* and *Face/Off*. He was preparing for a sell-out tour, called "Lose Your Head", to celebrate INXS's 20th anniversary and Michael Douglas had reportedly invited him to Hollywood to discuss future film roles.

Despite his commercial decline, Hutchence had been more in the media glare than ever in recent years because of his turbulent lifestyle, and as consort to a string of famous women. There were affairs with Kylie Minogue and the model Helena Christensen before he hit the tabloid headlines in 1995 over his liaison with Paula Yates, who had then been married to Bob Geldof for nine years. The two had first met much earlier, when Yates interviewed him on television and described him as "the sexiest man alive".

Caught in an increasingly tangled web of soap-opera complexity, Geldof and Yates at one point attempted a reconciliation, while Hutchence went back to Christensen and posed for romantic shots in *Hello!* magazine. Shortly afterwards Hutchence punched a paparazzo who had tracked him and Yates to a hotel. He was duly fined.

Last year Yates gave birth to Hutchence's daughter, named Heavenly Hiraani Tiger Lily. Then, after changing their partners, Geldof, Yates and Hutchence agreed to change houses. In a bizarre house-swap, the new couple moved into Geldof's Chelsea home while Yates's husband moved into Hutchence's one-bedroom house. Shortly afterwards, the police raided the couple's home for drugs.

Hutchence recently announced that he and Yates would marry in Tahiti in January, and he was reported to be house-hunting for them in Sydney. In an interview in October he described himself as "the luckiest man alive", and all who knew him were surprised by his death. After Kurt Cobain's suicide, Hutchence had remarked: "Pop eats its young, that's for sure." He is survived by Paula Yates and their daughter.

Michael Hutchence, rock star, was born on January 22, 1960. He was found dead in his hotel room in Sydney on November 22, 1997, aged 37

DUSTY SPRINGFIELD

•

*Shy, soulful, smoky-voiced singer whose songs and beehive hair
became enduring symbols of Swinging London*

The Times, March 4, 1999

Dusty Springfield was acknowledged on both sides of the Atlantic
as the finest female soul singer Britain has produced. Her croakily
erotic voice – which belied the shy, vulnerable convent girl who
produced it – created a string of hit records during the Sixties beat
boom. After three successful years teamed with her songwriter
brother Tom as two-thirds of the folk-music-based group the
Springfields, she made her 1963 solo debut with *I Only Want to Be with
You*, sung with jaunty fervour. It was an immediate hit, remaining in
the charts for 18 weeks, and it has endured as a pop classic.

More hits followed throughout the Sixties, including *Stay Awhile*,
I Just Don't Know What to do with Myself, *Losing You*, *In the Middle of
Nowhere*, and the poignant *You Don't Have to Say You Love Me*, which
in March 1966 took her to No 1. The following year she was back in
the Top Ten at No 4, with *I Close My Eyes and Count to Ten*.

Dusty Springfield took her enjoyment of her fame right down
to the wire in those heady years. As part of the swinging London
club scene, she found she had become a model for teenage girls,
who slavishly copied her startling beehive blonde hairstyle and dark
"panda" eye make-up.

On concert tours she played to packed houses, and adoring fans
writhed and screamed when the myopic star appeared hesitantly
from backstage to belt out her first number. The Sixties were her apogee.
She consistently won the top female singer award, outshining such
contemporaries as Lulu, Cilla Black and Sandie Shaw.

But the golden years did not last. Her career, spanning more
than four decades, was a turbulent one even by the standards of the
pop world. Persistent tabloid interest in her sexual proclivities –
largely engendered by her confessing that she was as much attracted
to women as to men – drove her to live in Los Angeles for much of

the Seventies. There, although she became something of an icon for gay men and lesbians, her talent was largely neglected. "I became bored with being a pop singer," she confessed. A rare success was *Son of a Preacher Man*, taken as a single from an otherwise stonily received LP *Dusty in Memphis*.

Despondent, and righting what was to be a lifelong weight problem, she followed a downward spiral of drug and alcohol abuse. Known for her impulsive candour during interviews, she once said: "I lost nearly all the Seventies in a haze of booze and pills. I couldn't have one or two drinks. I had to get loaded. Vodka and the pills helped ease my shyness. Then I got into cocaine and in seven months I was a brain-scrambled wreck."

But she went on to overcome her addictions and then revived her career, courtesy of the Pet Shop Boys, and enjoyed an inspired period in the late Eighties and Nineties. The group began by inviting her to sing on what was to become their worldwide triumph, *What Have I Done to Deserve This?* and went on to write much of her album *Reputation*.

In 1994, however, she discovered that she had breast cancer. She was forced to cancel her singing dates and undergo surgery and months of chemo- and radiotherapy at the Royal Marsden Hospital, London. After the initial shock, her attitude was typically wry: "Why me? Why not?" she said, and added: "I never expected to live this long anyway, so it's uncharted territory."

Dusty Springfield was born Mary Isobel Catherine Bernadette O'Brien in 1939 in Hampstead, of Irish parents. Her father was a tax consultant and her mother, as the singer once described her, was "a free spirit who married to escape spinsterhood; they both bitterly regretted it." Staunch Catholics, they stayed together for the children but quarrelled endlessly. Dusty recalled a troubled childhood. "I was so unhappy as a kid." She would challenge her hot-tempered father when he hit her, and she became "very jealous of my brother Dion. He was older and the blue-eyed boy."

She grew up at first in Buckinghamshire and then in Ealing, where she went to a convent school. On leaving, she took a part-time job in Bentalls department store, meanwhile joining a syrupy all-female vocal trio, the Lana Sisters, who sang mostly at airbases. In 1960 she and Dion, who was already writing songs, adopted the stage names Dusty and Tom Springfield, and launched themselves as the Springfields, a folk-singing duo. Dusty supplied the guitar accompaniment.

Success was elusive to begin with, but when they were joined by Tim Feild they quickly became one of the country's top vocal groups. They had two Top Five singles with *Island of Dreams* (1962) and *Say I Won't Be There* (1963), by which time Feild had been replaced by Mike Hurst. The Springfields had a million-seller in America with the country standard *Silver Threads and Golden Needles* (although it did nothing in Britain) before splitting up in 1963.

Inspired by the ear-thumping "wall of sound" style pioneered by the American producer Phil Spector, Dusty Springfield recorded her first solo hit, *I Only Want to Be with You*, which got to No 4. It was the first record ever played on a new television programme called *Top of the Pops*.

By 1967 she was in full flow, with a string of hits, including *Middle of Nowhere*, *Some of Your Lovin'*, and *The Look of Love*, which featured in the James Bond film *Casino Royale*. She was also a regular on the TV pop music show *Ready, Steady, Go*. At the time she used her celebrity to campaign on behalf of the then little-known American soul and Motown artists. Her eclectic taste in music tended to set her apart from most of her peers in this country. She became popular in America, where she made numerous appearances.

In all she had 16 hits almost successively during the 1960s before her career began to falter. She exiled herself to California for 15 years, living in a two-bedroom house with up to a dozen cats for company. She made sporadic visits to Britain, each time attempting a comeback. But renewed success eluded her until 1987, at the start of her collaboration with the Pet Shop Boys (the singer Neil Tennant and keyboard player Chris Low). Not only did she have a share in the duo's No 2 hit *What Have I Done to Deserve This?*, but she featured on the soundtrack of the film *Scandal*, about the Profumo affair, singing their theme tune *Nothing Has Been Proved*.

She was still bedevilled by her past, however. In 1991 she sued and won undisclosed damages in the High Court as the result of a sketch on a television show in which the comedian portrayed her performing while drunk.

Dusty Springfield, OBE, pop and soul singer, was born on April 16, 1939. She died of cancer on March 2, 1999, aged 59

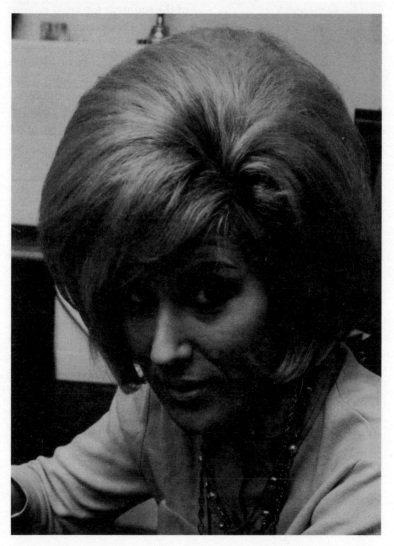

JOHN MARTYN

———— ● ————

Electrifying guitarist and singer whose music blurred the boundaries
between folk, jazz, rock and blues

The Times, January 30, 2009

John Martyn emerged from the British folk scene in the late 1960s to make some of the most hauntingly evocative and mesmerising music of his era.

A virtuoso guitarist with a laid-back but highly expressive voice, he made innovative records that defied categorisation and thrillingly blurred the boundaries between folk, jazz, blues and rock. At his height, every note he played or sang seemed to be imbued with a spacious elegance and sublime airiness all too rare in the hurly-burly of modern popular music.

Although he never attained huge commercial success, he was regarded by his contemporaries as a unique and inimitable talent. Among his collaborators were Eric Clapton, Steve Winwood, Dave

Gilmour and Phil Collins, while successive generations of younger musicians have since referenced his work – particularly such peerless 1970s albums as *Bless the Weather, Solid Air* and *One World.*

In truth, by the mid-1980s his best work was all behind him. He was beset by personal problems and debilitating bouts of alcoholism that took their toll on his health, and his later recordings lacked the timeless mastery and magic of his early work.

He became infamous for his erratic live performances, falling off the stage on more than one occasion. Yet such was the enduring power of his early recordings that his fans seemed prepared to indulge and forgive him.

Iain David McGeachy was born in New Maiden, Surrey, in 1948 to parents who were opera singers. He spent much of his childhood with a grandmother in Glasgow, where he attended Shawlands Academy.

By his mid-teens he was playing guitar in Scottish folk clubs, where he was helped considerably by the patronage of the singer and guitarist Hamish Imlach. By the time he was 18, he was playing professionally on the London folk club circuit and in 1967 he became the first signing in Chris Blackwell's expansion of Island Records to become a fully independent label.

His debut album, *London Conversation*, appeared in 1968 and was a relatively restrained recitation of the solo acoustic set that he was performing in folk clubs at the time. By the end of the same year, however, it had been followed by *The Tumbler*, a far more adventurous recording that included the jazzy tones of Harold McNair's flute and signposted what was to come.

Martyn's unique style was developed further on his next two albums, *Stormbringer* and *Road to Ruin*, both of which appeared in 1970 and were credited jointly to Martyn and his wife, Beverley Kutner.

Recorded in Woodstock in upstate New York and brilliantly produced by the folk-rock pioneer Joe Boyd – whose other acts included Fairport Convention and Nick Drake – *Stormbringer* featured a host of top US session men, including the Band's drummer, Levon Helm, and boasted a more expansive rock sound.

Road to Ruin pushed the folk-rock envelope even further and marked the first appearance of Martyn's longest-lasting collaborator, the double bass player Danny Thompson of Pentangle.

When neither album sold particularly well, Island – just starting to taste big success with Cat Stevens – concluded that it would be easier to market Martyn as a solo singer-songwriter than as a duo, and Beverley was unceremoniously relegated to the background, making only occasional "guest" appearances as a backing singer while raising a family.

It might have been unfair but it marked the start of Martyn's golden era. On *Bless the Weather* (1972) he combined a jazzy lilt with his folk-rock stylings, and on the track *Glistening Glyndebourne* he began to experiment with an echo unit that gave his guitar an extraordinary new sound, combining the warmth of an acoustic instrument with subtle layers of electronically enhanced complexity. Even better was to come with *Solid Air* in 1973. The title track, widely regarded as Martyn's masterpiece, was a tribute to his doomed friend Nick Drake, while *May You Never* – later covered by Eric Clapton – remains among his finest compositions. But the sound was extraordinary too, with Thompson's rolling double bass lines augmented by members of Fairport Convention and Martyn using his voice not merely to convey his lyrics but as another instrument in the mix.

Inside Out appeared later that same year and moved even farther in the direction of experimental rock, with greater use of guitar effects and featuring Steve Winwood and Chris Wood from Traffic among the performers.

It was followed by *Sunday Child* (1975), which included a wonderfully elegiac version of the traditional ballad *Spencer the Rover*, as if to show he had not totally lost touch with his folk roots.

Blackwell then suggested that Martyn should spend time in Jamaica checking out the island's music scene, and the result was *One World* (1977), a lush-sounding record that included a collaboration with the reggae producer Lee "Scratch" Perry on *Big Muff*. The record's dubby, echoing soundscapes have since been claimed as the forerunner of the "trip-hop" style that emerged in the 1990s with bands such as Portishead.

By the end of the 1970s Martyn's marriage was on the rocks, owing in part to his self-destructive drink and drug addictions and in part simply to the fact that he was barely ever at home.

Intense, autobiographical and cathartic, many of the songs on his next album, *Grace and Danger* (1980), dealt with the disintegration of the relationship. The record also featured Phil Collins, who hung around to produce his next album, *Glorious Fool* (1981).

Collins's involvement helped Martyn to his first Top 30 album, but its more mainstream sound did not find favour with his more longstanding fans. Thereafter, the flame of his once unique talent flickered more sporadically on albums such as *Well Kept Secret* (1982), *Sapphire* (1984) and *Piece by Piece* (1986). He later confessed that he could not even remember making some of them and by the end of the decade he found himself without a record label.

In the 1990s he went on to record for a variety of smaller labels and continued to tour. He often appeared in poor health and the worse for drink and cut a shambling, overweight figure unrecognisable from the handsome, curly-haired youth seen staring so hopefully out of his early album covers.

There were occasional flashes of the old spark on albums such as *And* (1996), *Glasgow Walker* (2000) and *On the Cobbles* (2004), but the record-buying public was more interested in reissues of his classic albums and retrospective box sets such as the aptly titled *Ain't No Saint* (2008).

His health suffered further when in 2003 his right leg was amputated below the knee. This rather sad period of his life was documented in a BBC film.

His contribution to British music was recognised in 2008 when he received the lifetime achievement award at the BBC Radio 2 Folk awards and he was appointed OBE in the 2009 New Year Honours.

Martyn last toured in November 2008, when he performed his album *Grace & Danger* in its entirety.

John Martyn, OBE, singer and guitarist, was born on September 11, 1948. He died on January 29, 2009, aged 60

SHANE MACGOWAN

———————•———————

Hard-drinking frontman of Celtic punk band the Pogues who was hailed for his raw talent and masterful songwriting

The Times, November 30, 2023

"It's a miracle every morning when you wake up," Shane MacGowan once observed – and he was not kidding.

MacGowan's dissolute and self-destructive lifestyle – he claimed that he had never been sober since he was 14 – led doctors and concerned friends alike to tell him that unless he gave up the drink and drugs he would not live long enough to get his bus pass.

He took no notice and not only stubbornly defied medical science to see in his 60th birthday but revelled in his notoriety and bragged of being an "alcoholic junkie republican".

Sinéad O'Connor was so distressed by his heroin addiction that she turned police informer and had him arrested "for his own good". The bust helped to wean him off narcotics but his appetite for binge drinking continued unabated.

As an unlikely rock'n'roll survivor he rivalled Keith Richards and Ozzy Osbourne but it came at a high cost. Bruised and bloodied, he was confined to a wheelchair after a bad fall from which his broken body never healed. Having lost all of his teeth by 2015, a documentary, *Shane MacGowan: A Wreck Reborn*, followed one Irish dentist as she took on the monumental task of replacing 28 dentures, which she dubbed "the Everest of dentistry".

His indestructible legacy, though, were the songs he wrote and recorded with his band the Pogues. He scribbled his lyrics on scraps of paper littering the floor amid the empty bottles at his King's Cross flat, but the street poetry of songs such as *Fairytale of New York*, *A Rainy Night in Soho* and *A Pair of Brown Eyes* are as vivid and memorable as almost anything in the modern pop canon.

He sang with a permanent slur: invariably drunk by the time he went on stage, he stumbled around while swigging from a bottle and had a disconcerting tendency to vomit mid-song. Typically, he prided himself on his timing, "puking in between a chorus and a verse so you don't miss a word".

Despite such antics, he remained a much-loved figure whose excesses were for the most part indulgently forgiven by his fans and the music industry.

At a Dublin concert to celebrate his 60th birthday, Bono, Johnny Depp, Nick Cave and the Irish president, Michael D Higgins, all joined him on stage.

"Shane is 60 years old," announced Irvine Welsh at the birthday bash most never expected him to see. "Say it again: Shane MacGowan is 60. Whatever is he still doing here?"

Welsh, the author of *Trainspotting* and a noted hell-raiser himself, added: "The reassuring presence continues. If you walk into a bar or party and the first thing you hear is that sniggering laugh, which sounds like Muttley on crystal meth, you know you are in for quite a night."

It was perhaps ironic that Shane Patrick Lysaght MacGowan's birth certificate recorded that he was born in Royal Tunbridge Wells, that most genteel of English towns, on Christmas Day, 1957, although in truth it was an accident.

His Irish parents, Maurice and Therese MacGowan, were visiting Maurice's sister for Christmas when Therese went into labour. After a few weeks spent "sleeping in a drawer" in his aunt's house, the family returned to the village of Silvermines in Tipperary, a community so cut off that there was only one bus a week to the nearest market town.

His father, who sported a huge white beard in later years that made him look like a member of the Dubliners, was an accountant. His mother, who died in a road accident on New Year's Day, 2017, was a typist and a talented amateur singer. At the age of 73 she got on stage in front of a sold-out audience in Dublin's biggest concert hall to duet with her son on *Fairytale of New York*, singing "You scumbag, you maggot,/You cheap lousy faggot", a part originally taken by Kirsty MacColl on the hit record.

MacGowan grew up steeped in the twin pillars of republicanism and Roman Catholicism. The family home in Tipperary had been a safe house from the Black and Tans during the war for Irish independence and an uncle had been the local IRA commandant.

He suggested that if he had not been a singer he might have become a priest. "I was a religious maniac and a total hedonist at the same time," he said.

However, according to his younger sister Siobhan, who still lives in Silvermines, the MacGowans imbued "a fierce sense of individuality" in their offspring and taught them "to question and think for ourselves".

He loved his early years in Ireland, surrounded by his mother's extended family. "It was open house – people would come around at all hours and there would be dancing and card-playing and boozing and singing," he recalled. "It was like living in a pub. I was smoking and drinking and gambling before I could talk."

By the mid-1960s, he was back in the more demure environs of Tunbridge Wells, where his father became a bookkeeper at the local C&A store.

At Holmewood House prep school, an elegant Decimus Burton country pile in the rolling Kent countryside, he came under the influence of the headmaster Bob Bairamian, who taught him classics and encouraged his precocious essay writing, which won him a scholarship to Westminster School. "He was very unusual indeed," Bairamian recalled. "Westminster asked whether I'd written his English paper. They said they'd never seen anything like this before."

Bullied for his looks and Irish accent at Westminster, he squandered his academic promise and spent his time truanting, drawn by the peep shows and strip joints to wander alone in Soho. He lasted two years before he was expelled for drug possession.

His frustrated creativity and hedonistic tendencies found a natural outlet on the London rock scene, playing in the punk band the Nipple Erectors. His Irish heritage was also a key part of his make-up and he began to fashion an innovative fusion of punk, Irish traditional songs and rebel yells, topped off with a reckless, alcohol-fuelled bonhomie.

He honed the style as a busker, scaring the life out of commuters at Finsbury Park Station, and formed Pogue Mahone (anglicised Gaelic for "kiss my arse"). The band's debut single, *Dark Streets of London*, was promptly banned by BBC radio when the meaning of the name became known.

As the group's popularity grew, so did MacGowan's notoriety as a hard drinker, although the story that when the group signed to Stiff Records in 1984 he asked to be paid with a crate of Guinness was a piece of clever myth-making on the part of an inventive marketing department.

Against MacGowan's wishes they were persuaded to change their name to the Pogues. Hit albums such as *Rum Sodomy & the Lash* and

If I Should Fall from Grace with God combined his original and evocative compositions – often about drunks and derelicts – with roaring, alcohol-drenched versions of trad Irish songs in an endearingly ramshackle but dynamic style that made them favourites at rock and folk festivals alike.

As the group's guitarist Philip Chevron put it, they looked like "a bunch of tumbledown wrecks". At a time when Madonna and Michael Jackson were ruling the pop roost, MacGowan's dishevelled lack of pretension was a whiskey breath of boozy, devil-may-care fresh air.

Scrapes and incidents followed him wherever he went. To the gossip columns of a dirt-hungry media his every ravaged excess was enthusiastically welcomed as X-rated copy, whether breaking an arm when he drunkenly fell into the path of a taxi after leaving a London restaurant or spitting on posters of Margaret Thatcher in the video for the Pogues' hit *A Pair of Brown Eyes*.

A brilliant collaboration with the Dubliners on *The Irish Rover* gave the Pogues a Top Ten single in 1987 but even better was that same year's *Fairytale of New York*.

The song was the perfect encapsulation of MacGowan's writing strengths. Poignant and romantic, yet brutally honest ("It was Christmas Eve babe/ In the drunk tank/ An old man said to me, won't see another one/And then he sang a song"), it was the festive song for those who cannot abide festive songs.

It should have been the Christmas No 1 but lost out to the Pet Shop Boys. No matter. Rereleased annually, *Fairytale of New York* charts again every Christmas and has become the UK's most-played Christmas song of the 21st century, ahead of Slade and John Lennon.

Fairytale of New York was the high watermark of the Pogues' commercial success and thereafter MacGowan's drinking, once the source of the band's roguish appeal, became a serious threat to the band's stability, as his performances vacillated wildly between the inspired and the incoherent.

In 1988 he collapsed at Heathrow Airport as the Pogues were flying to America for the biggest tour of their career, supporting Bob Dylan. They played on without him and when he returned to the fray it was never the same again. He was fired from the band in 1991, after his binge drinking on a tour of Japan rendered him incapable of taking the stage.

He re-emerged with a new group, the Popes, whose debut album featured Johnny Depp on guitar. However, the band were grounded when MacGowan fell off a bar stool and broke his hip while shooting a beer commercial. He later reunited with the Pogues until "we got a bit sick of each other again".

Those tasked with interviewing him deserved danger money. When Lynn Barber profiled him for *The Observer* in 2001, he plied her with gin and tonics for six hours and then tried to talk her into being the getaway driver while he and a friend robbed a bank.

She eventually made her way to her hotel room "completely blotto". When she came down for breakfast the next morning he was still sitting at the bar.

He met his long-term partner, Victoria Mary Clarke, in 1982, when she was 16. She wrote a biography of him – inevitably titled *A Drink with Shane MacGowan* – and made Sharon Osbourne, wife of Ozzy, her role model in attempting to keep her wayward partner out of trouble.

She did not always succeed and on several occasions thought she had lost him for good. On one occasion in New Orleans he went drinking on Bourbon Street and when he was not seen again for 48 hours she reported him missing. The police were getting ready to check the dumpsters when he turned up in the lobby of the wrong hotel asking for the key to his room.

After three decades together they married in 2018 at a quiet ceremony in Copenhagen attended by Depp, who sang at their reception.

"She's probably the only reason I'm alive," MacGowan said.

Shane MacGowan, singer and songwriter, was born on December 25, 1957. He died of viral encephalitis on November 30, 2023, aged 65

INDEX

PHOTO CREDITS

Front cover (Kurt Cobain): Minneapolis Star Tribune/ZUMAPRESS.com/ Alamy Stock Photo

Back cover (Chuck Berry): Album/Alamy Stock Photo

Back cover (Tina Turner): Roger Bamber/News UK/News Licensing

Back cover (Marc Bolan): Roger Bamber/News UK/News Licensing

Page 15 (David Cassidy): Stephen Markeson/News UK/News Licensing

Page 20 (Lemmy): Ilpo Musto/Shutterstock

Page 31 (Prince): David Boyle/News UK/News Licensing

Page 37 (Astrud Gilberto): Fremantle Media/Shutterstock

Page 47 (David Bowie): Steve Lewis/News UK/News Licensing

Page 48 (Kirsty MacColl): Michael Powell/News UK/News Licensing

Page 51 (Vangelis): ANL/Shutterstock

Page 61 (Chuck Berry): Mark Pepper/News UK/News Licensing

Page 62 (Bob Marley): Jonathan Player/Shutterstock

Page 64 (Olivia Newton-John): News UK/News Licensing

Page 69 (Michael Jackson): Tom Kidd/News UK/News Licensing

Page 77 (Chas Hodges): Adam Pensotti/News UK/News Licensing

Page 85 (Joni Sledge): Stephen Markeson/News UK/News Licensing

Page 86 (Joe Strummer): Arthur Steel/News UK/News Licensing

Page 95 (James Brown): Mike Schofield/News UK/News Licensing

Page 96 (Christine McVie): News UK/News Licensing

Page 109 (Leonard Cohen): Ibl/Shutterstock

Page 110 (Jimi Hendrix): David Magnus/Shutterstock

Page 117 (Amy Winehouse): David Bebber/News UK/News Licensing

Page 118 (George Michael): John Rogers/News UK/News Licensing

Page 131 (John Lennon): News UK/News Licensing

Page 132 (Tina Turner): Alan Weller/News UK/News Licensing

Page 145 (Robin Gibb): Phil Foster/News UK/News Licensing

Page 146 (Jet Black): Roger Bamber/News UK/News Licensing

Page 155 (Whitney Houston): Ian Derry/News UK/News Licensing

Page 156 (Jerry Lee Lewis): Alfred Harris/News UK/News Licensing

Page 165 (Freddie Mercury): Roger Bamber/News UK/News Licensing

Page 166 (Ronnie Spector): Daily Herald Archive/Contributor/Getty

Page 171 (BB King): TDC Photography/Shutterstock

Page 177 (David Crosby): Ben Houdijk/Shutterstock

Page 183 (Keith Moon): Duncan Atkinson/News UK/News Licensing

Page 185 (Sinéad O'Connor): Paul Rogers/News UK/News Licensing

Page 195 (Elvis Presley): Mgm/Kobal/Shutterstock

Page 203 (Aretha Franklin): Bryan Wharton/News UK/News Licensing

Page 204 (Genesis P-Orridge): Sheila Rock/Shutterstock

Page 211 (Les McKeown): Roger Bamber/News UK/News Licensing

Page 212 (Marvin Gaye): Eugene Adebari/Shutterstock

Page 214 (Meat Loaf): Steve Lewis/News UK/News Licensing

Page 220 (Syd Barrett): Stevens/ANL/Shutterstock

Page 227 (Brian Jones): David Magnus/Shutterstock

Page 228 (Charlie Watts): Francesco Guidicini/News UK/News Licensing

Page 234 (Keith Flint): Linus Moran/News UK/News Licensing

Page 243 (Pete Shelley): David Thorpe/News UK/News Licensing

Page 245 (Jim Morrison): Araldo Di Crollalanza/Shutterstock

Page 249 (Nina Simone): Media Press/Shutterstock

Page 253 (Alvin Stardust): Roger Bamber/News UK/News Licensing

Page 254 (Ray Charles): Michael Ward/News UK/News Licensing

Page 263 (Glen Campbell): Roger Bamber/News UK/News Licensing

Page 264 (George Harrison): John Haynes/News UK/News Licensing

Page 272 (Lou Reed): James Clarke/News UK/News Licensing

Page 277 (Ginger Baker): John Pickering/News UK/News Licensing

Page 283 (Janis Joplin): News UK/News Licensing

Page 289 (Phil May): Ian Dickson/Shutterstock

Page 285 (Fats Domino): Simon Wilkinson/News UK/News Licensing

Page 296 (Marc Bolan): Roger Bamber/News UK/News Licensing

Page 299 (Tom Petty): James Morgan/News UK/News Licensing

Page 309 (Steve Strange): News UK/News Licensing

Page 315 (Eddie Van Halen): Sipa/Shutterstock

Page 316 (Cilla Black): Peter Trievnor/News UK/News Licensing

Page 322 (Gerry Rafferty): Alan Messer/Shutterstock

Page 327 (Glenn Frey): Everett/Shutterstock

Page 332 (Ian Dury): News UK/News Licensing

Page 341 (Little Richard): Keith Waldegrave/Shutterstock

Page 342 (Terry Hall): Ilpo Musto/Shutterstock

Page 349 (Poly Styrene): Tony Eyles/News UK/News Licensing

Page 350 (Dennis Wilson): Sally Soames/News UK/News Licensing

Page 352 (Jeff Beck): News UK/News Licensing

Page 357 (Mike Nesmith): ANL/Shutterstock

Page 367 (Loretta Lynn): Jim Hobden/News UK/News Licensing

Page 371 (Captain Beefheart): Alan Messer/Shutterstock

Page 377 (Don Everly): Dezo Hoffman/Shutterstock

Page 378 (Frank Zappa): Harry Kerr/News UK/News Licensing

Page 385 (Kurt Cobain): Stephen Sweet/Shutterstock

Page 386 (Jerry Garcia): Nigel Skelsey/Shutterstock

Page 390 (Michael Hutchence): Ilpo Musto/Shutterstock

Page 397 (Dusty Springfield): Ian Yeomans/News UK/News Licensing

Page 398 (John Martyn): Estate Of Keith Morris/Contributor/Getty

Page 402 (Shane MacGowan): Tim Rooke/Shutterstock